Passages
from Antiquity
to Feudalism

First published by NLB 1974

© Perry Anderson, 1974

Verso Edition 1978

Verso Editions, 7 Carlisle Street, London w1

Printed in Great Britain by
Lowe & Brydone Printers Limited, Thetford, Norfolk

ISBN 86091 709 6

The transition from classical antiquity to feudalism has been less often studied within historical materialism than the transition from feudalism to capitalism. This essay considers some of the problems posed by the change from the ancient to the mediaeval world, for European development. It starts with a discussion of the general nature of the slave mode of production in the classical epoch, and then compares the respective social and political structures of Greek, Hellenistic and Roman societies. The reasons for the eventual fall of the Roman imperial system, which brought Antiquity to an end, are surveyed in the light of the regional divisions within the Empire, and the evolution of the Germanic tribes on its borders.

A review of the Dark Ages leads to a summary outline of the emergence of feudalism in Western Europe, as a new mode of production. The variations of feudal formation in the different lands of the mediaeval West from England to Italy and Germany to Spain, are contrasted—together with the special evolution of Scandinavia. The causes of both the notable growth, and ultimate crisis, of the Western feudal economy are appraised. Finally, the distinct pattern of development of Eastern Europe in the mediaeval epoch is traced, including some assessment of the significance of the Asian nomadic invasions for this half of the continent. The Balkans are treated as a separate sub-region of the East, defined by the survival of Byzantium. The work closes with reflections on the nature and fate of the Byzantine Empire, whose final disappearance conventionally marks a threshold of the early modern epoch in Europe.

Designed to provide elements for discussion, *Passages from Antiquity to Feudalism* is intended as a contribution to wider debate on the historical past of European civilisation. A sequel, *Lineages of the Absolutist State*, is available in a hardback edition.

Perry Anderson

Verso

Foreword

Some words are necessary to explain the scope and intention of this essay. It is conceived as a prologue to the longer study, whose subject-matter follows immediately on it: *Lineages of the Absolutist State*. The two books are articulated directly into each other, and ultimately suggest a single argument. The relationship between the two – antiquity and feudalism on the one hand, and absolutism on the other – is not immediately apparent, in the usual perspective of most treatments of them. Normally, ancient history is separated by a professional chasm from mediaeval history, which very few contemporary works attempt to span: the gulf between them is, of course, institutionally entrenched in both teaching and research. The conventional distance between mediaeval history and early modern history is (naturally or paradoxically?) much less: but it nevertheless has typically been enough to preclude any examination of feudalism and absolutism within, as it were, a single focus. The argument of these interlinked studies is that in certain important respects this is the way in which the successive forms which are its concern should be considered. The present essay explores the social and political world of classical antiquity, the nature of the transition from it to the mediaeval world, and the resultant structure and evolution of feudalism in Europe; regional divisions, both of the Mediterranean and of Europe, are a central theme throughout. Its sequel discusses Absolutism against the background of feudalism and antiquity, as their legitimate political heir. The reasons for preceding a comparative survey of the Absolutist State by an excursion through classical antiquity and feudalism will become evident in the course of the second work itself, and are summarized in its conclusions. These attempt to situate the specificity of

European experience as a whole within a wider international setting, in the light of the analyses of both volumes.

It is necessary, however, to stress at the outset the limited and provisional character of the accounts presented in each work. The scholarship and skills of the professional historian are absent from them. Historical writing in the proper sense is inseparable from direct research into the original records of the past – archival, epigraphic or archaeological. The studies below have no claim to this dignity. Rather than an actual writing of history as such, they are based simply on a reading of the available works of modern historians: a very different matter. The accompanying apparatus of references, therefore, is the opposite of that which denotes a work of scholarly historiography. He who possesses authority, does not cite it: the sources themselves – the primary materials of the past – speak through him. The type and extent of the notes which support the text in both these works merely indicate the secondary level at which they are situated. Historians themselves, of course, have occasion to produce works of comparison or synthesis without always necessarily having intimate acquaintance with the full range of evidence across the field concerned, although their judgement is likely to be tempered by their command of their specialism. In itself, the effort to describe or understand very broad historical structures or epochs needs no undue apology or justification: without it, specific and local researches fall short of their own potential significance. But it is nevertheless true that no interpretations are so fallible as those which rely on conclusions reached elsewhere as their elementary units of evidence: for they remain constantly open to invalidation by new discoveries or revisions of further primary investigation. What is generally accepted by historians of one generation can still be disproved by the research of the next. Any attempt to generalize on the foundations of existing opinions, however erudite the latter, must therefore inevitably be precarious and conditional. In this case, the limits of the essays involved are particularly great, because of the span of time covered. In effect, the broader the range of history surveyed, the more compressed the treatment accorded to any phase of it will tend to be. In this sense, the full and difficult complexity of the past – which can only be captured on the rich canvas painted by the historian – remains largely outside the scope of these studies. The analyses found below, for reasons of both competence and space, are rudimentary diagrams: no more. Brief sketches for another history, they are intended to propose elements for discussion, rather than to expound closed or comprehensive theses.

The discussion for which they are designed is primarily one within the field of historical materialism. The aims of the method chosen for the usage of Marxism in them are set out in the foreword to *Lineages of the Absolutist State*, where they become most clearly visible in the formal structure of the work. Here there is no need to do more than state the principles which have governed the use of sources, in both studies. The authorities drawn upon for this survey, as for any basically comparative enquiry, are naturally extremely diverse – varying greatly in both intellectual and political character. No special privilege has been granted to Marxist historiography as such. Despite the changes of recent decades, the great bulk of serious historical work in the 20th century has been written by historians foreign to Marxism. Historical materialism is not a finished science; nor have all its practitioners been of a similar calibre. There are fields of historiography which are dominated by Marxist research; there are more, in which non-Marxist contributions are superior in quality and quantity to Marxist; and there are perhaps even more, where no Marxist interventions exist at all. The only permissible criterion of discrimination, in a comparative survey which must consider works coming from such different horizons, is their intrinsic solidity and intelligence. Maximum awareness and respect for the scholarship of historians outside the boundaries of Marxism is not incompatible with rigorous pursuit of a Marxist historical enquiry: it is a condition of it. Conversely, Marx and Engels themselves can never be taken simply at their word: the errors of their writings on the past should not be evaded or ignored, but identified and criticized. To do so is not to depart from historical materialism, but to rejoin it. There is no place for any fideism in rational knowledge, which is necessarily cumulative; and the greatness of the founders of new sciences has never been proof against misjudgments or myths, any more than it has been impaired by them. To take 'liberties' with the signature of Marx is in this sense merely to enter into the freedom of Marxism.

Acknowledgments

I would like to thank Anthony Barnett, Robert Browning, Judith Herrin, Victor Kiernan, Tom Nairn, Brian Pearce and Gareth Stedman Jones for their critical comments on this essay, or its sequel. Given the nature of both, it is more than conventionally necessary to absolve them of any responsibility for the errors, of fact or interpretation, which these contain.

Part One

I. Classical Antiquity

The delimitation of East and West within Europe has long been a conventional one for historians. It goes back, in fact, to the founder of modern positive historiography, Leopold Ranke. The cornerstone of Ranke's first major work, written in 1824, was a 'Sketch of the Unity of the Latin and Germanic Nations', in which he drew a line across the continent excluding the Slavs of the East from the common destiny of the 'great nations' of the West which were to be the subject of his book. 'It cannot be maintained that these peoples too belong to the unity of our nations; their customs and constitution have ever separated them from it. In that epoch they exercised no independent influence, but merely appear subordinate or antagonistic: now and then lapped, so to speak, by the receding waves of the general movements of history.'[1] It was the West alone which had participated in the barbarian migrations, the mediaeval crusades, and the modern colonial conquests – for Ranke, the *drei grosse Atemzüge dieses unvergleichlichen Vereins*, 'the three deep breaths drawn by that incomparable union'.[2] A few years later, Hegel remarked that 'the Slavs have to some extent been drawn within the sphere of Occidental Reason', since 'sometimes, as an advanced guard – an intermediate nationality – they took part in the struggle between Christian Europe and unchristian Asia.' But the substance of his view of the history of the eastern region of the continent was closely similar to that of Ranke. 'Yet this entire body of peoples remains excluded from our consideration, because hitherto it has not appeared as an independent element in the series of phases that

1. Leopold Von Ranke, *Geschichte der Romanischen und Germanischen Völker von 1494 bis 1514*, Leipzig 1885, p. XIX.
2. Ranke, op. cit., p. XXX.

Reason has assumed in the world.'[3] A century and a half later, contemporary historians normally avoid such accents. Ethnic categories have given way to geographical terms: but the distinction itself, and the dating of it from the Dark Ages, remain virtually unaltered. Its application, in other words, starts with the emergence of feudalism, in that historical era when the classical relationship of regions within the Roman Empire – advanced East and backward West – began for the first time to be decisively reversed. This change of signs can be observed in virtually every treatment of the transition from Antiquity to the Middle Ages. Thus, the explanations proposed for the fall of the Empire itself in the most recent and monumental study of the decline of Antiquity, Jones's *Later Roman Empire*, revolve constantly round the structural differences between the East and West within it. The East, with its wealthy and numerous cities, developed economy, small-holding peasantry, relative civic unity and geographical distance from the main brunt of barbarian attacks, survived; the West, with its sparser population and weaker towns, magnate aristocracy and rent-racked peasantry, political anarchy and strategic vulnerability to the Germanic invasions, went under.[4] The end of Antiquity was then sealed by the Arab conquests, which sundered the two shores of the Mediterranean. The Eastern Empire became Byzantium, a political and social system distinct from the rest of the European continent. It was in this new geographical space which emerged in the Dark Ages that the polarity between East and West was to permute its connotation. Bloch pronounced the authoritative judgment that 'from the 8th century onwards there was a sharply demarcated group of societies in Western and Central Europe, whose elements, however diverse, were cemented solidly together by profound resemblances and constant relationships'. It was this region which gave birth to mediaeval Europe: 'The European economy in the Middle Ages – in the sense in which this adjective, borrowed from the old geographical nomenclature of the five "parts of the world", can be used to designate an actual human reality – is that of the Latin and Germanic bloc, edged by a few Celtic islets and Slav fringes, gradually won to a common culture . . . Thus understood, thus

3. G. W. F. Hegel, *The Philosophy of History*, London 1878, p. 363.
4. A. H. M. Jones, *The Later Roman Empire, 282–602*, Oxford 1964, Vol. II, pp. 1026–68.

delimited, Europe is a creation of the early Middle Ages.'[5] Bloch expressly excluded the regions that are today Eastern Europe from his social definition of the continent: 'The greater parts of the Slav East in no way belonged to it . . . It is impossible to consider their economic conditions and those of their Western neighbours together, in the same object of scientific study. Their wholly different social structure and very special path of development forbid such a confusion absolutely: to commit it would be like mixing Europe and Europeanized countries with China or Persia in an economic history of the 19th century.'[6] His successors have respected his injunctions. The formation of Europe, and the germination of feudalism, have generally been confined to the history of the Western half of the continent, excluding the Eastern half from survey. Duby's commanding study of the early feudal economy, which starts in the 9th century, is already entitled: *Rural Economy and Country Life in the Mediaeval West*.[7] The cultural and political forms created by feudalism in the same period – the 'secret revolution of these centuries'[8] – are the main focus of Southern's *The Making of the Middle Ages*. The generality of the title conceals an ellipse, implicitly identifying a specific time with a certain space; the first sentence declares: 'The formation of Western Europe from the late tenth to the early thirteenth century is the subject of this book'.[9] Here, the mediaeval world becomes Western Europe *tout court*. The distinction between East and West is thus reflected in modern historiography right from the outset of the post-classical age. Its origins, in effect, are coeval with those of feudalism itself. Any Marxist study of differential historical development within the continent must thus initially consider the general matrix of European feudalism. Only when this is established, will it be possible to see how far and in what way a divergent history is traceable in its Western and Eastern regions.

5. Marc Bloch, *Mélanges Historiques*, Paris 1963, Vol. I, pp. 123–4.
6. Bloch, op. cit., p. 124.
7. Georges Duby, *L'Economie Rurale et la Vie des Campagnes dans l'Occident Médiéval*, Paris 1962; English translation, London 1968.
8. R. W. Southern, *The Making of the Middle Ages*, London 1953, p. 13.
9. Southern, op. cit., p. 11.

I

The Slave Mode of Production

The genesis of capitalism has been the object of many studies inspired by historical materialism, ever since Marx devoted celebrated chapters of *Capital* to it. The genesis of feudalism, by contrast, has remained largely unstudied within the same tradition: as a distinctive *type of transition* to a new mode of production, it has never been integrated into the general corpus of Marxist theory. Yet, as we shall see, its importance for the global pattern of history is perhaps scarcely less than that of the transition to capitalism. Gibbon's solemn judgement on the fall of Rome and the end of Antiquity emerges, paradoxically, perhaps for the first time in its full truth today: 'a revolution which will ever be remembered, and is still felt by the nations of the Earth.'[1] By contrast with the 'cumulative' character of the advent of capitalism, the genesis of feudalism in Europe derived from a 'catastrophic', convergent collapse of two distinct anterior modes of production, the *recombination* of whose disintegrated elements released the feudal synthesis proper, which therefore always retained a hybrid character. The dual predecessors of the feudal mode of production were, of course, the decomposing slave mode of production on whose foundations the whole enormous edifice of the Roman Empire had once been constructed, and the distended and deformed primitive modes of pro-

1. *The History of the Decline and Fall of the Roman Empire*, Vol. I, 1896 (Bury edition), p. 1. Gibbon repented of this sentence in a manuscript note for a projected revision of his book, restricting its reference to the countries of Europe only, not those of the world. 'Have Asia and Africa, from Japan to Morocco, any feeling or memory of the Roman Empire?', he asked. (Op. cit., p. xxxv). He wrote too soon to see how the rest of the world was indeed to 'feel' the impact of Europe, and with it of the ultimate consequences of the 'revolution' he recorded; neither remote Japan nor adjacent Morocco were to be immune from the history it inaugurated.

duction of the Germanic invaders which survived in their new home-lands, after the barbarian conquests. These two radically distinct worlds had undergone a slow disintegration and creeping interpenetration in the last centuries of Antiquity.

To see how this had come about, it is necessary to look backwards at the original matrix of the whole civilization of the classical world. Graeco-Roman Antiquity had always constituted a universe centred on cities. The splendour and confidence of the early Hellenic *polis* and the later Roman Republic, which dazzled so many subsequent epochs, represented a meridian of urban polity and culture that was never to be equalled for another millenium. Philosophy, science, poetry, history, architecture, sculpture; law, administration, currency, taxation; suffrage, debate, enlistment – all these emerged or developed to levels of unexampled strength and sophistication. Yet at the same time this frieze of city civilization always had something of the effect of a *trompe l'oeil* facade, on its posterity. For behind this urban culture and polity lay no urban *economy* in any way commensurate with it: on the contrary, the material wealth which sustained its intellectual and civic vitality was drawn overwhelmingly from the countryside. The classical world was massively, unalterably rural in its basic quantitative proportions. Agriculture represented throughout its history the absolutely dominant domain of production, invariably furnishing the main fortunes of the cities themselves. The Graeco-Roman towns were never predominantly communities of manufacturers, traders or crafts-men: they were, in origin and principle, urban congeries of land-owners. Every municipal order from democratic Athens to oligarchic Sparta or senatorial Rome, was essentially dominated by agrarian pro-prietors. Their income derived from corn, oil and wine – the three great staples of the Ancient World, produced on estates and farms out-side the perimeter of the physical city itself. Within it, manufactures remained few and rudimentary: the range of normal urban commodities never extended much beyond textiles, pottery, furniture and glass-ware. Technique was simple, demand was limited and transport was exorbitantly expensive. The result was that manufactures in Antiquity characteristically developed not by increasing concentration, as in later epochs, but by decontraction and dispersal, since distance dictated relative costs of production rather than the division of labour. A graphic idea of the comparative weight of the rural and urban economies in the classical world is provided by the respective fiscal revenues yielded by each in the Roman Empire of the 4th century A.D., when city trade was finally subjected to an imperial levy for the first time by Constantine's *collatio lustralis*: income from this duty in the towns never amounted to more than 5 per cent of the land-tax.[2]

Naturally, the statistical distribution of output in the two sectors did not suffice to subtract economic significance from the cities of Antiquity. For in a uniformly agricultural world, the gross profits of urban exchange might be very small: but the net superiority they could yield to any given agrarian economy over any other might still be decisive. The precondition of this distinctive feature of classical civilization was its *coastal* character.[3] Graeco-Roman Antiquity was quintessentially Mediterranean, in its inmost structure. For the inter-local trade which linked it together could only proceed by water: marine transport was the sole viable means of commodity exchange over medium or long distances. The colossal importance of the sea for trade can be judged from the simple fact that it was cheaper in the epoch of Diocletian to ship wheat from Syria to Spain – one end of the Mediterranean to the other – than to cart it 75 miles over land.[4] It is thus no accident that the Aegean zone – a labyrinth of islands, harbours and promontories – should have been the first home of the city-state; that Athens, its greatest exemplar, should have founded its commercial fortunes on shipping; that when Greek colonization spread to the Near East in the Hellenistic epoch, the port of Alexandria should have become the major city of Egypt, first maritime capital in its history; and that eventually Rome in its turn, upstream on the Tiber, should have become a coastal metropolis. Water was the irreplaceable medium of communication and

2. A. H. M. Jones, *The Later Roman Empire*, Vol. I, p. 465. The tax was paid by *negotiatores*, or virtually all those engaged in commercial production of any sort in the towns, merchants and craftsmen alike. Despite its minimal returns, it proved intensely oppressive and unpopular to the urban population, so fragile was the city economy proper.

3. Max Weber was the first scholar to give full emphasis to this fundamental fact, in his two great, forgotten studies, 'Agrarverhältnisse im Altertum' and 'Die Sozialen Gründe des Untergangs der Antiken Kultur'. See *Gesammelte Aufsätze zur Sozial- und Wirtschaftsgeschichte*, Tübingen 1924, pp. 4 ff., 292 ff.

4. Jones, *The Later Roman Empire*, II, pp. 841–2.

trade which rendered possible urban growth of a concentration and sophistication far in advance of the rural interior behind it. The sea was the conductor of the improbable radiance of Antiquity. The specific combination of town and country that defined the classical world was in the last resort only operational because of the lake at the centre of it. The Mediterranean is the only large inland sea on the circumference of the earth: it alone offered marine speed of transport with terrestrial shelter from highest wind or wave, for a major geographical zone. The unique position of classical Antiquity within universal history cannot be separated from this physical privilege.

The Mediterranean, in other words, provided the necessary geographical setting for Ancient civilization. Its historical content and novelty, however, lay in the social foundation of the relationship between town and country within it. The slave mode of production was the decisive invention of the Graeco-Roman world, which provided the ultimate basis both for its accomplishments and its eclipse. The originality of this mode of production must be underlined. Slavery itself had existed in various forms throughout Near Eastern Antiquity (as it was later to do elsewhere in Asia): but it had always been one juridically impure condition – frequently taking the form of debt bondage or penal labour – among other mixed types of servitude, forming merely a very low category in an amorphous continuum of dependence and unfreedom that stretched well up the social scale above it.[5] Nor was it ever the predominant type of surplus extraction in these pre-Hellenic monarchies: it was a residual phenomenon that existed on the edges of the main rural work force. The Sumerian, Babylonian, Assyrian and Egyptian Empires – riverine states built on intensive, irrigated agriculture that contrasted with the light, dry-soil farming of the later Mediterranean world – were not slave economies, and their legal systems lacked any sharply separate conception of chattel property. It was the Greek city-states that first rendered slavery absolute in form and dominant in extent, thereby transforming it from an ancillary facility into a systematic mode of production. The classic Hellenic world never, of course, rested exclusively on the use of slave labour. Free peasants, dependent tenants, and urban artisans always

5. M. I. Finley, 'Between Slavery and Freedom', *Comparative Studies in Society and History*, VI, 1963–4, pp. 237–8.

coexisted with slaves, in varying combinations, in the different city-states of Greece. Their own internal or external development, more-over, could alter the proportions between the two markedly from one century to the next: every concrete social formation is always a specific combination of different modes of production, and those of Antiquity were no exception.[6] But the *dominant* mode of production in classical Greece, which governed the complex articulation of each local economy and gave its imprint to the whole civilization of the city-state, was that of slavery. This was to be true of Rome as well. The Ancient World as a whole was never continuously or ubiquitously marked by the pre-dominance of slave-labour. But its great *classical* epochs, when the civilization of Antiquity flowered – Greece in the 5th and 4th centuries B.C. and Rome from the 2nd century B.C. to the 2nd century A.D. – were those in which slavery was massive and general, amidst other labour systems. The solstice of classical urban culture always also witnessed the zenith of slavery; and the decline of one, in Hellenistic Greece or Christian Rome, was likewise invariably marked by the setting of the other.

The overall proportions of the slave population in the original homelands of the slave mode of production, post-archaic Greece, are not possible to calculate exactly, in the absence of any reliable statistics. The most reputable estimates vary greatly, but a recent assessment is that the ratio of slaves to free citizens in Periclean Athens was about 3 : 2;[7] the relative number of slaves in Chios, Aegina, or Corinth was

6. Throughout this text, the term 'social formation' will generally be preferred to that of 'society'. In Marxist usage, the purport of the concept of social forma-tion is precisely to underline the plurality and *heterogeneity* of possible modes of production within any given historical and social totality. Uncritical repetition of the term 'society', conversely, all too often conveys the assumption of an inherent unity of economy, polity or culture within a historical ensemble, when in fact this simple unity and identity does not exist. Social formations, unless specified otherwise, are thus here always concrete combinations of different modes of production, organized under the *dominance* of one of them. For this distinction, see Nicos Poulantzas, *Pouvoir Politique et Classes Sociales*, Paris 1968, pp. 10–12. Having made this clear, it would be pedantry to avoid the familiar term 'society' altogether, and no attempt will be made to do so here.

7. A. Andrewes, *Greek Society*, London 1967, p. 135, who reckons that the total slave labour-force was in the region of 80–100,000 in the 5th century, when the citizenry numbered perhaps some 45,000. This order of magnitude probably commands a wider consensus than lower or higher estimates. But all modern

at various times probably even larger; while the helot population always greatly outnumbered the citizenry of Sparta. In the 4th century B.C., Aristotle could remark as a matter of course that 'states are bound to contain slaves in large numbers', while Xenophon drew up a scheme to restore the fortunes of Athens by which 'the state would possess public slaves, until there were three for every Athenian citizen'.[8] In classical Greece, slaves were thus for the first time habitually employed in crafts, industry and agriculture beyond the household scale. At the same time, while the use of slavery became general, its *nature* correspondingly became absolute: it was no longer one relative form of servitude among many, along a gradual continuum, but a polar condition of complete loss of freedom, juxtaposed against a new and untrammelled liberty. For it was precisely the formation of a limpidly demarcated slave sub-population that conversely lifted the citizenry of the Greek cities to hitherto unknown heights of conscious juridical freedom. Hellenic liberty and slavery were indivisible: each was the structural condition of the other, in a dyadic system which had no precedent or equivalent in the social hierarchies of the Near Eastern Empires, ignorant alike of either the notion of free citizenship or servile property.[9] This profound juridical change was itself the social and ideological correlate of the economic 'miracle' wrought by the advent of the slave mode of production.

The civilization of classical Antiquity represented, as we have seen, the anomalous supremacy of town over country within an overwhelmingly rural economy: antithesis of the early feudal world which

---

histories of Antiquity are hampered by basic lack of reliable information as to the size of populations and social classes. Jones could compute the proportion of slaves to citizens in the 4th century, when the population of Athens had fallen, at 1:1 on the basis of the city's corn imports: *Athenian Democracy*, Oxford 1957, pp. 76–9. Finley, on the other hand, has argued that it may have been as high as 3 or 4:1 in peak periods of both the 5th and 4th centuries: 'Was Greek Civilization Based on Slave Labour?', *Historia*, VIII, 1959, pp. 58–9. The most comprehensive, if defective, modern monograph on the subject of ancient slavery, W. L. Westermann's *The Slave Systems of Greek and Roman Antiquity*, Philadelphia 1955, p. 9, arrives at something like the same gross figure as that accepted by Andrewes and Finley, of some 60–80,000 slaves at the outset of the Peloponnesian War.

8. Aristotle, *Politics*, VII, iv, 4; Xenophon, *Ways and Means*, IV, 17.

9. Westermann, *The Slave Systems of Greek and Roman Antiquity*, pp. 42–3; Finley, 'Between Slavery and Freedom', pp. 236–9.

succeeded it. The condition of possibility of this metropolitan grandeur in the absence of municipal industry was the existence of slave-labour in the countryside: for it alone could free a landowning class so radically from its rural background that it could be transmuted into an essentially urban citizenry that yet still drew its fundamental wealth from the soil. Aristotle expressed the resultant social ideology of late classical Greece with his casual prescription: 'Those who cultivate the land should ideally be slaves, not all recruited from one people nor spirited in temperament (so as to be industrious in work and immune to rebellion), or as a second best barbarian bondsmen of a similar character.'[10] It was characteristic of the fully developed slave mode of production in the Roman countryside that even management functions were delegated to slave supervisors and bailiffs, putting to work slave gangs in the fields.[11] The slave estate, unlike the feudal manor, permitted a permanent disjuncture between residence and revenue; the surplus product that provided the fortunes of the possessing class could be extracted without its presence on the land. The nexus binding the immediate rural producer to the urban appropriator of his product was not a customary one, and was not mediated through the locality of the land itself (as in later adscriptive serfdom). It was, on the contrary, typically the universal, commercial act of commodity purchase realized in the towns, where the slave trade had its typical markets. The slave labour of classical Antiquity thus embodied two contradictory attributes in whose unity lay the secret of the paradoxical urban precocity of the Graeco-Roman world. On the one hand, slavery represented the most radical rural degradation of labour imaginable – the conversion of men themselves into inert means of production by their deprivation of every social right and their legal assimilation to beasts of burden: in Roman theory, the agricultural slave was designated an *instrumentum vocale*, the speaking tool, one grade away from the livestock that constituted an *instru-*

10. *Politics*, VII, ix, 9.

11. The very ubiquity of slave labour at the height of the Roman Republic and Principate had the paradoxical effect of promoting certain categories of slaves to responsible administrative or professional positions, which in turn facilitated manumission and subsequent integration of the sons of skilled freedmen into the citizen class. This process was not so much a humanitarian palliation of classical slavery, as another index of the radical abstention of the Roman ruling class from any form of productive labour whatever, even of an executive type.

mentum semi-vocale, and two from the implement which was an *instrumentum mutum*. On the other hand, slavery was simultaneously the most drastic urban commercialization of labour conceivable: the reduction of the total person of the labourer to a standard object of sale and purchase, in metropolitan markets of commodity exchange. The destination of the numerical bulk of slaves in classical Antiquity was agrarian labour (this was not so everywhere or always, but was in aggregate the case): their normal assemblage, allocation and dispatch was effected from the marts of the cities, where many of them were also, of course, employed. Slavery was thus the economic hinge that joined town and country together, to the inordinate profit of the *polis*. It both maintained the captive agriculture that permitted the dramatic differentiation of an urban ruling class from its rural origins, and promoted the inter-city trade that was the complement of this agriculture in the Mediterranean. Slaves, among other advantages, were an eminently movable commodity in a world where transport bottlenecks were central to the structure of the whole economy.[12] They could be shifted without difficulty from one region to another; they could be trained in a number of different skills; in epochs of abundant supply, moreover, they acted to keep down costs where hired labourers or independent craftsmen were at work, because of the alternative labour they provided. The wealth and ease of the propertied urban class of classical Antiquity – above all, that of Athens and Rome at their zenith – rested on the broad surplus yielded by the pervasive presence of this labour system, that left none other untouched.

The price paid for this brutal and lucrative device was, nevertheless, a high one. Slave relations of production determined certain insurmountable limits to ancient forces of production, in the classical epoch. Above all, they ultimately tended to paralyze productivity in both agriculture and industry. There were, of course, certain technical improvements in the economy of classical Antiquity. No mode of production is ever devoid of material progress in its ascendant phase, and the slave mode of production in its prime registered certain important advances in the economic equipment deployed within the framework of its new social division of labour. Among them can be accounted the spread of more profitable wine and oil cultures; the

12. Weber, 'Agrarverhältnisse im Altertum', pp. 5–6.

introduction of rotary mills for grain and an amelioration in the quality of bread. Screw-presses were designed, glass-blowing developed and heating-systems refined; combination cropping, botanical knowledge and field drainage probably also advanced.[13] There was thus no simple, terminal halt to technique in the classical world. But at the same time, no major cluster of inventions ever occurred to propel the Ancient economy forward to qualitatively new forces of production. Nothing is more striking, in any comparative retrospect, than the overall technological stagnation of Antiquity.[14] It is enough to contrast the record of its eight centuries of existence from the rise of Athens to the fall of Rome, with the equivalent span of the feudal mode of production which succeeded it, to perceive the difference between a relatively static and dynamic economy. More dramatic still, of course, was the contrast within the classical world itself between its cultural and superstructural vitality and its infrastructural hebetude: the manual technology of Antiquity was exiguous and primitive not merely by the external standards of a posterior history, but above all by the measure of its own intellectual firmament – which in most critical respects always remained far higher than that of the Middle Ages to come. There is little doubt that it was the structure of the slave economy that was fundamentally responsible for this extraordinary disproportion. Aristotle, to later ages the greatest and most representative thinker of Antiquity, tersely summed up its social principle with his dictum: 'The best State will not make a manual worker a citizen, for the bulk of manual labour today is slave or foreign.'[15] Such a State represented the ideal norm of the slave mode of production, nowhere realized in any actual social formation in the Ancient World. But its logic was always immanently present in the nature of the classical economies.

Once manual labour became deeply associated with loss of liberty,

13. See especially F. Kiechle, *Sklavenarbeit und Technischer Fortschritt im römischen Reich*, Wiesbaden 1969, pp. 12–114; L. A. Moritz, *Grain-Mills and Flour in Classical Antiquity*, Oxford 1958; K. D. White, *Roman Farming*, London 1970, pp. 123–4, 147–72, 188–91, 260–1, 452.

14. The general problem is forcibly put, as usual, by Finley, 'Technical Innovation and Economic Progress in the Ancient World', *Economic History Review*, XVIII, No. 1, 1955, pp. 29–45. For the specific record of the Roman Empire, see F. W. Walbank, *The Awful Revolution*, Liverpool 1969, pp. 40–1, 46–7, 108–10.

15. *Politics*, III, iv, 2.

there was no free social rationale for invention. The stifling effects of slavery on technique were not a simple function of the low average productivity of slave-labour itself, or even of the volume of its use: they subtly affected all forms of labour. Marx sought to express the type of action which they exerted in a celebrated, if cryptic theoretical formula: 'In all forms of society it is a determinate production and its relations which assign every other production and its relations their rank and influence. It is a general illumination in which all other colours are plunged and which modifies their specific tonalities. It is a special ether which defines the specific gravity of everything found within it.'[16] Agricultural slaves themselves had notoriously little incentive to perform their economic tasks competently and conscientiously, once surveillance was relaxed; their optimal employment was in compact vine-yards or olive-groves. On the other hand, many slave craftsmen and some slave cultivators were often notably skilled, within the limits of prevailing techniques. The structural constraint of slavery on technology thus lay not so much in a direct intra-economic causality, although this was important in its own right, as in the mediate social ideology which enveloped the totality of manual work in the classical world, contaminating hired and even independent labour with the stigma of debasement.[17] Slave-labour was not in general less productive than free, indeed in some fields it was more so; but it set the pace of both, so that no great divergence ever developed between the two, in a common economic space that excluded the application of culture to technique for inventions. The divorce of material work from the sphere of liberty was so rigorous that the Greeks had no word in their language even to express the concept of labour, either as a social function or as personal conduct. Both agricultural and artisanal work were essentially deemed 'adaptations' to nature, not transformations of it; they were forms of service. Plato too implicitly barred artisans from the *polis* altogether: for him 'labour remains alien to any human value and in certain respects seems even to be the antithesis of what is

16. *Grundrisse der Kritik der Politischen Okonomie*, Berlin 1953, p. 27.

17. Finley points out that the Greek term *penia*, customarily opposed to *ploutos* as 'poverty' to 'wealth', in fact had the wider pejorative meaning of 'drudgery' or 'compulsion to toil', and could cover even prosperous smallholders, whose labour fell under the same cultural shadow: M. I. Finley, *The Ancient Economy*, London 1973, p. 41.

essential to man'.[18] Technique as premeditated, progressive instru-
mentation of the natural world by man was incompatible with wholesale assimilation of men to the natural world as its 'speaking instruments'. Productivity was fixed by the perennial routine of the
instrumentum vocalis, which devalued all labour by precluding any
sustained concern with devices to save it. The typical path of expansion
in Antiquity, for any given state, was thus always a 'lateral' one –
geographical conquest – not economic advance. Classical civilization
was in consequence inherently *colonial* in character: the cellular city-
state invariably reproduced itself, in phases of ascent, by settlement and
war. Plunder, tribute and slaves were the central objects of aggrandisement, both means and ends to colonial expansion. Military power was
more closely locked to economic growth than in perhaps any other
mode of production, before or since, because the main single origin of
slave-labour was normally captured prisoners of war, while the raising
of free urban troops for war depended on the maintenance of production at home by slaves; battle-fields provided the manpower for corn-
fields, and *vice-versa*, captive labourers permitted the creation of citizen
armies. Three great cycles of imperial expansion can be traced in
classical Antiquity, whose successive and variant features structured
the total pattern of the Graeco-Roman world: Athenian, Macedonian
and Roman. Each represented a certain solution to the political and
organizational problems of overseas conquest, which was integrated
and surpassed by the next, without the underlying bases of a common
urban civilization ever being transgressed.

18. J. P. Vernant, *Mythe et Pensée chez les Grecs*, Paris 1965, pp. 192, 197–9,
217. Vernant's two essays, 'Prométhée et la Fonction Technique' and 'Travail et
Nature dans la Grèce Ancienne' provide a subtle analysis of the distinctions
between *poiesis* and *praxis*, and the relations of the cultivator, craftsman and
money-lender to the *polis*. Alexandre Koyré once tried to argue that the technical
stagnation of Greek civilization was not due to the presence of slavery or the
devaluation of labour, but to the absence of physics, rendered impossible by its
inability to apply mathematical measurement to the terrestrial world: 'Du Monde
de l'À Peu Près à l'Univers de la Précision', *Critique*, September 1948, pp. 806–8.
By doing so, he explicitly hoped to avoid a sociological explanation of the
phenomenon. But as he himself implicitly admitted elsewhere, the Middle Ages
equally knew no physics, yet produced a dynamic technology: it was not the
itinerary of science, but the course of the relations of production, which printed
out the fate of technique.

2

Greece

The emergence of the Hellenic city-states in the Aegean zone predates
the classical epoch proper, and only its outlines can be glimpsed from
the unwritten sources available. After the collapse of Mycenean civilization about 1200 B.C., Greece experienced a prolonged 'Dark Age' in which
literacy disappeared and economic and political life regressed to a rudimentary household stage: the primitive and rural world portrayed in
the Homeric epics. It was in the succeeding epoch of Archaic Greece,
from 800 to 500 B.C., that the urban pattern of classical civilization first
slowly crystallized. At some time before the advent of historical
records, local kingships were overthrown by tribal aristocracies, and
cities were founded or developed under the domination of these nobilities. Aristocratic rule in Archaic Greece coincided with the reappear-
ance of long-distance trade (mainly with Syria and the East), the
adumbration of coinage (invented in Lydia in the 7th century), and the
creation of an alphabetic script (derived from Phoenicia). Urbanization
proceeded steadily, spilling out overseas into the Mediterranean and
Euxine, until by the end of the colonization period in the mid 6th
century, there were some 1,500 Greek cities in the Hellenic homelands
and abroad – virtually none of them more than 25 miles inland from
the coastline. These cities were essentially residential nodes of concentration for farmers and landowners: in the typical small town of this
epoch, the cultivators lived within the walls of the city and went out to
work in the fields every day, returning at night – although the territory
of the cities always included an agrarian circumference with a wholly
rural population settled in it. The social organization of these towns
still reflected much of the tribal past from which they had emerged:
their internal structure was articulated by hereditary units whose kin

nomenclature represented an urban translation of traditional rural divisions. Thus the inhabitants of the cities were normally organized – in descending order of size and inclusiveness – into 'tribes', 'phratries' and 'clans'; 'clans' being exclusive aristocratic groups, and 'phratries' perhaps originally their popular clienteles.[1] Little is known of the formal political constitutions of the Greek cities in the Archaic age, since – unlike that of Rome at a comparable stage of development – they did not survive into the classical epoch itself, but it is evident that they were based on the privileged rule of a hereditary nobility over the rest of the urban population, typically exercised through the government of an exclusive aristocratic council over the city.

The rupture of this general order occurred in the last century of the Archaic Age, with the advent of the 'tyrants' (c. 650–510 B.C.). These autocrats broke the dominance of the ancestral aristocracies over the cities: they represented newer landowners and more recent wealth, accumulated during the economic growth of the preceding epoch, and rested their power to a much greater extent on concessions to the unprivileged mass of city-dwellers. The tyrannies of the 6th century, in effect, constituted the critical transition towards the classical *polis*. For it was during their general period of sway that the economic and military foundations of Greek classical civilization were laid. The tyrants were the product of a dual process within the Hellenic cities of the later archaic period. The arrival of coinage and the spread of a money economy were accompanied by a rapid increase in the aggregate population and trade of Greece. The wave of overseas colonization from the 8th to the 6th centuries was the most obvious expression of this development; while the higher productivity of Hellenic wine and olive cultivation, more intensive than contemporary cereal agriculture, perhaps gave Greece a relative advantage in commercial exchanges within the Mediterranean zone.[2] The economic opportunities afforded by this growth created a stratum of newly enriched agrarian proprietors, drawn from outside the ranks of the traditional nobility, and in some cases probably benefiting from auxiliary commercial enterprises. The fresh wealth of this group was not matched by any

1. A. Andrewes, *Greek Society*, London 1967, pp. 76–82.
2. See the arguments in William McNeill, *The Rise of the West*, Chicago 1963, pp. 201, 273.

equivalent power in the city. At the same time, the increase of population and the expansion and disruption of the archaic economy provoked acute social tensions among the poorest class on the land, always most liable to become degraded or subjected to noble estate-owners, and now exposed to new strains and uncertainties.[3] The combined pressure of rural discontent from below and recent fortunes from above forced apart the narrow ring of aristocratic rule in the cities. The characteristic outcome of the resultant political upheavals within the cities was the emergence of the transient tyrannies of the later 7th and 6th centuries. The tyrants themselves were usually comparative upstarts of considerable wealth, whose personal power symbolized the access of the social group from which they were recruited to honours and position within the city. Their victory, however, was generally possible only because of their utilization of the radical grievances of the poor, and their most lasting achievement was the economic reforms in the interests of the popular classes which they had to grant or tolerate to secure their power. The tyrants, in conflict with the traditional nobility, in effect objectively blocked the monopolization of agrarian property that was the ultimate tendency of its unrestricted rule, and which was threatening to cause increasing social distress in Archaic Greece. With the single exception of the landlocked plain of Thessaly, small peasant farms were preserved and consolidated throughout Greece in this epoch. The different forms in which this process occurred have largely to be reconstructed from their later effects, given the lack of documented evidence from the pre-classical period. The first major revolt against aristocratic dominance that led to a successful tyranny, supported by the lower classes, occurred in Corinth in the mid 7th century, where the Bacchiadae family was evicted from its traditional grip over the city, one of the earliest trading centres to flourish in Greece. But it was the Solonic reforms in Athens that furnish the clearest and best recorded example of what was probably something like a general pattern of the time. Solon, not himself a tyrant, was vested with supreme power to mediate the bitter social struggles between the rich

3. W. G. Forrest, *The Emergence of Greek Democracy*, London 1966, pp. 55, 150–6, who emphasizes the new economic growth in the countryside; A. Andrewes, *The Greek Tyrants*, London 1956, pp. 80–1, who stresses the social depression of the small farmer class.

and the poor which erupted in Attica at the turn of the 6th century. His decisive measure was to abolish debt bondage on the land, the typical mechanism whereby small-holders fell prey to large landowners and became their dependent tenants, or tenants became captives of aristocratic proprietors.[4] The result was to check the growth of noble estates and to stabilize the pattern of small and medium farms that henceforward characterized the countryside of Attica.

This economic order was accompanied by a new political dispensation. Solon deprived the nobility of its monopoly of office by dividing the population of Athens into four income classes, according the top two rights to the senior magistracies, the third access to lower administrative positions, and the fourth and last a vote in the Assembly of the citizenry, which henceforward became a regular institution of the city. This settlement was not destined to last. In the next thirty years, Athens experienced swift commercial growth, with the creation of a city currency and the multiplication of local trade. Social conflicts within the citizenry were rapidly renewed and aggravated, culminating in the seizure of power by the tyrant Peisistratus. It was under this ruler that the final shape of the Athenian social formation emerged. Peisistratus sponsored a building programme which provided employment for urban craftsmen and labourers, and presided over a flourishing development of marine traffic out of the Piraeus. But above all, he provided direct financial assistance to the Athenian peasantry, in the form of public credits which finally clinched their autonomy and security on the eve of the classical *polis*.[5] The staunch survival of small and medium farmers was assured. This economic process – whose inverse non-occurence was later to define the contrasting social history of Rome – seems to have been common throughout Greece, although the events behind it are nowhere so documented outside Athens. Elsewhere, the average size of rural holdings might sometimes be bigger, but only in Thessaly did large aristocratic estates predominate. The

4. It is uncertain whether the poor peasantry in Attica were tenants or owners of their farms before Solon's reforms. Andrewes argues that they may have been the former (*Greek Society*, pp. 106–7), but subsequent generations had no memory of an actual redistribution of land by Solon, so this seems improbable.

5. M. I. Finley, *The Ancient Greeks*, London 1963, p. 33, regards Peisistratus's policies as more important for the economic independence of the Attic peasantry than Solon's reforms.

economic basis of Hellenic citizenry was to be modest agrarian property. Approximately concomitant with this social settlement in the age of the tyrannies, there was a significant change in the military organization of the cities. Armies were henceforward composed essentially of hoplites, heavily armoured infantry which were a Greek innovation in the Mediterranean world. Each hoplite equipped himself with weaponry and armour at his own expense: such a soldiery thus presupposed a reasonable economic livelihood, and in fact hoplite troops were always drawn from the medium farmer class of the cities. Their military efficacy was to be proved by the startling Greek victories over the Persians in the next century. But it was their pivotal position within the political structure of the city-states that was ultimately most important. The precondition of later Greek 'democracy' or extended 'oligarchy' was a self-armed citizen infantry.

Sparta was the first city-state to embody the social results of hoplite warfare. Its evolution forms a curious pendant to that of Athens in the pre-classical epoch. For Sparta did not experience a tyranny, and its omission of this normal transitional episode lent a peculiar character to its economic and political institutions thereafter, blending advanced and archaic features in a *sui generis* mould. The city of Sparta at an early date conquered a relatively large hinterland in the Peloponnese, first in Laconia to the east and then in Messenia to the west, and enslaved the bulk of the inhabitants of both regions, who became state 'helots'. This geographical aggrandisement and social subjection of the surrounding population was achieved under monarchic rule. In the course of the 7th century, however, after either the initial conquest of Messenia or the subsequent repression of a Messenian rebellion, and as a consequence, certain radical changes in Spartan society occurred – traditionally attributed to the mythical figure of the reformer Lycurgus. According to Greek legend, the land was divided up into equal portions, which was distributed to the Spartans as *kleroi* or allotments, tilled by helots who were collectively owned by the State; these 'ancient' holdings were later reputed to be inalienable, while more recent tracts of land were deemed personal property that could be bought or sold.[6] Each citizen had to pay fixed subscriptions in kind to commensal

6. The reality of an original land division, or even a later inalienability of the *kleroi*, has been doubted: for example, see A. H. M. Jones, *Sparta*, Oxford 1967,

syssitia, served by helot cooks and waiters: those who became unable to do so automatically lost citizenship and became 'inferiors', a misfortune against which the possession of inalienable lots may have been purposefully designed. The upshot of this system was to create an intense collective unity among the Spartiates, who proudly designated themselves *hoi homoioi* – the 'Equals', although complete economic equality was never at any time a feature of the actual Spartan citizenry.[7]

The political system which emerged on the basis of the *kleroi* farms was a correspondingly novel one for its time. Monarchy never entirely disappeared, as it did in the other Greek cities, but it was reduced to a hereditary generalship and restricted by a dual incumbency, vested in two royal families.[8] In all other respects, the Spartan 'kings' were merely members of the aristocracy, participants without special privileges in the thirty-man council of elders or *gerousia* which originally ruled the city; the typical conflict between monarchy and nobility in the early archaic age was here resolved by an institutional compromise between the two. During the 7th century, however, the rank-and-file citizenry came to constitute a full city Assembly, with rights of decision over policies submitted to it by the council of elders, which itself became an elective body; while five annual magistrates or ephors henceforward wielded supreme executive authority, by direct election from the whole citizenry. The Assembly could be over-ruled by a veto of the *gerousia*, and the ephors were endowed with an exceptional concentration of arbitrary power. But the Spartan Constitution which thus crystallized in the pre-classical epoch was nevertheless the most socially advanced of its time. It represented, in effect, the first hoplite franchise to be achieved in Greece.[9] Its introduction is often, indeed, dated from the role of the new heavy infantry in conquering or crushing the Messenian subject population; and Sparta was thereafter, of course, always famed for the matchless discipline and prowess of its

---

pp. 40–3. Andrewes, although cautious, accords more credit to Greek beliefs: *Greek Society*, pp. 94–5.

7. The size of the *kleroi* which underpinned Spartan social solidarity has been much debated, with estimates varying from 20 to 90 acres of arable: see P. Oliva, *Sparta and Her Social Problems*, Amsterdam-Prague 1971, pp. 51–2.

8. For the structure of the constitution, see Jones, *Sparta*, pp. 13–43.

9. Andrewes, *The Greek Tyrants*, pp. 75–6.

hoplite soldiery. The unique military qualities of the Spartiates, in their turn, were a function of the ubiquitous helot labour which relieved the citizenry of any direct role in production at all, allowing it to train professionally for war on a full-time basis. The result was to produce a body of perhaps some 8–9,000 Spartan citizens, economically self-sufficient and politically enfranchised, which was far wider and more egalitarian than any contemporary aristocracy or later oligarchy in Greece. The extreme conservatism of the Spartan social formation and political system in the classical epoch, which made it appear backward and retarded by the 5th century, was in fact the product of the very success of its pioneering transformations in the 7th century. The earliest Greek state to achieve a hoplite constitution, it became the last ever to modify it: the primal pattern of the archaic age survived down to the very eve of Sparta's final extinction, half a millennium later.

Elsewhere, as we have seen, the city-states of Greece were slower to evolve towards their classical form. The tyrannies were usually necessary intermediate phases of development: it was their agrarian legislation or military innovations which prepared the Hellenic *polis* of the 5th century. But one further and completely decisive innovation was necessary for the advent of classical Greek civilization. This was, of course, the introduction on a massive scale of chattel slavery. The conservation of small and medium property on the land had solved a mounting social crisis in Attica and elsewhere. But by itself it would have tended to arrest the political and cultural development of Greek civilization at a 'Boeotian' level, by preventing the growth of a more complex social division of labour and urban superstructure. Relatively egalitarian peasant communities could congregate physically in towns; they could never in their simple state create a luminous city-civilization of the type that Antiquity was now for the first time to witness. For this, generalized and captive surplus labour was necessary, to emancipate their ruling stratum for the construction of a new civic and intellectual world. 'In the broadest terms, slavery was basic to Greek civilization in the sense that, to abolish it and substitute free labour, if it had occurred to anyone to try this, would have dislocated the whole society and done away with the leisure of the upper classes in Athens and Sparta.'[10]

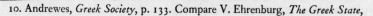

10. Andrewes, *Greek Society*, p. 133. Compare V. Ehrenburg, *The Greek State*,

Thus it was not fortuitous that the salvation of the independent peasantry and the cancellation of debt bondage were promptly followed by a novel and steep increase in the use of slave-labour, both in the towns and countryside of classical Greece. For once the extremes of social polarization were blocked within the Hellenic communities, recourse to slave imports was logical to solve labour shortages for the dominant class. The price of slaves – mostly Thracians, Phrygians and Syrians – was extremely low, not much more than the cost of a year's upkeep;[11] and so their employment became generalized throughout native Greek society, until even the humblest artisans or small farmers might often possess them. This economic development, too, had first been anticipated in Sparta; for it was the previous creation of mass rural helotry in Laconia and Messenia that had permitted the bonded fraternity of the Spartiates to emerge, the first major slave population of pre-classical Greece and the first hoplite franchise. But here as elsewhere, early Spartan priority arrested further evolution: helotry remained an 'undeveloped form' of slavery,[12] since helots could not be bought, sold or manumitted, and were collective rather than individual property. Full commodity slavery, governed by market exchange, was ushered into Greece in the city-states that were to be its rivals. By the 5th century, the apogee of the classical *polis*, Athens, Corinth, Aegina and virtually every other city of importance contained a voluminous slave population, frequently outnumbering the free citizenry. It was the establishment of this slave economy – in mining, agriculture and crafts – which permitted the sudden florescence of Greek urban civilization. Naturally, its impact – as was seen above – was not simply economic. 'Slavery, of course, was not merely an economic necessity, it was vital to the whole social and political life of the citizenry'.[13] The classical *polis* was based on the new conceptual discovery of liberty, entrained by the systematic institution of slavery: the free citizen now stood out in full relief, against the background of

London 1969, p. 96: 'Without metics or slaves, the *polis* could hardly have existed at all'.

11. Andrewes, *Greek Society*, p. 135.

12. Oliva, *Sparta and Her Social Problems*, pp. 43–4. Helots also possessed their own families, and were on occasion used for military duties.

13. Victor Ehrenburg, *The Greek State*, p. 97.

slave labourers. The first 'democratic' institutions in classical Greece are recorded in Chios, during the mid 6th century: it was also Chios that tradition held to be the first Greek city to import slaves on a large scale from the barbarian East.[14] In Athens, the reforms of Solon had been succeeded by a sharp increase in the slave population in the epoch of the tyranny; and this in turn was followed by a new constitution devised by Cleisthenes, which abolished the traditional tribal divisions of the population with their facilities for aristocratic clientage, reorganized the citizenry into local territorial 'demes', and instituted balloting by lot for an expanded Council of Five Hundred to preside over the affairs of the city, in combination with the popular Assembly. The 5th century saw the generalization of this 'probouleutic' political formula in the Greek city-states: a smaller Council proposed public decisions to a larger Assembly that voted on them, without rights of initiative (although in more popular states, the Assembly was later to gain these). The variations in the composition of the Council and Assembly, and in the election of the magistrates of the State who conducted its administration, defined the relative degree of 'democracy' or 'oligarchy' within each *polis*. The Spartan system, dominated by an authoritarian ephorate, was notoriously antipodal to the Athenian, which came to be centred in the full Assembly of citizens. But the essential line of demarcation did not pass within the constituent citizenry of the *polis*, however it was organized or stratified: it divided the citizenry – whether the 8,000 Spartiates or 45,000 Athenians – from the non-citizens and unfree beneath them. The community of the classical *polis*, no matter how internally class-divided, was erected above an enslaved work-force which underlay its whole shape and substance.

These city-states of classical Greece were engaged in constant rivalry and aggression against each other: their typical path of expansion, after the colonization process had come to an end in the late 6th century, was military conquest and tribute. With the expulsion of Persian forces from Greece in the early 5th century, Athens gradually achieved preeminent power among the competing cities of the Aegean basin. The Athenian Empire that was built up in the generation from Themistocles to Pericles appeared to contain the promise, or threat, of the political unification of Greece under the rule of a single *polis*. Its

14. Finley, *The Ancient Greeks*, p. 36.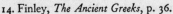

material basis was provided by the peculiar profile and situation of Athens itself, territorially and demographically the largest Hellenic city-state – although only some 1,000 square miles in extent and perhaps 250,000 in population. The Attic agrarian system exemplified the general pattern of the time, perhaps in a particularly pronounced form. By Hellenic standards, big landed property was an estate of 100–200 acres.[15] In Attica, there were few large estates, even wealthy landowners possessing a number of small farms rather than concentrated latifundia. Holdings of 70 or even 45 acres were above average, while the smallest plots were probably not much more than 5 acres; three-quarters of the free citizenry owned some rural property down to the end of the 5th century.[16] Slaves provided domestic service, field labour – where they typically tilled the home farms of the rich – and artisanal work; they were probably outnumbered by free labour in agriculture and perhaps in the crafts, but constituted a much larger group than the total citizenry. In the 5th century, there were perhaps some 80,000–100,000 slaves in Athens, to some 30–40,000 citizens.[17] A third of the free population lived in the city itself. Most of the rest were settled in villages in the immediate hinterland. The bulk of the citizenry were formed by the 'hoplite' and 'thete' classes, in respective proportions of perhaps 1:2, the latter being the poorest section of the population, which was incapable of equipping itself for heavy infantry duty. The division between hoplites and thetes was technically one of income, not occupation or residence: hoplites might be urban craftsmen, while perhaps half the thetes were poor peasants. Above these two rank-and-file classes were two much smaller orders of richer citizens, the elite of which formed an apex of some 300 wealthy families at the summit of Athenian society.[18] This social structure, with its acknowledged stratification but absence of dramatic crevasses within the citizen body, provided the foundation of Athenian political democracy.

By the mid 5th century, the Council of Five Hundred which supervised the administration of Athens was selected from the whole citizenry by sortition, to avoid the dangers of autocratic predominance

15. Forrest, *The Emergence of Greek Democracy*, p. 46.

16. M. I. Finley, *Studies in Land and Credit in Ancient Athens 500–200 B.C.*, New Brunswick, pp. 58–9.

17. Westermann, *The Slave Systems of Greek and Roman Antiquity*, p. 9.

18. A. H. M. Jones, *Athenian Democracy*, Oxford 1957, pp. 79–91.

and clientage associated with elections. The only major elective posts in the State were ten military generalships, which accordingly went as a rule to the upper stratum of the city. The Council no longer presented controversial resolutions to the Assembly of Citizenry, which by now concentrated full sovereignty and political initiative within itself, merely preparing its agenda and submitting key issues for its decision. The Assembly itself held a minimum of 40 sessions a year, at which average attendance was probably well over 5,000 citizens: a quorum of 6,000 was necessary for deliberations on even many routine matters. All important political questions were directly debated and determined by it. The judicial system which flanked the legislative centre of the *polis* was composed of jurors selected by lot from the citizenry and paid for their duties, to enable the poor to serve, as were councillors; a principle extended in the 4th century to attendance at the Assembly itself. There was virtually no permanent officialdom whatever, administrative positions being distributed by sortition among councillors, while the diminutive police-force was composed of Scythian slaves. In practice, of course, the direct popular democracy of the Athenian constitution was diluted by the informal dominance of professional politicians over the Assembly, recruited from traditionally wealthy and well-born families in the city (or later from the newly rich). But this social dominance never became legally entrenched or solidified, and was always liable to upsets and challenges because of the demotic nature or the polity in which it had to be exercised. The contradiction between the two was basic to the structure of the Athenian *polis*, and found striking reflection in the unanimous condemnation of the city's unprecedented democracy by the thinkers who incarnated its unexampled culture – Thucydides, Socrates, Plato, Aristotle, Isocrates, or Xenophon. Athens never produced any democratic political theory: virtually all Attic philosophers or historians of note were oligarchic by conviction.[19] Aristotle condensed the quintessence of their outlook in his brief and pregnant proscription of all manual workers from the citizenry of the ideal State.[20] The slave mode of production which

19. Jones, *Athenian Democracy*, pp. 41–72, documents this divergence, but fails to see its implications for the structure of Athenian civilization as a whole, contenting himself with defending the democracy of the *polis* against the thinkers of the city.

20. Politics, III, iv, 2, cited above.

underlay Athenian civilization necessarily found its most pristine ideological expression in the privileged social stratum of the city, whose intellectual heights its surplus labour in the silent depths below the *polis* made possible.

The structure of the Athenian social formation, thus constituted, was not in itself sufficient to generate its imperial primacy in Greece. For this, two further and specific features of the Athenian economy and society, which set it apart from any other Hellenic city-state of the 5th century, were necessary. Firstly, Attica contained the richest silver mines in Greece, at Laureion. Worked mainly by massed gangs of slaves – some 30,000 or so – it was the ore of these mines that financed the construction of the Athenian fleet which triumphed over the Persian ships at Salamis. Athenian silver was from the beginning the condition of Athenian naval power. Moreover, it made possible an Attic currency which – alone among Greek coinages of the time – became widely accepted abroad, as a medium of interlocal trade, contributing greatly to the commercial prosperity of the city. This was further enhanced by the exceptional concentration of 'metic' foreigners in Athens, who were debarred from landownership but came to dominate trading and industrial enterprise in the city, making it the focal point of the Aegean. The maritime hegemony which thus accrued to Athens bore a functional relation to the political complexion of the city. The hoplite class of medium farmers which provided the infantry of the *polis* numbered some 13,000 – a third of the citizenry. The Athenian fleet, however, was manned by sailors recruited from the poorer class of thetes below them; rowers were paid money wages, and were on service eight months a year. Their numbers were virtually equal to those of the foot-soldiers (12,000), and it was their presence which helped to ensure the democratic breadth of the Athenian polity, in contrast to those Greek city-states where the hoplite category alone provided the social basis of the *polis*.[21] It was the monetary and naval superiority of Athens which gave the edge to its imperialism; as it was also these which fostered its democracy. The citizenry of the city was largely exempt

21. Tradition held that it was the sailors' victory at Salamis that had rendered the demands of the thetes for political rights irresistible, much as the soldiers' campaigns against Messenia had once probably gained the Spartan hoplites their franchise.

from any form of direct taxation: in particular, ownership of land –
which was legally confined to citizens – bore no fiscal burden whatever,
a critical condition of peasant autonomy within the *polis*. Athenian
public revenues at home were derived from state property, indirect
taxes (such as harbour dues), and obligatory financial 'liturgies'
offered to the city by the wealthy. This clement fiscality was comple-
mented by public pay for jury service and ample naval employment, a
combination which helped to ensure the notable degree of civic peace
which marked Athenian political life.[22] The economic costs of this
popular harmony were displaced into Athenian expansion abroad.

The Athenian Empire which emerged in the wake of the Persian
Wars was essentially a marine system, designed for the coercive subjugation of the Greek city-states of the Aegean. Settlement proper
played a secondary if by no means negligible role in its structure. It is
significant that Athens was the only Greek state to create a special class
of overseas citizens or 'cleruchs', who were given colonial lands
confiscated from rebellious allies abroad and yet – unlike all other
Hellenic colonists – retained full juridical rights in the mother city
itself. The steady plantation of cleruchies and colonies overseas in the
course of the 5th century enabled the city to promote more than 10,000
Athenians from thete to hoplite condition, by endowment of lands
abroad, thereby greatly strengthening its military power at the same
stroke. The brunt of Athenian imperialism, however, did not lie with
these settlements. The ascent of Athenian power in the Aegean created
a political order whose real function was to coordinate and exploit
already urbanized coasts and islands, by a system of monetary tribute
levied for the maintenance of a permanent navy, nominally the common defender of Greek liberty against Oriental menaces, in fact the
central instrument of imperial oppression by Athens over its 'allies'.
In 454 the central treasury of the Delian League, originally created to
fight Persia, had been transferred to Athens; in 450, Athenian refusal
to permit the dissolution of the League after peace with Persia converted it into a *de facto* Empire. At its height in the 440's, the Athenian
imperial system embraced some 150 – mainly Ionian – cities, which
paid an annual cash sum to the central treasury in Athens, and were

22. M. I. Finley, *Democracy Ancient and Modern*, London 1973, pp. 45, 48–9;
see also his remarks in *The Ancient Economy*, pp. 96, 173.

prevented from keeping fleets themselves. The total tribute from the Empire was actually reckoned to be 50 per cent larger than Attic internal revenues, and undoubtedly financed the civic and cultural superabundance of the Periclean *polis*.[23] At home, the navy for which it paid provided stable employment for the most numerous and least well-off class of citizens, and the public works which it funded were the most signal embellishments of the city, among them the Parthenon. Abroad, Athenian squadrons policed Aegean waters, while political residents, military commanders and itinerant commissioners ensured docile magistracies in the subject states. Athenian courts exercised powers of judicial repression over citizens of allied cities suspected of disloyalty.[24]

But the limits of Athenian external power were soon reached. It probably stimulated trade and manufactures in the Aegean, where use of Attic coinage was extended by decree and piracy was suppressed, although the major profits from commercial growth accrued to the metic community in Athens itself. The imperial system also enjoyed the sympathy of the poorer classes of the allied cities, because Athenian tutelage generally meant the installation of democratic regimes locally, congruent with those of the imperial city itself, while the financial burden of tribute fell on the upper classes.[25] But it was incapable of achieving an institutional inclusion of these allies into a unified political system. Athenian citizenship was so wide at home that it was impracticable ever to extend it abroad to non-Athenians, for to do so would have functionally contradicted the direct residential democracy of the mass Assembly, only feasible within a very small geographical compass. Thus, despite the popular overtones of Athenian rule, the 'democratic' domestic foundation of Periclean imperialism necessarily generated 'dictatorial' exploitation of its Ionian allies, who inevitably tended to be thrust rapaciously downwards into colonial servitude: there was no

23. R. Meiggs, *The Athenian Empire*, Oxford 1972, pp. 152, 258–60.
24. Meiggs, *The Athenian Empire*, pp. 171–4, 205–7, 215–16, 220–33.
25. This sympathy is convincingly demonstrated by G. E. M. De Ste Croix, 'The Character of the Athenian Empire', *Historia*, Bd. III, 1954–5, pp. 1–41. There were some oligarchic allies in the Delian League – Mytilene, Chios or Samos – and Athens did not intervene systematically in its constituent cities; but local conflicts were typically used as opportunities for the forcible establishment of popular systems.

basis for equality or federation, such as a more oligarchic constitution might have permitted. At the same time, however, the democratic nature of the Athenian *polis* – whose principle was direct participation, not representation – precluded the creation of a bureaucratic machinery that could have held down an extended territorial empire by administrative coercion. There was scarcely any separate or professional State apparatus in the city, whose political structure was essentially defined by its rejection of specialized bodies of officials – civilian or military – apart from the ordinary citizenry: Athenian democracy signified, precisely, the refusal of any such division between 'state' and 'society'.[26] There was thus no basis for an imperial bureaucracy either. Athenian expansionism consequently broke down relatively soon, both because of the contradictions of its own structure, and because of the resistance, thereby facilitated to it, from the more oligarchic cities of mainland Greece, led by Sparta. The Spartan League possessed the converse advantages of Athenian liabilities: a confederation of oligarchies, whose strength was based squarely on hoplite proprietors rather than an admixture with demotic sailors, and whose unity did not therefore involve either monetary tribute or a military monopoly by the hegemon city of Sparta itself, whose power was therefore always intrinsically less of a threat to the other Greek cities than that of Athens. The lack of any substantial hinterland rendered Athenian military power – both in recruitment and resources – too thin to resist a coalition of terrestrial rivals.[27] The Peloponnesian War joined the attack of its peers to the revolt of its subjects, whose propertied classes rallied to the mainland oligarchies once it had started. Even so, however, Persian gold was

26. For Ehrenburg, this was its great weakness. The identity of State and Society was necessarily a contradiction, because the state had to be single while society always remained plural, because divided into classes. Hence either the State could reproduce these social divisions (oligarchy) or society could absorb the state (democracy): neither solution respected an institutional distinction that was for him unalterable, and hence both bore the seed of destruction within them: *The Greek State*, p. 89. It was, of course, for Marx and Engels just in this structural refusal that the greatness of Athenian democracy lay.

27. In general, the lines of division between 'oligarchy' and 'democracy' correlated fairly closely with maritime vs. mainland orientations in classical Greece; the same seaward factors which obtained in Athens were present in its Ionian zone of influence, while most of Sparta's allies in the Peloponnese and Boeotia were more narrowly rooted in the soil. The main exception, of course, was Corinth, the traditional commercial rival of Athens.

necessary to finance a Spartan fleet capable of ending Athenian mastery of the sea, before the Athenian Empire was finally broken on land by Lysander. Thereafter there was no chance of the Hellenic cities generating a unified imperial state from within their midst, despite their relatively rapid economic recovery from the effects of the long Peloponnesian war: the very parity and multiplicity of urban centres in Greece neutralized them collectively for external expansion. The Greek cities of the 4th century sank into exhaustion, as the classical *polis* experienced increasing difficulties of finance and conscription, symptoms of impending anachronism.

3

The Hellenistic World

The second major cycle of colonial conquest thus derived from the rural northern periphery of Greek civilization, with its greater demographic and peasant reserves. The Macedonian Empire was in origin a tribal monarchy of the mountainous interior, a backward zone which had preserved many of the social relations of post-Mycenaean Greece. The Macedonian royal state, precisely because it was morphologically much more primitive than the city-states of the South, was not subject to their impasse and so proved able to overleap their limits in the new epoch of their decline. Its territorial and political basis permitted an integrated international expansion, once it was allied to the far more developed civilization of Greece proper. Macedonian kingship was hereditary, yet subject to confirmation by a military assembly of the warriors of the realm. All land was technically the property of the monarch, but in practice a tribal nobility held estates from and claimed kinship with him, forming an entourage of royal 'companions' which provided his counsellors and governors. The majority of the population were free tenant peasants, and there was relatively little slavery.[1] Urbanization was minimal, the capital of Pella itself a recent and slender foundation. The ascent of Macedonian power in the Balkans in the reign of Philip II acquired an early and decisive thrust with the annexation of the Thracian gold mines – the bullion equivalent of the Attic silver mines in the previous century – which provided Macedonia with the indispensable finance for external aggression.[2] The success of

1. N. G. L. Hammond, *A History of Greece to 322 B.C.*, Oxford 1959, pp. 535–6.

2. The income yielded by the Thracian gold mines was greater than that of the Laureion silver mines in Attica; Arnaldo Momigliano, *Filippo Il Macedone*, Florence 1934, pp. 49–53 – the most lucid study of the early phase of Macedonian expansion, which in general has attracted comparatively little modern research.

Philip's armies in over-running the Greek city-states and unifying the Hellenic peninsula was essentially due to its military innovations, which reflected the distinct social composition of the tribal interior of Northern Greece. Cavalry – an aristocratic arm always previously subordinated to hoplites in Greece – was renovated and linked elastically to infantry, while infantry shed some of its heavy hoplite armour for greater mobility and the massed use of the long lance in battle. The result was the famous Macedonian phalanx, flanked by horse, victorious from Thebes to Kabul. Macedonian expansion, of course, was not merely due to the skills of its commanders and soldiers, or its initial access to precious metals. The precondition of its eruption into Asia was its prior absorption of Greece itself. The Macedonian monarchy consolidated its advances in the peninsula by creating new citizens from Greeks and others in the conquered regions, and urbanizing its own rural hinterland – demonstrating its capacity for extended territorial administration. It was the political and cultural impetus it acquired from the integration of the most advanced city centres of the epoch that then enabled it to accomplish in a few years the lightning conquest of the whole of the Near East, under Alexander. Symbolically, the irreplaceable fleet which transported and supplied the invincible troops in Asia was always Greek. The unitary Macedonian Empire which emerged after Gaugamela, stretching from the Adriatic to the Indian Ocean, did not survive Alexander himself, who died before any coherent institutional framework could be given to it. The social and administrative problems it posed could already be glimpsed from his attempts to fuse Macedonian and Persian nobilities by official intermarriage: but it was left to his successors to provide solutions to them. The internecine struggles of these contending Macedonian generals – the Diadochi – ended with the partition of the Empire into four main zones, Mesopotamia, Egypt, Asia Minor and Greece, the first three henceforward generally outclassing the last in political and economic importance. The Seleucid dynasty ruled Syria and Mesopotamia; Ptolemy founded the Lagid realm in Egypt; and half a century later, the Attalid kingdom of Pergamum became the dominant power in Western Asia Minor. Hellenistic civilization was essentially the product of these new Greek monarchies of the East.

The Hellenistic States were hybrid creations, which nevertheless shaped the whole historical pattern of the Eastern Mediterranean for centuries thereafter. On the one hand, they presided over the most imposing surge of city-foundations that hitherto seen in classical Antiquity: major Greek cities sprang up, by spontaneous initiative or royal patronage, throughout the Near East, making it henceforward the most densely urbanized region of the Ancient World, and durably hellenizing the local ruling classes everywhere they were planted.[3] If the number of these foundations was less than that of Archaic Greek colonization, their size was infinitely greater. The largest city of classical Greece was Athens, with a total population of some 80,000 in the 5th century B.C. The three greatest urban centres of the Hellenistic world – Alexandria, Antioch and Seleucia – may have had up to of 500,000 inhabitants. The distribution of the new foundations was uneven, since the centralized Lagid State in Egypt was suspicious of any *polis* autonomy and did not sponsor many new cities, while the Seleucid State actively multiplied them, and in Asia Minor the local gentry created its own cities in imitation of Hellenic example elsewhere.[4] Everywhere, these new urban foundations were settled with Greek and Macedonian soldiers, administrators, and merchants, who arrived to furnish the dominant social stratum in the epigone monarchies of the Diadochi. The proliferation of Greek cities in the East was accompanied by an upswing of international trade and commercial prosperity. Alexander had dethesaurized Persian royal bullion, releasing accumulated Achaemenid hoards into the exchange system of the Near East, and thereby financing a steep increase in the volume of market transactions in the Mediterranean. The Attic monetary standard was now generalized throughout the Hellenistic world, with the exception of Ptolemaic Egypt, facilitating international trade and shipping.[5] The triangular sea-way between Rhodes, Antioch and Alexandria became the axis of the new mercantile space created by the Hellenistic East.

3. The majority of the new cities were created from below, by the local land-owners; but the largest and most important were, of course, official foundations of the new Macedonian rulers. A. H. M. Jones, *The Greek City from Alexander to Justinian*, Oxford 1940, pp. 27–50.

4. For the contrast between Lagid and Seleucid policies, see M. Rostovtsev, *The Social and Economic History of the Hellenistic World*, Oxford 1941, Vol. I, pp. 476 ff.

5. F. M. Heichelheim, *An Ancient Economic History*, Vol. III, Leyden 1970, p. 10.

Banking was developed to levels of sophistication never later surpassed in Antiquity, by the Lagid administration in Egypt. The urban
pattern of the Eastern Mediterranean was thus successfully set by
Greek emigration and example.

Yet at the same time, the anterior Near Eastern social formations –
with their very different economic and political traditions – imper-
viously resisted Greek patterns in the countryside. Thus slave-labour
notably failed to spread to the rural interior of the Hellenistic East.
Contrary to popular legend, the Alexandrine campaigns had not been
accompanied by mass enslavements, and the proportion of the slave
population does not seem to have risen appreciably in the path of
Macedonian conquests.[6] Agrarian relations of production were consequently left relatively unaffected by Greek rule. The traditional agricultural systems of the great riverine cultures of the Near East had
combined landlords, dependent tenants and peasant proprietors with
ultimate or immediate royal property of the soil. Rural slavery had
never been economically very important. Regal claims to a monopoly
of land were centuries old. The new Hellenistic States inherited this
pattern, quite alien to that of the Greek homelands, and preserved it
with little alteration. The main variations between them concerned the
degree to which royal property over the land was actually enforced by
the dynasties of each realm. The Lagid State in Egypt – the wealthiest
and most rigidly centralized of the new monarchies – exacted its claims
to a legal monopoly of land, outside the boundaries of the few *poleis*,
to the full. The Lagid rulers leased out virtually all land in small plots
on short-term leases to a miserable peasantry, rack-rented directly by
the State, without any security of tenure and subject to forced labour
for irrigation works.[7] The Seleucid dynasty in Mesopotamia and Syria,
which presided over a much larger and more rambling territorial
complex, never attempted such a rigorous control of agrarian exploitation. Royal lands were granted to nobles or administrators in the
provinces, and autonomous villages of peasant proprietors were

6. Westermann, *The Slave Systems of Greek and Roman Antiquity*, pp. 28–31.
7. For descriptions of this system, see Rostovtsev, *The Social and Economic History of the Hellenistic World*, Vol. I, pp. 274–300; there is an analytic survey of the various forms of labour usage in Lagid Egypt in K. K. Zel'in, M. K. Trofimova, *Formy Zavisimosti v Vostochnom Sredizemnomor'e Ellenisticheskovo Perioda*, Moscow 1969, pp. 57–102.

tolerated, side by side with the dependent *laoi* tenants who formed the bulk of the rural population. Significantly, it was only in Attalid Pergamum, the most westerly of the new Hellenistic States, which lay immediately across the Aegean from Greece itself, that agricultural slave-labour was used on royal and aristocratic estates.[8] The geographical limits of the mode of production pioneered in classical Greece were those of the adjacent regions of Asia Minor.

If the towns were Greek in model, while the countryside remained Oriental in pattern, the structure of the States which integrated the two was inevitably syncretic, a mixture of Hellenic and Asian forms in which the secular legacy of the latter was unmistakeably predominant. The Hellenistic rulers inherited the overwhelmingly autocratic traditions of the riverine civilizations of the Near East. The Diadochi monarchs enjoyed unlimited personal power, as had their Oriental predecessors before them. Indeed, the new Greek dynasties introduced an ideological surcharge on the pre-existent weight of royal authority in the region, with the establishment of officially decreed worship of rulers. The divinity of kings had never been a doctrine of the Persian Empire which Alexander had overthrown: it was a Macedonian innovation, first instituted by Ptolemy in Egypt, where age-long cult of the Pharaohs had existed prior to Persian absorption, and which therefore naturally provided fecund soil for ruler-worship. The divinization of monarchs soon became a general ideological norm throughout the Hellenistic world. The typical administrative mould of the new royal States revealed a similar development – a fundamentally Oriental structure refined by Greek improvements. The leading military and civilian personnel of the State were recruited from Macedonian or Greek emigrants, and their descendants. There was no attempt to achieve an ethnic fusion with the indigenous aristocracies of the type that Alexander had briefly envisaged.[9] A considerable bureaucracy –

8. Rostovtsev, *The Social and Economic History of the Hellenistic World*, Vol. II, pp. 806, 1106, 1158, 1161. Slaves were also widely employed in the royal mines and industries of Pergamum. Rostovtsev thought that there continued to be an abundance of slaves in the Greek homelands themselves during the Hellenistic epoch (op. cit. pp. 625–6, 1127).

9. Alexander's own cosmopolitanism has often been exaggerated, on slender evidence; for an effective critique of the claims made for it, see E. Badian, 'Alexander the Great and the Unity of Mankind', in G. T. Griffith, *Alexander the Great; the Main Problems*, Cambridge 1966, pp. 287–306.

the imperial instrument that classical Greece had so completely lacked –
was created, often with ambitious administrative tasks allocated to it
– above all in Lagid Egypt, where management of much of the whole
rural and urban economy devolved on it. The Seleucid realm was
always more loosely integrated, and its administration comprised a
larger proportion of non-Greeks than the Attalid or Lagid bureaucracies;[10] it was also more military in character, as befitted its far-flung
extent, by contrast with the scribal functionaries of Pergamum or
Egypt. But in all these States, the existence of centralized royal
bureaucracies was accompanied by the absence of any developed legal
systems to stabilize or universalize their functions. No impersonal law
could emerge where the arbitrary will of the ruler was the sole source
of all public decisions. Hellenistic administration in the Near East never
achieved unitary legal codes, merely improvizing with coexistent
systems of Greek and local provenance, all subject to the personal
interference of the monarch.[11] By the same token, the bureaucratic
machinery of the State was itself condemned to a formless and random
summit of the 'king's friends', the shifting group of courtiers and commanders who made up the immediate entourage of the ruler. The
ultimate amorphousness of Hellenistic state-systems was reflected in
their lack of any territorial appellations: they were simply the lands of
the dynasty that exploited them, which provided their only designation.

In these conditions, there could be no question of genuine political
independence for the cities of the Hellenistic East: the days of the
classical *polis* were now long past. The municipal liberties of the Greek
cities of the East were not negligible, compared with the despotic outer
framework into which they were inserted. But these new foundations
were lodged in an environment very dissimilar to that of their homelands, and consequently never acquired the autonomy or vitality of
their originals. The countryside below and the State above them
formed a milieu which checked their dynamic and adapted them to the
secular ways of the region. Their fate is perhaps best exemplified by
Alexandria, which became the new maritime capital of Lagid Egypt,

10. Iranians may have outnumbered Greeks and Macedonians in the Seleucid
State institutions, in fact; C. Bradford Welles, *Alexander and the Hellenistic
World*, Toronto 1970, p. 87.

11. P. Petit, *La Civilisation Hellénistique*, Paris 1962, p. 9; V. Ehrenburg, *The
Greek State*, pp. 214–17.

and within a few generations the greatest and most flourishing Greek city in the Ancient World: the economic and intellectual pivot of the Eastern Mediterranean. But the wealth and culture of Alexandria under its Ptolemaic rulers was gained at a price. No free citizenry could emerge amidst a countryside peopled by dependent peasant *laoi*, or a kingdom dominated by an omnipresent royal bureaucracy. Even in the city itself, financial and industrial activities – once the domain of metics in classical Athens – were not correspondingly released by the disappearance of the old *polis* structure. For most of the main urban manufactures – oil, textiles, papyrus, or beer – were royal monopolies. Taxes were farmed to private entrepreneurs, but under strict State control. The characteristic conceptual polarization of liberty and slavery, which had defined the cities of the classical Greek epoch, was thus fundamentally absent from Alexandria. Suggestively, the Lagid capital was simultaneously the scene of the most fecund episode in the history of Ancient technology: the Alexandrine Museum was the progenitor of most of the few significant innovations of the classical world, and its pensionary Ctesibius one of the rare notable inventors of Antiquity. But even here, the main royal motive in founding the Museum and promoting its research, was the quest for military and engineering improvements, not economic or labour-saving devices, and most of its work reflected this characteristic emphasis. The Hellenistic Empires – eclectic compounds of Greek and Oriental forms – extended the space of the urban civilization of classical Antiquity by diluting its substance, but by the same token they were unable to surmount its indigenous limits.[12] From 200 B.C. onwards, Roman imperial power was advancing eastwards at their expense, and by the

12. The syncretism of the Hellenistic States scarcely warrants the dithyrambs of Heichelheim, for whom they represent 'miracles of economic and administrative organization' whose unconscionable destruction by a barbarian Rome arrested history for the next millennium and a half. See *An Ancient Economic History*, Vol. III, pp. 185–6, 206–7. Rostovtsev is somewhat more temperate, but he too ventured the judgment that Roman conquest of the Eastern Mediterranean was a regrettable disaster which disintegrated and 'de-hellenized' it, while 'unnaturally' compromising the integrity of Roman civilization itself: *The Social and Economic History of the Hellenistic World*, Vol. II, pp. 70–3. The remote ancestry of such attitudes goes back, of course, as far as Winckelmann and the Graecian cult of the German Enlightenment, when they were of some intellectual importance.

middle of the 2nd century its legions had trampled down all serious barriers of resistance in the East. Symbolically, Pergamum was the first Hellenistic realm to be incorporated into the new Roman Empire, when its last Attalid ruler disposed of it in his will as a personal bequest to the Eternal City.

4

Rome

The rise of Rome marked a new cycle of urban-imperial expansion, which represented not just a geographical shift in the centre of gravity of the Ancient world to Italy, but a socio-economic development of the mode of production which had been pioneered in Greece that rendered possible a far greater and more lasting dynamism than that which had produced the Hellenistic epoch. The early growth of the Roman Republic followed the normal course of any ascendant classical city-state: local wars with rival cities, annexation of land, subjection of 'allies', foundation of colonies. In one critical respect, however, Roman expansionism distinguished itself at the outset from Greek experience. The constitutional evolution of the city conserved aristocratic political power right down and into the classical phase of its urban civilization. Archaic monarchy was overthrown by a nobility in the earliest epoch of its existence, at the end of the 6th century B.C., in a change strictly comparable to the Hellenic pattern. But thereafter, unlike the Greek cities, Rome never knew the upheaval of tyrant rule, breaking aristocratic dominance and leading to a subsequent democratization of the city, based on a secure small and medium agriculture. Instead a hereditary nobility kept unbroken power through an extremely complex civic constitution, which underwent important popular modifications through the course of a prolonged and fierce social struggle within the city, but was never abrogated or replaced. The Republic was dominated by the Senate, which was controlled for the first two centuries of its existence by a small group of patrician clans; membership of the Senate, which was cooptive, was for life. Annual magistrates, of which the two highest were consuls, were elected by 'assemblies of the people', comprising the whole citizenry of Rome, but organized into unequal 'centuriate' units weighted to ensure a majority of the propertied classes. The consulates were the supreme executive offices of the State, and was legally monopolized by the closed order of patricians down to 366 B.C.

This original structure embodied the political dominion of the traditional aristocracy pure and simple. It was subsequently altered and qualified in two important respects, after successive struggles which provide the nearest Roman equivalent of the Greek phases of 'tyranny' and 'democracy', but which each time fell decisively short of the comparable outcome in Greece Firstly, recently enriched 'plebeians' forced the 'patrician' nobility to concede access to one of the two annual consular offices from 366 B.C. onwards; although it was not until nearly two hundred years later, in 172 B.C., that both consuls were for the first time plebeians. This slow change led to a broadening of the composition of the Senate itself, since former consuls automatically became senators. The result was the social formation of a widened nobility, including both 'patrician' and 'plebeian' families, rather than the political overthrow of the system of aristocratic rule itself, such as had occurred during the age of tyrants in Greece. Chronologically and sociologically overlapping this contest within the wealthiest strata of the Republic, was the struggle of the poorer classes to gain increased rights within it. Their pressure early resulted in the creation of the tribunate of the plebs, a corporate representation of the popular mass of the citizenry. The tribunes were elected each year by a 'tribal' assembly which, unlike the 'centuriate' assembly, was in principle genuinely egalitarian: the 'tribes' were actually, as in Archaic Greece, territorial rather than kin divisions of the population, four in the city itself and seventeen outside it (an indication of the degree of urbanization at that date). The tribunate formed a secondary and parallel executive agency, designed to protect the poor from the oppression of the rich. Eventually, in the early 3rd century, the tribal assemblies which elected the tribunes gained legislative powers, and the tribunes themselves nominal rights of veto over the acts of the consuls and the decrees of the Senate.

The direction of this evolution corresponded to the process that had led to the democratic *polis* in Greece. But here too, the process was arrested before it could impend a new political constitution for the city.

The tribunate and tribal assembly were simply added to the central existing institutions of the Senate, Consulates and Centuriate Assembly: they did not signify an internal abolition of the oligarchic complex of power which guided the Republic, but external accretions to it, whose practical significance was often much less than their formal potential. For the struggle of the poorer classes had generally been led by wealthy plebeians, who championed the popular cause to further their own parvenu interests: and this continued to be true even after the newly rich had gained access to the ranks of the senatorial order itself. The tribunes, normally men of considerable fortunes, thus became for long periods docile instruments of the Senate itself.[1] Aristocratic supremacy within the Republic was not seriously shaken. A plutocracy of wealth now merely enlarged a nobility of birth, both using extensive 'clientage' systems to ensure a deferent following among the urban masses, and lavish customary bribes to secure election to the annual magistracies through the centuriate assembly. The Roman Republic thus retained traditional oligarchic rule, through a composite constitution, down to the classical epoch of its history.

The resultant social structure of the Roman citizenry was thus inevitably distinct from that which had been typical of classical Greece. The patrician nobility had early on striven to concentrate landed property in its hands, reducing the poorer free peasantry to debt bondage (as in Greece), and appropriating the *ager publicus* or common lands which they used for pasturage and cultivation. The tendency to abase the peasantry by debt bondage to the condition of dependent tenants was checked, although the problem of debts themselves persisted:[2] but the expropriation of the *ager publicus* and the depression of

1. P. A. Brunt, *Social Conflicts in the Roman Republic*, London 1971, pp. 58, 66–7. This short work is a masterly survey of the class struggles of the Republic, in the light of modern historical research.

2. Brunt, *Social Conflicts in the Roman Republic*, pp. 55–7. The legal institution of debt bondage – the *nexum* – was abolished in 326 B.C. Brunt perhaps minimizes the consequences of this abolition a shade, in his emphasis on the fact that the *nexum* could be later revived in other, informal versions. The history of the Roman social formation would certainly have been very different if a juridically dependent peasantry had been consolidated under a landlord class, during the Republic. In the event, rural indebtedness led to concentration of agrarian property in the hands of the nobility, but not to a tied labour force at its disposal. Slavery was to provide the manpower for its estates, producing a very distinct social configuration.

medium and small farmers was not. There was no economic or political upheaval to stabilize the rural property of the ordinary citizenry of Rome, comparable to that which had occurred in Athens or, in a different way, Sparta. When the Gracchi eventually attempted to follow the path of Solon and Peisistratus, it was too late: by then, the 2nd century B.C., much more radical measures than those enacted in Athens were necessary to save the situation of the poor – nothing less than a redistribution of land, demanded by both Gracchi brothers – with correspondingly less chance of them ever being implemented over aristocratic opposition. In fact, no durable or substantial agrarian reform ever occurred in the Republic, despite constant agitation and turbulence over the question in the final epoch of its existence. The political dominance of the nobility blocked all efforts to reverse the relentless social polarization of property on the land. The result was a steady erosion of the modest farmer class that had provided the backbone of the Greek polis. The Roman equivalent of the hoplite category – men who could equip themselves with armour and weaponry necessary for infantry service in the legions – were the *assidui* or 'those settled on the land', who possessed the necessary property qualification to bear their own arms. Below them were the *proletarii*, propertyless citizens, whose service to the State was merely to rear children (*proles*). The increasing monopolization of land by the aristocracy was thus translated into a steady decline in the numbers of the *assidui*, and an inexorable increase in the size of the *proletarii* class. Moreover, Roman military expansionism also tended to thin the ranks of the *assidui* who provided the conscripts and casualties for the armies with which it was conducted. The result was that by the end of the 3rd century B.C., the *proletarii* were probably already an absolute majority of citizens, and had to be themselves called up to deal with the emergency of Hannibal's invasion of Italy; while the property qualification for the *assidui* was twice reduced, until in the next century it had sunk below a subsistence minimum on the land.[3]

Small-holders never disappeared generally or completely in Italy;

3. Brunt, *Social Conflicts in the Roman Republic*, pp. 13–14. Even after Marius had done away with the property qualifications for conscription, however, the legions remained overwhelmingly rural in composition. Brunt: 'The Army and the Land in the Roman Revolution', *The Journal of Roman Studies*, 1962, p. 74.

but they were increasingly driven into the more remote and precarious recesses of the country, in marshy or mountainous regions unappealing to engrossing landowners. The structure of the Roman polity in the Republican epoch thus came to diverge sharply from any Greek precedent. For while the countryside became chequered with large noble domains, the city conversely became populated with a proletarianized mass, deprived of land or any other property. Once fully urbanized, this large and desperate underclass lost any will to return to a small-holder condition, and could often be manipulated by aristocratic cliques against projects for agrarian reform backed by the *assidui* farmers.[4] Its strategic position in the capital of an expanding empire ultimately obliged the Roman ruling class to pacify its immediate material interests with public grain distributions. These were, in effect, a cheap substitute for the land distribution which never occurred: a passive and consumer proletariat was preferable to a recalcitrant and producer peasantry, for the senatorial oligarchy which controlled the Republic.

It is now possible to consider the implications of this configuration for the specific course of Roman expansionism. For the growth of Roman civic power was consequently distinguished from Greek examples in two fundamental respects, both related directly to the internal structure of the city. Firstly, Rome proved able to widen its own political system to include the Italian cities it subjugated in the course of its peninsular expansion. From the start, it had – unlike Athens – exacted troops for its armies, not money for its treasury, from its allies; thereby lightening the burden of its domination in peace, and binding them solidly to it in time of war. In this, it followed the example of Sparta, although its central military control of allied troops was always much greater. But Rome was also able to achieve an ultimate integration of these allies into its own polity which no Greek city had ever envisaged. It was the peculiar social structure of Rome which

4. Tiberius Gracchus, tribunal champion of a Lex Agraria, denounced the impoverishment of the small-holders: 'The men who fight and die for Italy share the air and light, but nothing else . . . They fight and perish to support others in wealth and luxury, and although they are styled the masters of the world, have not a single clod of earth that is their own'. (Plutarch, *Tiberius and Caius Gracchus*, IX, 5). Idol of the small peasantry, he was lynched by an urban mob inflamed against him by senatorial patrons.

permitted this. Even the most oligarchic Greek *polis* of the classical epoch basically rested on a median body of propertied citizens, and precluded extreme economic disparities of wealth and poverty within the city. The political authoritarianiam of Sparta – the exemplar of Hellenic oligarchy – did not mean a class polarization within the citizenry: in fact, as we have seen, it was accompanied by marked economic egalitarianism in the classical epoch, probably including allocation of inalienable state holdings to each Spartiate precisely to ensure hoplites against the type of 'proletarianization' which overtook them in Rome.[5] The classical Greek *polis*, whatever its degree of relative democracy and oligarchy, retained a civic unity rooted in the rural property of its immediate locality: it was for the same reason territorially inelastic – incapable of an extension without loss of identity. The Roman Constitution, by contrast, was not merely oligarchic in form: it was much more deeply aristocratic in content, because behind it lay an economic stratification of Roman society of quite another order. It was this which rendered possible an extension of Republican citizenship outwards to comparable ruling classes in the allied cities of Italy, who were socially

5. The decline of Sparta after the Peloponnesian War was accompanied, conversely, by a dramatically widened economic gulf between wealthy and impoverished citizens, amidst demographic contraction and political demoralization. But the traditions of martial equality remained so fierce and deep that in the 2nd century B.C., Sparta gave birth to the astonishing episodes of the radical kings Agis II, Cleomenes III and – above all – Nabis, at the very close of its history. Nabis's social programme for the revival of Sparta included the exile of nobles, abolition of the ephorate, enfranchisement of local subjects, emancipation of slaves and distribution of confiscated lands to the poor: probably the most coherent and far-reaching set of revolutionary measures ever formulated in Antiquity. This last explosion of Hellenic political vitality is too often tucked away as an aberrant or marginal postscript to classical Greece: in fact, it casts a revealing retrospective light on the nature of the Spartan polity at its height. In one of the most dramatic confrontations of Antiquity, at the exact point of intersection between the eclipse of Greece and the ascent of Rome, Nabis confronted Quinctus Flaminnius – commanding the armies sent to stamp out the example of Spartan subversion – with these pregnant words: 'Do not demand that Sparta conform to your own laws and institutions . . . You select your cavalry and infantry by their property qualifications and desire that a few should excel in wealth and the common people be subject to them. Our law-giver did not want the state to be in the hands of a few, whom you call the Senate, nor that any one class should have supremacy in the State. He believed that by equality of fortune and dignity there would be many to bear arms for their country.' Livy, *Histories*, XXXIV, xxxi, 17–18.

akin to the Roman nobility itself, and had benefited from Roman conquests overseas. The Italian cities finally revolted against Rome in 91 B.C., when their demand for the Roman franchise was refused – something no Athenian or Spartan ally had ever requested. Even then, their war aim was a peninsular Italian state with a capital and Senate, in avowed imitation of the unitary Roman order itself, rather than any return to scattered municipal independence.[6] The Italian rebellion was militarily defeated in the long and bitter struggle of the so-called Social War. But amidst the subsequent turmoil of the Civil Wars between the Marian and Sullan factions within the Republic, the Senate could concede the basic political programme of the allies, because the character of the Roman governing class and its Constitution facilitated a viable extension of citizenship to the other Italian cities, ruled by an urban gentry similar in character to the Senatorial class itself, with the wealth and leisure to participate in the political system of the Republic, even from a distance. The Italian gentry by no means consummated its political aspirations for central office within the Roman State immediately, and its ulterior ambitions after the grant of citizenship were to be a powerful force for social transformations at a later date. But their civic integration nevertheless represented a decisive step for the future structure of the Roman Empire as a whole. The relative institutional flexibility which it demonstrated gave Rome a signal advantage in its imperial ascent: it meant an avoidance of either of the two poles between which Greek expansion had divided and foundered – premature and impotent closure of the city-state or meteoric royal triumphalism at the expense of it. The political formula of Republican Rome marked a notable advance in comparative efficacy.

Yet the decisive innovation of Roman expansion was ultimately economic: it was the introduction of the large-scale slave *latifundium* for the first time in Antiquity. Greek agriculture had, as we have seen, employed slaves widely; but it was itself confined to small areas, with a meagre population, for Greek civilization always remained precariously coastal and insular in character. Moreover, and above all, the

6. P. A. Brunt, 'Italian Aims at the Time of the Social War', *The Journal of Roman Studies*, 1965, pp. 90–109. Brunt believes that the century of peace in Italy after the defeat of Hannibal was one of the reasons which convinced the allies of the advantages of political unity.

slave-tilled farms of Attica or Messenia were usually of very modest size – perhaps an average of some 30 to 60 acres, at most. This rural pattern was, of course, linked to the social structure of the Greek *polis*, with its absence of huge concentrations of wealth. Hellenistic civilization had, by contrast, witnessed enormous accumulations of landed property in the hands of dynasties and nobles, but no widespread agricultural slavery. It was the Roman Republic which first united large agrarian property with gang-slavery in the countryside on a major scale. The advent of slavery as an organized mode of production inaugurated, as it had in Greece, the classical phase proper of Roman civilization, the apogee of its power and culture. But whereas in Greece it had coincided with the stabilization of small farms and a compact citizen corps, in Rome it was systematized by an urban aristocracy which already enjoyed social and economic dominion over the city. The result was the new rural institution of the extensive slave *latifundium*. The manpower for the enormous holdings which emerged from the late 3rd century onwards was supplied by the spectacular series of campaigns which won Rome its mastery of the Mediterranean world: the Punic, Macedonian, Jugurthine, Mithridatic and Gallic wars, which poured military captives into Italy to the profit of the Roman ruling class. At the same time, successive ferocious struggles fought on the soil of the peninsula itself – the Hannibalic, Social and Civil Wars – delivered into the grasp of the senatorial oligarchy or its victorious factions large territories expropriated from the defeated victims of these conflicts, especially in Southern Italy.[7] Moreover, these same external and internal wars dramatically accentuated the decline of the Roman peasantry, which had once formed the robust small-holder base of the city's social pyramid. Constant warfare involved endless mobilization; the *assidui* citizenry called to the legions year after year died in thousands under their standards, while those who survived them were unable to maintain their farms at home, which were increasingly absorbed by the nobility. From 200 to 167 B.C., 10 per cent or more of all free Roman adult males were permanently conscripted: this gigantic military effort was only possible because the civilian economy behind it could be manned to such an extent by slave-labour, releasing corresponding

7. Where the two most irreconcilable foes of Rome, during both the Hannibalic and Social Wars, the Samnites and Lucanians, were concentrated.

manpower reserves for the armies of the Republic.[8] Victorious wars in their turn provided more slave-captives to pump back into the towns and estates of Italy.

The final outcome was the emergence of slave-worked agrarian properties of a hitherto unknown immensity. Prominent nobles like Lucius Domitius Ahenobarbus could own over 200,000 acres in the 1st century B.C. These latifundia represented a new social phenomenon, which transformed the Italian countryside. They did not, of course, necessarily or invariably form consolidated blocks of land, farmed as single units.[9] The typical pattern was for the latifundist to possess a large number of medium-sized *villa* estates, sometimes contiguous but perhaps equally often distributed across the country, designed for optimal surveillance by various bailiffs and agents. Even such dispersed holdings, however, were notably larger than their Greek predecessors, often exceeding 300 acres (500 *iugera*) in extent; while consolidated estates like the Younger Pliny's seat in Tuscany might be 3,000 acres or more in size.[10] The rise of the Italian latifundia led to a great extension of pastoral ranching, and the inter-cropping of wine and olives with cereal cultivation. The influx of slave-labour was so

8. P. A. Brunt, *Italian Manpower 225 B.C.–A.D. 14*, Oxford 1971, p. 426.

9. This was true throughout the Empire too, even after concentrated blocks of land grouped into *massae* became more frequent. Failure to understand this fundamental aspect of Roman latifundism has been relatively common. A recent example is the major Russian study of the later Empire: E. M. Shtaerman, *Kriẓis Rabovladel'cheskoro Stroya v Zapadnykh Provintsiyakh Rimskoi Imperii*, Moscow 1957. Shtaerman's whole analysis of the social history of the 3rd century rests on an unreal counterposition of the medium *villa* and the extensive *latifundium*, the former being designated the 'ancient form of property' and identified with the municipal oligarchies of the epoch, the latter becoming a 'proto-feudal' phenomenon, characteristic of an extra-municipal aristocracy. See *Kriẓis Rabovladel'-cheskovo Stroya*, pp. 34–45, 116–17. In fact, *latifundia* were always mainly composed of *villae*, and 'municipal' limitations on landed property were never of great importance; while conversely the extra-territorial *saltus* estates outside municipal boundaries were probably always a negligible proportion of imperial territory as a whole. (For the latter, on which Shtaerman lays exaggerated emphasis, see Jones, *The Later Roman Empire*, II, pp. 712–13).

10. See K. D. White, 'Latifundia', *Bulletin of the Institute of Classical Studies*, 1967, No. 14, pp. 76–7. White emphasizes that latifundia could be either large-scale mixed farms, like Pliny's Tuscan estate, or stock-breeding ranches. The latter were most frequent in Southern Italy, the former in the more fertile lands of the Centre and North.

great that by the late Republic, not only was Italian agriculture recast
by it, but trade and industry were overwhelmingly invaded by it too:
perhaps 90 per cent of the artisans in Rome itself were of slave origin.[11]
The nature of the gigantic social upheaval that Roman imperial expansion involved, and the basic motor-force that sustained it, can be seen
from the sheer demographic transformation that it wrought. Brunt
estimates that in 225 B.C. there were some 4,400,000 free persons in
Italy, to 600,000 slaves; by 43 B.C., there were perhaps 4,500,000 free
to 3,000,000 slave inhabitans – indeed there may actually have been a
net decline in the total size of the free population, while the slave
population quintupled.[12] Nothing like this had ever been seen in the
Ancient World before. The full potential of the slave mode of production was the first time unfolded by Rome, which organized and took it
to a logical conclusion that Greece had never experienced. The
predatory militarism of the Roman Republic was its main lever of
economic accumulation. War brought lands, tributes and slaves; slaves,
tribute and lands supplied the *materiél* for war.

But the historical significance of the Roman conquests in the
Mediterranean basin was, of course, by no means reducible simply to
the spectacular fortunes of the senatorial oligarchy. The march of the
legions accomplished a change much deeper than this, for the whole
history of Antiquity. Roman power integrated the Western Mediterranean and its northern hinterlands into the classical world. This was
the decisive achievement of the Republic, which in contrast with its
diplomatic caution in the East, from the outset unleashed its annexa-
tionist drive essentially in the West. Greek colonial expansion in the
Eastern Mediterranean, as has been seen, took the form of a proliferation of urban foundations, first created from above by the Macedonian
rulers themselves, then soon imitated from below by the local gentry
of the region; and it occurred in a zone with an extremely long prior
history of developed civilization, stretching back much further than
that of Greece itself. Roman colonial expansion in the Western Mediter-

11. Brunt, *Social Conflicts in the Roman Republic*, pp. 34–5.

12. Brunt, *Italian Manpower*, pp. 121–5, 131. For the enormous scale of the
treasure looted abroad by the Roman ruling class, apart from the accumulation of
slaves, see A. H. M. Jones, 'Rome', *Troisieme Conference International d'Histoire
Economique* (Munich 1965), 3, Paris 1970, pp. 81–2 – a paper on the economic
character of Roman imperialism.

ranean differed basically in both context and character. Spain and Gaul – later Noricum, Rhaetia and Britain – were remote and primitive lands peopled by Celtic tribal communities – many with no history of contact at all with the classical world. Their integration into it posed problems of an altogether different order from that of the Hellenization of the Near East. For not only were they socially and culturally backward: they also represented interior land-masses of a type that classical Antiquity had hitherto never been able to organize economically. The original matrix of the city-state was the narrow littoral and the sea, and classical Greece had never relinquished it. The Hellenistic epoch had seen the intensive urbanization of the riparian cultures of the Near East, long based on fluvial irrigation and now partly reoriented towards the sea (a modification symbolized by the shift from Memphis to Alexandria). But the desert lay close behind the whole Southern and Eastern coast-line of the Mediterranean, so that the depth of settlement was never very great either in the Levant or North Africa. The Western Mediterranean, however, offered neither a littoral nor an irrigative system to the advancing Roman frontiers. Here, for the first time, classical Antiquity was confronted with great interior land-masses, devoid of previous urban civilization. It was the Roman city-state, that had developed the rural slave-latifundium, that proved capable of mastering them. The river-routes of Spain or Gaul assisted this penetration. But the irresistible impetus which carried the legions to the Tagus, the Loire, the Thames and the Rhine, was that of the slave mode of production fully unleashed on the land, without constrictions or impediments. It was in this epoch that probably the major single advance in the agrarian technology of classical Antiquity was registered: the discovery of the rotary mill for grinding corn, which in its two main forms was first attested in Italy and Spain in the mid-2nd century B.C.,[13] concomitant with Roman expansion in the Western Mediterranean, and sign of its rural dynamism. The successful organization of large-scale agrarian production by slave-labour was the precondition of the permanent conquest and colonization of the great Western and Northern hinterlands. Spain and Gaul remained, with Italy, the Roman provinces most deeply marked by slavery down to the final

13. L. A. Moritz, *Grain-Mills and Flour in Classical Antiquity*, Oxford 1958, pp. 74, 105, 115–16.

end of the Empire.[14] Greek trade had permeated the East: Latin agriculture 'opened up' the West. Naturally, towns were founded by the Romans in the Western Mediterranean too, characteristically built along the banks of navigable rivers. The creation of a slave-worked rural economy itself depended on the implantation of a prosperous network of cities which represented the terminal points for its surplus produce, and its structural principle of articulation and control. Cordoba, Lyon, Amiens, Trier and hundreds of other towns were constructed. Their number never equalled that of the much older and more densely populated Eastern Mediterranean society, but it was far larger than that of the cities founded by Rome in the East.

For Roman expansion into the Hellenistic zone followed a very different course from its pattern in the Celtic backlands of the West. It was for a long time much more hesitant and uncertain, oriented towards blocking interventions to check major disruptions of the existing state system (Philip V, Antiochus III), and creating client realms rather than conquered provinces.[15] Thus it was characteristic than even after the rout of the last great Seleucid army at Magnesia in 198, no Eastern territory was annexed for another fifty years; and it was not until 129 B.C. that Pergamum passed peacefully into Roman administration, by the testament of its loyal monarch rather than by a senatorial volition, to become the first Asian province of the Empire. Thereafter, once the immense riches available in the East were fully realized in Rome, and army commanders gained escalating imperial powers abroad, aggression became more rapid and systematic, in the

14. Jones, 'Slavery in the Ancient World', pp. 196, 198. Jones later tended to subtract Gaul, confining the zones of high-density slavery to Spain and Italy: *The Later Roman Empire*, II, pp. 793–4. But in fact there are good reasons for sustaining his original judgment. Southern Gaul was noted for its closeness to Italy in social and economic structure from the early Imperial period onwards: Pliny regarded it as virtually an extension of the peninsula – *Italia verius quam provincia*, 'more Italy than a province'. The assumption of slave latifundia in the Narbonensis thus seems a safe one. Northern Gaul, in contrast, was much more primitive and less urbanized in character. But it was precisely there – in the Loire region – that the great Bacaudae rebellions were to break out in the later Empire, expressly described by contemporary accounts as risings of rural slaves: see note 82 below. It seems plausible that Gaul as a whole should therefore be aligned with Spain and Italy as a major region of slave agriculture.

15. E. Badian, *Roman Imperialism in the Late Republic*, Oxford 1968, pp. 2–12, contrasts Roman policies in the East and West very sharply.

1st century B.C. But the Republican regimes generally administered the profitable Asian provinces which their generals now seized from their Hellenistic rulers, with a minimum of social change or political interference, professing to have 'liberated' them from their royal despots, and contenting themselves with the lush tax returns of the region, There was no widespread introduction of agrarian slavery in the Eastern Mediterranean; the numerous war prisoners enslaved there were shipped westwards for employment in Italy itself. Royal estates were appropriated by Roman administrators and adventurers, but their labour systems were left effectively intact. The main innovation of Roman rule in the East occurred in the Greek cities throughout the region, where property qualifications were now imposed for municipal office – to align them more closely with the oligarchic norms of the Eternal City itself; in practice, this merely gave juridical codification to the *de facto* power of the local notabilities who dominated these towns already.[16] A few specifically Roman urban colonies were created in the East by Caesar and Augustus, to settle Latin proletarians and veterans in Asia. But these left very little mark. Significantly, when a new wave of cities were built under the Principate (above all, in the Antonine epoch), they were essentially Greek foundations, consonant with the previous cultural character of the region. There was never any attempt to Romanize the Eastern provinces; it was the West which underwent the full brunt of Latinization. The language frontier – running from Illyricum to Cyrenaica – demarcated the two basic zones of the new imperial order.

The Roman conquest of the Mediterranean in the last two centuries of the Republic, and the massive expansion of the senatorial economy which it promoted, was accompanied at home by a superstructural development without precedent in the Ancient world. For it was in this period that Roman civil law emerged in all its unity and singularity. Gradually developed from 300 B.C. onwards, the Roman legal system became essentially concerned with regulation of informal relationships of contract and exchange between private citizens. Its fundamental orientation lay in economic transactions – purchase, sale, hire, lease, inheritance, security – and their familial concomitants – matrimonial or testamentary. The public relationship of the citizen to the State, and

16. Jones, *The Greek Cities from Alexander to Justinian*, pp. 51–8, 160.

the patriarchal relationship of the head of the family to his dependants, were marginal to the central development of legal theory and practice; the first was considered too mutable to be subject to systematic jurisprudence, while the second covered most of the inferior domain of crime.[17] The real thrust of Republican jurisprudence was concerned with neither of these: it was not public or criminal law, but civil law governing suits between disputing parties over property, that formed the peculiar province of its remarkable advance. The development of a general legal theory as such was wholly new in Antiquity. It was the creation, not of State functionaries or of practising lawyers, but of specialized and aristocratic jurists who remained outside the process of litigation itself, furnishing opinions to the judiciary in actual court-cases only on questions of legal principle rather than matters of fact. Republican jurists, who had no official status, evolved a series of abstract 'contractual figures' applicable to the analysis of particular acts of commercial and social intercourse. Their intellectual bent was analytic rather than systematic, but the cumulative result of their work was the appearance, for the first time in history, of an organized body of civil jurisprudence as such. The economic growth of commodity exchange in Italy attendant on the construction of the Roman imperial system, founded on the extensive use of slavery, thus found its juridical reflection in the creation of an unexampled commercial law in the later Republic. The great, decisive accomplishment of the new Roman law was thus, appropriately enough, its invention of the concept of 'absolute property' – dominium ex jure Quiritium.[18] No prior legal system had ever known the notion of an unqualified private property: ownership in Greece, Persia or Egypt had always been 'relative', in other words conditional on superior or collaterial rights of other authorities and parties, or obligations to them. It was Roman jurisprudence that for the first time emancipated private ownership from

17. For a clear discussion of the emergence and nature of the jurisprudence of this period, see F. H. Lawson, 'Roman Law', in J. P. Balsdon (ed.), The Romans, London 1965, pp. 102–110 ff.

18. The importance of this achievement is given due emphasis in the best modern study of Roman law: H. F. Jolowicz, Historical Introduction to the Study of Roman Law, Cambridge 1952, pp. 142–3, 426. Full private property was 'quiritary' because it was an attribute of Roman citizenship as such: it was absolute, but not universal.

any extrinsic qualifications or restraints, by developing the novel distinction between mere 'possession' – factual control of goods, and 'property' – full legal title to them. The Roman law of property, of which an extremely substantial sector was naturally devoted to owner- ship of slaves, represented the pristine conceptual distillation of the commercialized production and exchange of commodities within an enlarged State system, which Republican imperialism had made pos- sible. Just as Greek civilization had been the first to disengage the absolute pole of 'liberty' from the political continuum of relative conditions and rights that had always prevailed before it, so Roman civilization was the first to separate the pure colour of 'property' from the economic spectrum of opaque and indeterminate possession that had typically preceded it. Quiritary ownership, the legal consum- mation of the extensive slave economy of Rome, was a momentous arrival, destined to outlive the world and age that had given birth to it.

The Republic had won Rome its Empire: it was rendered anachronis- tic by its own victories. The oligarchy of a single city could not hold the Mediterranean together in a unitary polity – it had been outgrown by the very scale of its success. The final century of Republican conquest, which took the legions to the Euphrates and the Channel, was accompanied by spiralling social tensions within Roman society itself – the direct outcome of the very triumphs that were being regularly won abroad. Peasant agitation for land had been stifled by the suppression of the Gracchi. But it now reappeared in new and menacing forms, within the army itself. Constant conscription had steadily weakened and reduced the whole small-holder class as such: but its economic aspirations lived on and now found expression in the mounting pressures from the time of Marius onwards for allocations of land to discharged veterans – the bitter survivors of the military duties that lay so heavily on the Roman peasantry. The senatorial aristocracy profited enormously from the financial sacking of the Mediterranean that succeeded progressive annexations by Rome, making boundless fortunes in tribute, extortion, land and slaves: but it was utterly unwill- ing to provide even a modicum of compensation to the soldiery whose fighting yielded these unheard-of gains to it. Legionaries were meanly paid and brusquely dismissed, without any solatium for long periods of service in which they not only risked their lives but often lost their property at home too. To have paid them bounties on discharge would have meant taxing the possessing classes, however slightly, and this the ruling aristocracy refused to consider. The result was to create an inherent tendency within the later Republican armies to a deflection of military loyalty away from the State, towards successful generals who could guarantee their soldiers plunder or donatives by their personal power. The bond between legionary and commander came increasingly to resemble that between patron and client in civilian life: from the epoch of Marius and Sulla onwards, soldiers looked to their generals for economic rehabilitation, and generals used their soldiers for political advancement. Armies came to be instruments of popular commanders, and wars started to become private ventures of ambitious consuls: Pompey in Bithynia, Crassus in Parthia, Caesar in Gaul determined their own strategic plans of conquest or aggression.[19] The factional rivalries which had traditionally rent municipal politics were consequently transferred onto a military stage, much vaster than the narrow confines of Rome itself. The inevitable result was to be the outbreak of full-scale civil wars.

At the same time, if peasant distress was the subsoil of the military turbulence and disorder of the late Republic, the plight of the urban masses acutely sharpened the crisis of senatorial power. With the extension of the Empire, the capital city of Rome itself increased uncontrollably in size. Growing rural drift from the land was combined with massive imports of slaves, to produce a vast metropolis. By the time of Caesar, Rome probably contained a population of some 750,000 – surpassing even the largest cities of the Hellenistic world. Hunger, disease and poverty squeezed the crowded slums of the capital, filled with artisans, labourers and petty-shopkeepers, whether slave, manumitted or freeborn.[20] The urban mob had been skilfully mobilized by noble manoeuvres against agrarian reformers in the 2nd century – an operation repeated once again with the abandonment of Catiline by the Roman plebs, which succumbed in time-honoured fashion to oligarchic propaganda against an 'incendiary' enemy of the State, to

19. The novelty of this development is emphasized by Badian, *Roman Imperialism in the Late Republic*, pp. 77–90.

20. P. A. Brunt, 'The Roman Mob', *Past and Present*, 1966, pp. 9–16.

whom only Etrurian small-holders remained faithful to the end. But this was the last such episode. Thereafter, the Roman proletariat seems to have broken away irreversibly from senatorial tutelage; its mood became increasingly threatening and hostile to the traditional political order in the closing years of the Republic. Given the virtual absence of any solid or serious police force in a teeming city of three-quarters of a million inhabitants, the immediate mass pressure which urban riots could bring to bear in crises of the Republic was considerable. Orchestrated by the tribune Clodius, who armed sections of the city's poor in the 50's, the urban proletariat obtained a free grain dole for the first time in 53 B.C. – henceforward a permanent fact of Roman political life: the number of its recipients had risen to 320,000 by 46 B.C. Moreover, it was popular clamour that gave Pompey the extraordinary army commands which set in motion the final military disintegration of the senatorial state; popular enthusiasm for Caesar that rendered him so menacing to the aristocracy a decade later; and popular welcome that ensured him his triumphal reception in Rome after the crossing of the Rubicon. After Caesar's death, it was once again the popular uproar in the streets of Rome at the absence of his heir that forced the Senate to plead for Augustus's acceptance of renewed consular and dictatorial powers in 22–19 B.C., the definitive entombment of the Republic.

Finally, and perhaps most fundamentally of all, the self-protective immobilism and haphazard misgovernment of the Roman nobility in the conduct of its rule over the provinces rendered it increasingly unfit to manage a cosmopolitan empire. Its exclusive privileges were incompatible with any progressive unification of its overseas conquests. The provinces as such were still helpless to put up any serious resistance to its rapacious egoism. But Italy itself, the first province to achieve formal civic parity after a violent rebellion in the previous generation, was not. The Italian gentry had won juridical integration into the Roman community, but had not hitherto broken into the inner circle of senatorial office and power. With the eruption of the final round of civil wars between the Triumvirs, its opportunity for decisive political intervention had come. The provincial gentry of Italy flocked to Augustus, self-proclaimed defender of its traditions and prerogatives against the ominous and outlandish orientalism of Marcus Antonius and his camp.[21] It was their adhesion to his cause, with the famous oath of allegiance sworn by '*tota Italia*' in 32, which ensured the victory of Actium. It is significant that each of the three civil wars which determined the fate of the Republic followed the same geographical pattern: they were all won by the side which controlled the West, and lost by the party based on the East, despite its much greater wealth and resources. Pharsala, Philippi and Actium were all fought out in Greece, the advance-post of the defeated hemisphere. The dynamic centre of the Roman imperial system was shown once again to be in the Western Mediterranean. But whereas Caesar's original territorial base had been the barbarian provinces of Gaul, Octavian forged his political bloc in Italy itself – and his victory proved in consequence less praetorian and more lasting.

The new Augustus garnered supreme power by uniting behind him the multiple forces of discontent and disintegration within the later Republic. He was able to rally a desperate urban plebs and weary peasant conscripts against a small and hated governing elite, whose opulent conservatism exposed it to ever greater popular contumely: and above all, he relied on the Italian provincial gentry who now sought their share of office and honour in the system which they had helped to build up. A stable, universal monarchy emerged from Actium, because it alone could transcend the narrow municipalism of the senatorial oligarchy in Rome. The Macedonian monarchy had been suddenly superimposed on a vast, alien continent and had failed to produce a unified ruling class to govern it *post facto*, despite Alexander's possible awareness that this was the central structural problem it faced. The Roman monarchy of Augustus, by contrast, punctually arrived when its hour struck, neither too early nor too late: the critical passage from city-state to universal empire – the familiar cyclical transition of classical Antiquity – was accomplished with signal success under the Principate.

The most dangerous tensions of the later Republic were now lowered by a series of astute policies, designed to restabilize the whole Roman

21. The role of the Italian landowning class in Augustus's ascent to power is one of the central themes of the most famous study of the period: R. Syme, *The Roman Revolution*, Oxford 1960, pp. 8, 286–90, 359–65, 384, 453.

social order. First and foremost, Augustus provided allotments of land for the thousands of soldiers demobilized after the civil wars, financing many of them out of his personal fortune. These grants – like those of Sulla before them – were probably mostly at the expense of other small-holders, who were evicted to make room for home-coming veterans, and hence did little to improve the social situation of the peasantry as a whole or alter the general pattern of agrarian property in Italy;[22] but they did effectively pacify the demands of the critical minority of the peasant class in arms, the key section of the rural population. Pay on active service had already been doubled by Caesar, an increase maintained under the Principate. More important still, from A.D. 6 onwards, veterans received regular cash bounties on discharge, worth thirteen years' wages, which were paid out of a specially created military treasury financed by modest sales and inheritance taxes on the pro-pertied classes of Italy. Such measures had been resisted to the death by the senatorial oligarchy, to their undoing: with the inauguration of the new system, discipline and loyalty returned to the army, which was trimmed from 50 to 28 legions, and converted into a permanent, pro-fessional force.[23] The result was to make possible the most significant change of all: conscription was lifted by the time of Tiberius, thereby relieving the Italian small-holders of the secular burden that had provoked such widespread suffering under the Republic – probably a more tangible benefit than any of the land allotment schemes.

In the capital, the urban proletariat was calmed with distributions of corn that were allowed to rise again from their Caesarian levels, and

22. The problem of the land settlements granted to army veterans by Caesar, the Triumvirate and Augustus has given rise to a number of different interpreta-tions. Jones believes that these did, in fact, redistribute agrarian property to peasant-soldiers sufficiently to pacify rural discontent in Italy henceforward – hence the relative social peace of the Principate, after the storms of the late Republic: A. H. M. Jones, *Augustus*, London 1970, pp. 141–2. Brunt, on the other hand, argues persuasively that the land allotments were often merely confiscations of the small plots of soldiers or supporters of the defeated armies in the civil wars, transferred to the rank-and-file of the victorious troops, without breaking up the large estates – appropriated by landowner officers – or thereby altering much the total pattern of property in the countryside. 'The Roman Revolution may then have affected no permanent changes in the agrarian society of Italy'. See 'The Army and the Land in the Roman Revolution', p. 84; *Social Conflicts in the Roman Republic*, pp. 149–50.

23. Jones, *Augustus*, pp. 110–111 ff.

which were now better assured since the incorporation of the granary of Egypt into the Empire. An ambitious building programme was launched, which provided considerable plebeian employment, and the municipal services of the city were greatly improved, by the creation of effective fire-brigades and water-supplies. At the same time, praetorian cohorts and urban police were henceforward always stationed in Rome to quell tumults. In the provinces, meanwhile, the random and un-bridled extortions of the Republican tax-farmers – one of the worst abuses of the old regime – were phased out, and a uniform fiscal system composed of a land-tax and poll-tax, and based on accurate censuses, was instituted: the revenues of the central state were increased, while peripheral regions no longer suffered the pillage of publicans. Pro-vincial governors were henceforward paid regular salaries. The judicial system was overhauled to expand its appellate facilities against arbitrary decisions very greatly, both for Italians and provincials. An imperial postal service was created to link the far-flung provinces of the Empire together for the first time with a regular communications system.[24] Roman colonies and municipalities and Latin communities were planted in outlying zones, with a heavy concentration in the Western provinces. Domestic peace was restored after a generation of destructive civil strife, and with it provincial prosperity. On the frontiers, the successful conquest and integration of the critical cor-ridors between East and West – Rhaetia, Noricum, Pannonia and Illyria – achieved the final geo-strategic unification of the Empire. Illyria, in particular, was henceforward the central military link of the imperial system in the Mediterranean.[25]

Within the new borders, the advent of the Principate meant the promotion of Italian municipal families into the ranks of the senatorial order and upper administration, where they now formed one of the bastions of Augustus's power. The Senate itself ceased any longer to

24. Jones, *Augustus*, pp. 140–1, 117–20, 95–6, 129–30.
25. Syme, *The Roman Revolution*, p. 390. The Augustan attempt to conquer Germany, at a time when major Teutonic migrations into the country were arriving from the Baltic, was the one important external failure of the reign; the frontier of the Rhine proved – contrary to official expectations at the time – definitive. For a recent revaluation of Roman strategic objectives in this epoch, see C. M. Wells, *The German Policy of Augustus*, Oxford 1972, pp. 1–13, 149–61, 246–50.

be the central authority in the Roman State: it was not deprived of power or prestige, but it was henceforward a generally obedient and subordinate tool of successive emperors, reviving politically only during dynastic disputes or interregna. But while the Senate as an institution became a stately shell of its former self, the senatorial order itself – now purged and renovated by the reforms of the Principate – continued to be the ruling class of the Empire, largely dominating the imperial state machine even after equestrian appointments became normal to a wider range of positions within it. Its capacity for cultural and ideological assimilation of newcomers to its ranks was remarkable: no representative of the old patrician nobility of the Republic ever gave such powerful expression to its outlook on the world as a once modest provincial from Southern Gaul under Trajan, Tacitus. Senatorial oppositionism survived for centuries after the creation of the Empire, in quiescent reserve or refusal of the autocracy installed by the Principate. Athens, which had known the most untrammelled democracy of the Ancient World, produced no important theorists or defenders of it. Paradoxically yet logically Rome, which had never experienced anything but a narrow and oppressive oligarchy, gave birth to the most eloquent threnodies for freedom in Antiquity. There was no real Greek equivalent to the Latin cult of *Libertas*, intense or ironic in the pages of Cicero or Tacitus.[26] The reason is evident from the contrasting structure of the two slave-owning societies. In Rome, there was no social conflict between literature and politics: power and culture were concentrated in a compact aristocracy under the Republic and the Empire. The narrower the circle that enjoyed the characteristic municipal freedom of Antiquity, the purer was the vindication of liberty it bequeathed to posterity, still memorable and formidable over fifteen hundred years later.

The senatorial ideal of *libertas* was, of course, suppressed and negated

26. For the changing connotations of this concept, see Ch. Wirszubski, *Libertas as a Political Idea at Rome during the Late Republic and Early Empire*, Cambridge 1950, which traces the evolution of *libertas* through Cicero, when it was still an active, public ideal, to its dying fall in the subjective and quietist ethic of Tacitus. Wirszubski points out the contrasting connotations of *libertas* and *eleutheria*, pp. 13–14. The latter was tainted with popular rule; it was never compatible with the aristocratic dignity that was inseparable from the former, and so received no comparable honour in Greek political thought.

by the imperial autocracy of the Principate, and the resigned acquies-
cence of the propertied classes of Italy to the new dispensation, the
alien visage of their own rule in the epoch to come. But it was never
altogether cancelled, for the political structure of the Roman monarchy
that now encompassed the whole Mediterranean world was never that
of the Hellenistic monarchies of the Greek East which preceded it. The
Roman imperial state rested on a system of civil laws, not mere royal
caprice, and its public administration never interfered greatly with the
basic legal framework handed down by the Republic. In fact, the
Principate for the first time elevated Roman jurists to official positions
within the State, when Augustus selected prominent jurisconsults for
advisers and conferred imperial authority on their interpretations of
the law. The Emperors themselves, on the other hand, were henceforward to legislate by edicts, adjudications and rescripts to questions
or petitions from subjects. The development of an autocratic public
law through imperial decretals, of course, rendered Roman legality
much more complex and composite than it had been under the Republic. The political distance travelled from Cicero's *legum servi sumus ut
liberi esse possimus* ('We obey laws in order to be free') to Ulpian's
quod principi placuit legis habet vicem ('The ruler's will has force of
law') speaks for itself.[27] But the key tenets of civil law – above all, those
governing economic transactions – were left substantially intact by this
authoritarian evolution of public law, which by and large did not
trespass upon the inter-citizen domain. The possessing classes continued to be juridically guaranteed in their property by the precepts
established in the Republic. Beneath them, criminal law – essentially
designed for the lower classes – remained as arbitrary and repressive as
it had always been: a social safeguard for the whole ruling order. The
Principate thus preserved the classical legal system of Rome, while
superimposing on it the new innovatory powers of the Emperor in the
realm of public law. Ulpian was later to formulate the distinction which
articulated the whole juridical corpus under the Empire with char-

27. It is important not to antedate the successive phases in this evolution. The
constitutional maxim that the Emperor was *legibus solutus* did not mean that he
was above all laws during the Principate, but rather that he could override those
restrictions from which dispensation was legally possible. It was only under the
Dominate that the phrase came to acquire a wider significance. See Jolowicz,
Historical Introduction to the Study of Roman Law, p. 337.

acteristic clarity: private law – *quod ad singulorum utilitatem pertinet* –
was in particular separate from public law – *quod ad statum rei Romanae
spectat*. The former suffered no real eclipse from the extension of the
latter.[28] It was, indeed, the Empire which produced the great syste-
matizations of civil jurisprudence in the 3rd century, in the work of the
Severan prefects Papinian, Ulpian and Paulus, that transmitted Roman
law as a codified body to later ages. The solidity and stability of the
Roman imperial State, so different from anything the Hellenistic world
produced, was rooted in this heritage.

The subsequent history of the Principate was largely that of the
increasing 'provincialization' of central power within the Empire.
Once the monopoly of central political office enjoyed by the Roman
aristocracy proper had been broken, a gradual process of diffusion
integrated a wider and wider ambit of the Western landed classes outside Italy itself into the imperial system.[29] The origin of the successive
dynasties of the Principate was a straightforward record of this
evolution. The Roman patrician Julio-Claudian house (Augustus to
Nero) was followed by the Italian municipal Flavian line (Vespasian to
Domitian); succession then passed a series of Emperors with a provincial Spanish or Southern Gallic background (Trajan to Marcus
Aurelius). Spain and Gallia Narbonensis were the oldest Roman
conquests in the West, whose social structure was consequently closest
to that of Italy itself. The composition of the Senate reflected much the
same pattern, with a growing intake of rural dignitaries from Trans-
padane Italy, Southern Gaul and Mediterranean Spain. The imperial
unification of which Alexander had once dreamed appeared symbolically accomplished by the epoch of Hadrian, the first Emperor to
tour his whole immense domain from end to end in person. It was
formally consummated by Caracalla's decree of A.D. 212 granting
Roman citizenship to nearly all free inhabitants throughout the
Empire. Political and administrative unification was matched by
external security and economic prosperity. The Dacian kingdom was

28. Individual Emperors such as Nero arbitrarily confiscated senatorial
fortunes, of course. Such exactions were the mark of those rulers most detested
by the aristocracy; but they did not acquire continuous or institutional form, and
did not substantially affect the collective nature of the landowning class.

29. R. Syme, *Tacitus*, II, Oxford 1958, pp. 585–606, documents the 'rise of the
provincials' in the first century of the Empire.

conquered and its gold mines annexed; the Asian frontiers were extended and consolidated. Agricultural and artisanal techniques slightly improved: screw presses promoted oil production, kneading-machines facilitated the manufacture of bread, glass-blowing became widespread.[30] Above all, the new *pax romana* was accompanied by a buoyant surge of municipal rivalry and urban embellishments in virtually all the provinces of the Empire, exploiting the architectural discovery by Rome of the arch and the vault. The Antonine epoch was perhaps the peak period for city construction in Antiquity. Economic growth was accompanied by the flowering of Latin culture in the Principate, when poetry, history and philosophy blossomed after the relative intellectual and aesthetic austerity of the early Republic. To the Enlightenment this was a Golden Age, in Gibbon's words 'the period in the history of the world during which the condition of the human race was most happy and prosperous'.[31]

For some two centuries, the tranquil magnificence of the urban civilization of the Roman Empire concealed the underlying limits and strains of the productive basis on which it rested. For, unlike the feudal economy which succeeded it, the slave mode of production of Antiquity possessed no natural, internal mechanism of self-reproduction, because its labour-force could never be homeostatically stabilized within the system. Traditionally, the supply of slaves largely depended on foreign conquests, since prisoners of war probably always provided the main source of servile labour in Antiquity. The Republic had sacked the whole Mediterranean for its manpower, to install the Roman imperial system. The Principate halted further expansion, in the three available remaining sectors of possible advance, Germany, Dacia and Mesopotamia. With the final closure of the imperial frontiers after Trajan, the well of war captives inevitably dried up. The commercial slave-trade could not make up for the shortages that resulted, since it had always itself been largely parasitic on military operations for its stocks. The barbarian periphery along the Empire continued to provide slaves, bought by dealers at the frontiers, but not in sufficient numbers

30. F. Kiechle, *Sklavenarbeit und Technischer Fortschritt*, pp. 20–60, 103–5. Kiechle's book aims to disprove Marxist theories of slavery in Antiquity; in fact, the evidence assembled, and somewhat over-pitched, by him is quite expectable within the canons of historical materialism.

31. *The History of the Decline and Fall of the Roman Empire*, I, p. 78.

to solve the supply problem in conditions of peace. The result was that prices started to climb sharply upwards; by the 1st and 2nd centuries A.D., they were 8 to 10 times the levels of the 2nd and 1st centuries B.C.[32] This steep rise in costs increasingly exposed the contradictions and risks of slave labour for its proprietors. For each adult slave represented a perishable capital investment for the slave-owner, which had to be written off *in toto* at death, so that the renewal of forced labour (unlike wage-labour) demanded a heavy preliminary outlay in what had become an increasingly tight market. For, as Marx pointed out, 'the capital paid for the purchase of a slave does not belong to the capital by means of which profit, surplus-labour, is extracted from him. On the contrary, it is capital which the slave-owner has parted with, it is a deduction from the capital which he has available for actual production.'[33] In addition, of course, the maintenance of slave offspring was an unproductive financial charge on the owner, which inevitably tended to be minimized or neglected. Agricultural slaves were housed in barrack-like *ergastula*, in conditions approximating to those of rural prisons. Female slaves were few, being generally unprofitable to owners because there was a lack of ready employment for them, beyond domestic tasks.[34] Hence the sexual composition of the rural slave-population was always drastically lopsided, and was compounded by the virtual absence of conjugality within it. The result must have been a customarily low rate of reproduction, which would have diminished the size of the labour-force from generation to generation.[35] To counteract this fall, slave-breeding seems to have been increasingly practised by landowners in the later Principate, who granted premia to women-slaves for child-bearing.[36] Although there is little evidence as

32. Jones, 'Slavery in the Ancient World', pp. 191–4.

33. Marx, *Capital*, Moscow 1962, III, pp. 788–9. Marx was referring to the use of slavery within the capitalist mode of production of the 19th century, and – as will be pointed out – it is dangerous to extrapolate his remarks backwards without further ado to Antiquity. But in this case, the nub of his comment applies *mutatis mutandis* to the slave mode of production as such. The same point was later made by Weber: 'Agrarverhältnisse im Altertum', p. 18 ff.

34. Brunt, *Italian Manpower*, pp. 143–4, 707–8.

35. Classically emphasized by Weber in 'Die Sozialen Gründe des Untergangs der Antiken Kultur', pp. 297–9, 'Agrarverhältnisse im Altertum', p. 19: 'The cost of maintaining wives and rearing children would have lain like dead ballast on the investment capital of the owner.'

36. Columella recommended bonuses for slave maternity in the 1st century

to the scale of slave-breeding in the Empire, it may have been this resort which for a time mitigated the crisis in the whole mode of production after the closure of the frontiers: but it could not provide a long-term solution to it. Nor, meanwhile, was the rural free population increasing, to compensate for losses in the slave sector. Imperial anxieties about the demographic situation in the countryside were revealed as early as Trajan, who instituted public loans to landowners for the upkeep of local orphans, an omen of shortages to come.

Nor could the dwindling volume of labour be compensated by increases in its productivity. Slave agriculture in the late Republic and early Empire was more rational and profitable to landowners than any other form of exploitation of the soil, partly because slaves could be utilized full-time, where tenants were unproductive for considerable stretches of the year.[37] Cato and Columella carefully enumerate all the different indoor and out of season tasks to which they could be set when there were no fields to be tilled or crops to be gathered. Slave artisans were just as proficient as free craftsmen, since they tended to determine the general level of skills in any trade by their employment in it. On the other hand, not only did the efficiency of the *latifundia* depend on the quality of their *vilicus* bailiffs (always the weak link

A.D., but there are few recorded cases of systematic breeding. Finley has argued that since slave-breeding was successfully practised by planters in the U.S. South during the 19th century, where the slave population actually increased after the abolition of the slave trade, there is no reason why the same conversion should not have occurred in the Roman Empire after the closure of the frontiers: see *The Journal of Roman Studies*, XLVIII, 1958, p. 158. But the comparison is a faulty one. Southern cotton planters were supplying the raw material for the central manufacturing industry of a world capitalist economy: their labour costs could be geared to the international levels of profit, unprecedented in character, realized by this capitalist mode of production after the industrial revolution of the early 19th century. Even so, the condition of their slave-breeding was probably the national integration of the South into the larger wage-labour economy of the United States as a whole. No comparable rates of reproduction were achieved in Latin America, where slave mortality was catastrophic throughout, the population in the case of Brazil dwindling to a fifth of its 1850 level by the time slavery was formally abolished. See C. Van Woodward's instructive essay, 'Emancipation and Reconstruction. A Comparative Study', *13th International Congress of Historical Sciences*, Moscow 1970, pp. 6–8. Slavery in classical Antiquity, of course, was far more primitive than that of South America. There was no objective possibility of any precursor of the Southern U.S. experience.

37. K. D. White, 'The Productivity of Labour in Roman Agriculture', *Antiquity*, XXXIX, 1965, pp. 102–7.

in the *fundus*), but supervision of slave-labourers was notoriously difficult in the more extensive cereal crops.[38] Above all, however, certain inherent limits of slave productivity could never be overcome. The slave mode of production was by no means devoid of technical progress; as we have seen, its extensive ascent in the West was marked by some significant agricultural innovations, in particular the introduction of the rotary mill and the screw press. But its dynamic was very restricted one, since it rested essentially on the annexation of labour rather than the exploitation of land or the accumulation of capital; thus unlike either the feudal or capitalist modes of production which were to succeed it, the slave mode of production possessed very little objective impetus for technological advance, since its labour-additive type of growth constituted a structural field ultimately resistant to technical innovations, although not initially exclusive of them. Thus, while it is not wholly accurate to say that Alexandrine technology remained the unchanging basis of work-processes in the Roman Empire, or that no labour-saving devices of any kind were ever introduced in the four centuries of its existence, the boundaries of the Roman agrarian economy were soon reached, and rigidly fixed.

The insuperable social obstacles to further technical progress – and the fundamental limits of the slave mode of production – were, in fact, strikingly illustrated by the fate of the two major inventions which were recorded under the Principate: the water-mill (Palestine at the turn of the 1st century A.D.) and the reaping machine (Gaul in the 1st century A.D.). The immense potential of the water-mill – basic to later feudal agriculture – is evident enough: for it represented the first applied use of inorganic power in economic production: as Marx

38. It was in such arable farming that Marx's comments on slave efficiency were perhaps most justified: 'The labourer here is, to use a striking expression of the ancients, distinguishable only as instrumentum vocale, from an animal as instrumentum semi-vocale, and from an instrument as instrumentum mutum. But he himself takes care to let both beast and implement feel that he is none of them, but is a man. He convinces himself with immense satisfaction, that he is a different being, by treating the one unmercifully and damaging the other *con amore*.' *Capital*, Moscow 1961, I, p. 196. It should always be remembered, however, that Marx in *Capital* was essentially concerned with the use of slaves in the capitalist mode of production (the American South), not with the slave mode of production as such. He never fully theorized the function of slavery in Antiquity. Moreover, modern research has radically revised many of his judgments of American slavery itself.

commented, with its appearance, 'the Roman Empire handed down the elementary form of all machinery in the water-wheel'.[39] The Empire, however, made no general use of the invention itself. It was in practice ignored under the Principate; in the later Empire, its incidence was somewhat more frequent, but it never seems to have become a normal instrument of Ancient agriculture. Likewise, the wheeled harvester introduced to accelerate reaping in the rainy climate of the North, was never adopted on any scale outside Gaul.[40] Here, the lack of interest was a reflection of a wider failure to alter the methods of Mediterranean dry-soil agriculture – with its scratch-plough and two-field system – on the heavy, moist lands of Northern Europe, which needed new instruments of labour to be fully exploited. Both cases amply demonstrate that mere technique itself is never a prime mover of economic change: inventions by individuals can remain isolated for centuries, so long as the social relations have not emerged which alone can set them to work as a collective technology. The slave mode of production had little space or time for the mill or the harvester: Roman agriculture as a whole remained innocent of them to the end. Significantly, the only major treatises of applied invention or technique to have survived from the Roman Empire were military or architectural – designed essentially for its complex of weaponry and fortifications, and its repertoire of civic ornamentation.

There was no urban salvation for the malady of the countryside, however. The Principate presided over an unprecedented range of city-building in the Mediterranean. But the quantitative expansion in the number of large and medium towns in the first two centuries of the Empire was never accompanied by any qualitative modification of the structure of overall production within it. Neither industry nor trade could ever accumulate capital or experience growth beyond the strict limits set by the economy of classical Antiquity as a whole. The regionalization of manufactures, because of transport costs, thwarted any industrial concentration and development of a more advanced division of labour in manufactures. A population overwhelmingly

39. *Capital*, I, p. 348.

40. For the water-mill in late Antiquity, see Moritz, *Grain-Mills and Flour*, pp. 137–9; Jones, *The Later Roman Empire* II, 1047–8. For the harvester, see White, *Roman Farming*, pp. 452–3.

composed of subsistence peasants, slave labourers and urban paupers narrowed consumer markets down to a very slender scale. Apart from the tax-farms and public contracts of the Republican epoch (whose role declined greatly in the Principate, after the Augustan fiscal reforms), no commercial companies ever developed, and funded debts did not exist: the credit system remained rudimentary. The propertied classes maintained their traditional disdain for trade. Merchants were a despised category, frequently recruited from freedmen. For manumission of administrative and domestic slaves remained a widespread practice, regularly thinning the higher ranks of the urban slave population; while the contraction of external supplies must have gradually diminished the stock of servile artisans in the cities. The economic vitality of the towns was always limited and derivative: its course reflected rather than offset that of the countryside. There were no civic springs for a reversal of the relationship between the two. Moreover, once the Principate had been consolidated, the character of the imperial State apparatus itself tended to stunt commercial enterprise. For the State was by far the largest single consumer of the Empire, and was the one real focus for mass production of necessities, which might have given birth to a dynamic manufacturing sector. The provisioning policy and peculiar structure of the imperial State precluded this, however. Throughout classical Antiquity, ordinary public works – roads, buildings, aqueducts, drains – were typically executed by slave-labour. The Roman Empire, with its massively enlarged State machine, saw a corresponding extension of this principle: for the entire armaments and a considerable proportion of the procurements supply for its military and civilian apparatus came to be furnished autarchically by its own industries, manned by sub-military personnel or hereditary state slaves.[41] The one truly large-scale manufacturing sector was thus to a

41. For some comments on the tradition of slave-employment in public works, see Finley, *The Ancient Economy*, p. 75. The imperial mints and textile factories (providing uniforms for the state apparatus, mandatory for civilians as well as military from Constantine onwards) were staffed with state slaves; so was the huge corps of manual labourers in the *cursus publicus* or imperial postal service, which provided the central communications system of the Empire. The weapons establishments were maintained by hereditary workers with military status, who were branded to prevent escape from their condition. In practice, there was not much social difference between the two social groups. Jones, *The Later Roman Empire*, II, pp. 830–7.

great extent subtracted from commodity exchange altogether. The permanent and direct use by the Roman State of slave-labour – a structural feature which lasted right down and into the Byzantine Empire – was one of the central pillars of the political economy of late Antiquity. The infrastructure of slavery found one of its most concentrated expressions within the imperial superstructure itself. Thus the State could expand, but the urban economy received little benefit from its growth: if anything, its size and weight tended to suffocate private commercial initiative and entrepreneurial activity. There was thus no increase of production in either agriculture or industry within the imperial borders to offset the silent decline in its servile manpower, once external expansion had ceased.[42]

The result was an incipient crisis in the whole economic and social system, by the early 3rd century, that soon developed into a pervasive breakdown of the traditional political order, amidst fierce external

42. Finley has recently proposed an ingenious reinterpretation of the recession of slavery towards the end of the Principate. He argues that the interval between the closure of the frontiers (effectively A.D. 14) and the onset of the decline of slavery (post A.D. 200) is too long for the former to account for the latter. He suggests that the basic mechanism was rather to be found in the decay of the meaning of citizenry within the Empire, which led to the juridical distinction between the two classes of *honestiores* and *humiliores*, and the depression of the free peasantry to dependent status, under the crushing political and fiscal weight of the imperial State. Once enough indigenous labour was reduced to an exploitable dependent condition (whose later shape was the colonate), imports of allogenous captive labour became unnecessary, and slavery tended to die away: see his analysis in *The Ancient Economy*, pp. 85–7 ff. This explanation, however, suffers from the very difficulty it attributes to the account it rejects. For the political elimination of any true popular citizenry, and the economic decline of the free peasantry, were consummated long before the diminution of slavery: they were largely the work of the later Republican period. Even the distinction between *honestiores* and *humiliores* dates from the early 2nd century at latest – a hundred years before the crisis of the slave economy proper, which Finley himself concedes should be dated from the 3rd century. A tinge of subtle animus against the Roman imperial State may perhaps be detected beneath the surface of Finley's arguments, which effectively renders the autocracy of the Empire responsible for the mutations of its economy. A materialist analysis, which starts from the internal contradictions of the slave mode of production itself, remains preferable. It is possible that the chronological gap to which Finley rightly draws attention was due to the mitigating effects of home-breeding and frontier-purchase in the intervening period.

attacks on the Empire. The sudden dearth of sources, one of the symptoms of the crisis of the mid-3rd century, makes it very difficult retrospectively to trace its exact course or mechanisms.[43] It looks as if serious strains were already surfacing in the closing years of the Antonine age. Germanic pressure on the Danubian frontiers had led to the lengthy Marcomannic wars; the silver *denarius* had been devalued by 25 per cent by Marcus Aurelius; the first major outbreak of social brigandage had erupted, with the menacing seizure of large regions of Gaul and Spain by the armed bands of the deserter Maternus, who even sought to invade Italy itself during the disastrous reign of Commodus.[44] The accession, after a brief civil war, of the Severan house brought an African dynasty to power: regional rotation of the imperial office seemed to have functioned once again, as civic order and prosperity were apparently restored. But soon inflation became mysteriously rampant, as the currency was devalued again and again. By mid century, there was a complete collapse of the silver coinage, which reduced the *denarius* to 5 per cent of its traditional value, while by the end of the century, corn prices had rocketed to levels 200 times over their rates in the early Principate.[45] Political stability degenerated apace with monetary stability. In the chaotic fifty years from 235 to

43. The great watershed of the mid 3rd century remains the most obscure phase of Roman imperial history, incomparably less documented and studied than the fall of the 4th or 5th centuries. Most existing discussions are very defective. Rostovtsev provides an extended description in *The Social and Economic History of the Roman Empire*, Oxford 1926, pp. 417–48. But his account is vitiated by the insistent anachronism of his analytic concepts, which incongrously turn municipal landowners into a 'bourgeoisie' and imperial legions into 'peasant armies' arrayed against it, and interpret the whole crisis in terms of the polarity between them. Meyer Reinhold has written an effective Marxist criticism of these unhistorical themes of Rostovtsev's work: 'Historian of the Ancient World: A Critique of Rostovtseff', *Science and Society*, Fall 1946, X, No. 4, pp. 361–91. On the other hand, the most conspicuous Marxist treatment of this epoch, E. V. Shtaerman's *Kriẓis Rabovladel'cheskovo Stroya*, also suffers from serious weaknesses, stemming from Shtaerman's rigid counterposition of median slave *villa* – the ancient form of a property' – and the extensive *latifundium* – a 'proto-feudal' development of an extra-municipal aristocracy. See above, note 9, p. 61.

44. For Maternus, see the recent and thoughtful remarks of M. Mazza, *Lotte Sociale e Restauraẓione Autoritaria nel Terẓo Secolo D.C.*, Catania 1970, pp. 326–7.

45. F. Millar, *The Roman Empire and its Neighbours*, London 1967, pp. 241–2. There is an over-extended discussion of the great inflation in Mazza, *Lotte Sociale e Restauraẓione Autoritaria*, pp. 316–408.

284, there were no less than 20 Emperors, eighteen of whom died violent deaths, one a captive abroad, the other a victim of the plague – all fates expressive of the times. Civil wars and usurpations were virtually uninterrupted, from Maximinus Thrax to Diocletian. They were compounded by a devastating sequence of foreign invasions and attacks along the frontiers, stabbing deep into the interior. Franks and other Germanic tribes repeatedly ravaged Gaul, sacking their way into Spain; Alamanni and Iuthungi marched into Italy, Carpi raided into Dacia and Moesia; Heruli overran Thrace and Greece; Goths crossed the sea to pillage Asia Minor; Sassanid Persia occupied Cilicia, Cappadocia and Syria; Palmyra detached Egypt; Mauri and Blemmyes nomads harrassed North Africa. Athens, Antioch and Alexandria at different moments fell into enemy hands; Paris and Tarragona were put to the torch; Rome itself had to be refortified. Domestic political turmoil and foreign invasions soon brought successive epidemics in their train, weakening and reducing the populations of the Empire, already diminished by the destructions of war. Lands were deserted, and supply shortages in agrarian output developed.[46] The tax system disintegrated with the depreciation of the currency, and fiscal dues reverted to deliveries in kind. City construction came to an abrupt halt, archaeologically attested throughout the Empire; in some regions, urban centres withered and contracted.[47] In Gaul, where a breakaway imperial state was maintained with a capital at Trier for fifteen years, there were full-scale rural uprisings by the exploited masses in 283–4, the first of the Bacaudae insurrections which were to recur in the history of the Western provinces. Under intense internal and external pressure, for some fifty years – from 235 to 284 – Roman society looked as if it might collapse.

By the late 3rd and early 4th century, however, the imperial state had altered and recovered. Military security was gradually restored by

46. Roger Rémondon, *La Crise de l'Empire Romaine*, Paris 1964, pp. 85–6. Rémondon tends to attribute the labour crisis in the countryside essentially to rural exodus into the towns, as a consequence of general urbanization; but in fact one of the most solidly established phenomena of the epoch was the decline in city construction.

47. Millar, *The Roman Empire and Its Neighbours*, pp. 243–4, particularly emphasizes the sudden cessation of urban development, as the central evidence for the depth of the crisis.

a martial series of Danubian and Balkan generals who successively seized the purple: Claudius II routed the Goths in Moesia, Aurelian drove back the Alamanni from Italy and subdued Palmyra, Probus annihilated the Germanic invaders of Gaul. These successes paved the way for the reorganization of the whole structure of the Roman State in the epoch of Diocletian, proclaimed Emperor in 284, which were to make possible the precarious revival of the next hundred years. First and foremost, the imperial armies were massively enlarged by the reintroduction of conscription: the number of legions was effectively doubled in the course of the century, bringing total troops strengths up to over 450,000 or so. From the late 2nd and early 3rd century onwards, increasing numbers of soldiers were stationed in guard-posts along highways to maintain internal security and police the countryside.[48] Later, from the time of Gallienus in the 260's onwards, crack field armies were increasingly redeployed in depth behind the imperial frontiers for greater mobility against external attacks, leaving second-class *limitanei* units to guard the outer perimeter of the Empire. Large numbers of barbarian volunteers were incorporated into the Army, henceforward providing many of its elite regiments. More important, all top military commands were now entrusted to men of equestrian rank only; the senatorial aristocracy was thereby displaced from its traditionally pivotal role in the political system, as supreme imperial power increasingly passed to the professional officer corps of the army. Diocletian himself also systematically shut senators out of the civil administration.[49] Provinces multiplied twice over, as they were divided into smaller and more manageable units, and the officialdom set over

48. Millar, *The Roman Empire and its Neighbours*, p. 6. The multiplication of these *stationes* was a symptom of the increasing social unrest of the period from Commodus to Carinus. However, interpretations of the Tetrarchy as basically an emergency junta for the restoration of the political order at home, sketched by Shtaerman and Mazza, are unduly strained. Shtaerman regards Diocletian's regime as the product of a reconciliation between the two types of estate-owner, whose conflict she believes characterized the epoch, in which the extensive latifundists had the upper hand, against the threat of a social upheaval from below. See *Kriẓis Rabovladel'cheskovo Stroya*, pp. 479–80, 499–501, 508–9. A Russian critic has pointed out, among other objections, that Shtaerman's whole scheme curiously overlooks the massive external invasions which form the main background to the Tetrarchy: V. N. D'yakov, *Vestnik Drevnei Istorii*, 1958, IV, p. 126.

49. See especially M. Arnheim, *The Senatorial Aristocracy in the Later Roman Empire*, Oxford 1972, pp. 39–48.

them was increased proportionately, to create closer bureaucratic control. A new fiscal system was established, after the debacle of the mid century, fusing the principles of a land and poll tax into a single unit, calculated on the basis of new and comprehensive censuses. Annual budgetary estimates were introduced for the first time in the Ancient World, which could adjust tax levels to current expenditures – that predictably moved steeply upwards. The formidable material expansion of the State machine that was the result all these measures inevitably contradicted the ideological attempts of Diocletian and his successors to stabilize the social structure of the later Empire beneath it. Decrees penning large groups of the population into caste-like hereditary guilds after the turbulence of the past half century can have had little practical efficacy;[50] social mobility probably increased some-what, because of the enlargement of new military and bureaucratic avenues of promotion within the State.[51] Transient efforts to fix administrative prices and wages throughout the Empire were even less realistic. On the other hand, the imperial autocracy itself successfully prised away all traditional restraints imposed by senatorial opinion and custom on the exercise of personal power. The 'Principate' gave way to the 'Dominate', as Emperors from Aurelian onwards styled them-selves *dominus et deus* and enforced the Oriental ceremonial of full-length abasement before the royal presence, the *proskynesis* with which Alexander had once inaugurated the Hellenistic Empires of the Near East.

The political complexion of the Dominate has thus often been interpreted as signifying a shift of the whole centre of gravity of the Roman imperial system to the Eastern Mediterranean, shortly to be consummated by the rise of Constantinople, the new Rome on the shores of the Bosphorus. There is no doubt that in two fundamental

50. R. Macmullen, 'Social Mobility and the Theodosian Code', *The Journal of Roman Studies*, LIV, 1964, pp. 49–53. The traditional view (for example of Rostovtsev) that Diocletian imposed a virtual caste structure on the later Empire has been discredited: it is evident that the imperial bureaucracy was incapable of implementing official decrees and policing the guilds.

51. The best brief analysis of social scent through the State machine is Keith Hopkins, 'Elite Mobility in the Roman Empire', *Past and Present* No. 32, December 1965, pp. 12–26, which stresses the necessary limits of this process: the majority of new dignitaries in the later Empire were always coopted from the provincial landowning class.

respects, the Eastern provinces now prevailed within the Empire. Economically, the crisis of the developed slave mode of production had naturally hit the West, where it was more deeply rooted, much harder and left it comparatively worse off: it now no longer possessed any native dynamism to offset the traditional wealth of the East, and manifestly started to drop back as the poorer half of the Mediterranean. Culturally, too, its thrust was increasingly spent. Greek philosophy and history were already reascendant by the close of the Antoinine epoch: the literary language of Marcus Aurelius, let alone Dio Cassius, was no longer Latin. Far more important, of course, was the slow growth of the new religion which was to capture the Empire. Christianity was born in the East, and spread steadily through it during the 3rd century, while the West remained by comparison relatively immune. Yet these critical changes were not, despite appearances, commensurately reflected in the political structure of the State itself. For no Hellenization of the governing summit of the imperial polity really occurred, still less any thorough-going Orientalization of it. The orbital rotation of dynastic power curiously stopped short of the Graeco-Levantine East.[52] The Severan house of Africa seemed as if it might effect a smooth transmission of the imperial office to a new region once again, when the Syrian family into which Septimius Severus had married engineered the accession of a local youth, falsely presented as his grandson, who became the Emperor Elagabalus in 218. The cultural exoticism of this adolescent – religious and sexual – rendered his brief reign notorious in Roman memories ever afterwards. He was rapidly ousted by a deeply affronted senatorial opinion, under whose tutelage his colourless cousin Alexander Severus – another minor, who had been educated in Italy – succeeded, before being assassinated in 235. Thereafter, only one Easterner ever became Roman Emperor again, an extremely atypical representative of the region: Julius Philippus, an Arab from the Transjordanian desert. Strikingly, no Greek from either

52. This fundamental fact has often been missed. Millar's blandly ecumenical list of successive dynasties is, in fact, seriously misleading: *The Roman Empire and its Neighbours*, p. 3. He later comments that it was merely 'an accident of fate' that Elagabalus and his cousin should have become the first Emperors from the Greek East, 'rather than any senators from the prosperous bourgeoisie of Asia Minor' (p. 49). In fact, no Greek from Asia Minor was ever to become ruler of the undivided Empire.

Asia Minor or Greece itself, no other Syrian, and not a single Egyptian ever achieved the imperial purple. The richest and most urbanized regions of the Empire failed to secure any direct lien on the apex of the State which governed them. They remained interdicted by the irreducibly *Roman* character of the Empire, founded and constructed from the West, which was always culturally far more homogeneous than the heteroclite East, in which at least three major cultures – Greek, Syriac and Egyptian – disputed the legacy of Hellenistic civilization, not to speak of the other and notable minorities of the region.[53] By the 3rd century, Italians were no longer a majority of the Senate, of which perhaps a third was recruited from the Greek-speaking East generally. But so long as the Senate exercised any power in the selection and control of Emperors, it chose representatives of the landed classes of the Latin West. Balbinus (Spain) and Tacitus (Italy) were among the last senatorial candidates to achieve the imperial dignity in the 3rd century.

For at the same time, the locus of political power ceased to be the capital, to become the military camp of the frontier areas. Gallienus was the last ruler in this epoch to reside in Rome. The Emperors were henceforward to be made and unmade beyond the range of senatorial influence, by factional struggles between military commanders. This political change was accompanied by a new, and decisive, regional shift in dynastic composition. From the mid 3rd century onwards, imperial power passed with arresting regularity to generals from the backward zone that had once been generically designated Illyricum, and now formed the block of provinces comprised by Pannonia, Dalmatia and Moesia. The predominance of these Danubian-Balkan Emperors remained a constant down to and even beyond the fall of the Roman State in the West. Decius, Claudius Gothicus, Aurelian, Probus, Diocletian, Constantine, Galerius, Jovian, Valentinian and Justinian were among them;[54] their common regional origin all the more remark-

53. There were thus four local literary languages in the East – Greek, Syriac, Coptic and Aramaic – where there was no other written language besides Latin anywhere in the West.

54. Syme suggests that Maximinus Thrax – probably from Moesia, not Thrace – and possibly even Tacitus should be added to the list: *Emperors and Biography, Studies in the Historia Augusta*, Oxford 1971, pp. 182–6, 246–7. The few other emperors of this epoch seem all to have been Westerners. Tribonianus Gallus,

able for the lack of kinship otherwise between them. Down to the turn of the 6th century, the only significant Emperor from outside this zone was a Spaniard from the Far West of the Empire, Theodosius. The most obvious reason for the rise of these Pannonian or Illyrian rulers was the role played by the Danubian and Balkan provinces in the supply of recruits for the army: they were by now a traditional reservoir of professional soldiers and officers for the legions. But there were also deeper reasons for the new prominence of this region. Pannonia and Dalmatia were the key conquests of the Augustan expansion, for they completed the basic geographical cordon of the Empire by closing the gap between its Eastern and Western sectors. Henceforward, they always operated as the central strategic bridge linking the two halves of the imperial territory. All overland troop movements along the East–West axis had to pass through this zone, which consequently became the critical fulcrum of many major civil wars of the Empire, by contrast with the typical navally-routed contests in Greece of the Republican period. Control of the passes of the Julian Alps permitted rapid descent and swift resolution of conflicts in Italy. Vespasian's victory in 69 was won from Pannonia, Septimius's triumph in 193, Decius's usurpation in 249, Diocletian's seizure of power in 285, Constantius's assumption in 351. Beyond the strategic importance of this zone, however, was its special social and cultural position within the Empire. Pannonia, Dalmatia and Moesia were intractable regions whose proximity to the Greek world had never led to their inclusion within it. They were among the last continental provinces to be Romanized, and their conversion to conventional *villa* agriculture was necessarily much later than in Gaul, Spain or Africa, and more incomplete.[55] The slave mode of production never achieved the same scale in them as in the other Latin provinces of the Western mainland, although it is possible that it eventually registered advances there while it was receding in older regions: Pannonia was singled out as a major slave exporter in a survey of the Empire in the later 4th century.[56] The crisis

---

Valerian and Gallienus were from Italy, Macrinus was from Mauretania, and Carus probably from Southern Gaul.

55. P. Oliva, *Pannonia and the Onset of Crisis in the Roman Empire*, Prague 1962, pp. 248–58, 345–50.

56. Shtaerman, *Kriᶎis Rabovladel'cheskovo Stroya*, p. 354.

of slave agriculture was consequently not so early or so sharp, and the number of peasant free-holders and tenants more considerable, in a rural pattern nearer to that of the East. The vitality of the region, amidst the decline further West, was doubtless not unconnected with this variant formation. But at the same time, its pivotal political role was inseparable from its Latinity. Linguistically, it was Roman and not Greek – the crude, easternmost extremity of Latin civilization. It was thus not merely its territorial location which determined its importance, at the inland juncture between East and West: it was also its position on the right side of the cultural border, which alone made possible its unexpected preeminence in an imperial system that was still in its deepest nature and origin a Roman order. The dynastic shift to the Danubian and Balkan backlands represented the furthest possible move eastwards of the Roman political system, to keep the Empire together, that was compatible with the maintenance of its integral Latin character.

The military and bureaucratic vigour of the new Pannonian and Illyrian rulers had accomplished the restabilization of the imperial State by the early 4th century. But the administrative restoration of the Empire was bought at the price of a serious and growing fissure within its overall structure of power. For the political unification once more of the Mediterranean now brought with it a social division within the dominant classes. The senatorial aristocracy of Italy, Spain, Gaul and Africa remained by far the most economically powerful stratum in the West, by reason of the traditional concentration of its wealth. But it was now divorced from the military apparatus of command that was the source of imperial political power, which had passed to often parvenu officers from the impoverished Balkans. A structural antagonism was thus introduced into the whole ruling order of the Dominate, which had never existed in the Principate, and was ultimately to have fatal consequences. It was taken to its extreme by Diocletian's stony discrimination against senatorial candidates for virtually any senior office, military or civilian. In this exacerbated form, the conflict was not destined to last. Constantine reversed his predecessor's policy towards the traditional nobility in the West and systematically courted it with appointments to provincial governorships and administrative honours, if not to army commands – from which its relegation was to be permanent. The Senate itself was enlarged and a new patrician elite created within it. At the same time, the composition of the aristocracy across the Empire as a whole was drastically modified by the great institutional change of Constantine's reign, the Christianization of the State, after the conversion of Constantine and his victory over Maxentius at the Milvian Bridge. Characteristically, the new Eastern religion only conquered the Empire once it was adopted by a Caesar in the West. It was an army marching from Gaul that imposed a creed originated in Palestine, signal and paradoxical accident, or symptom, of the political dominance of the Latin homelands of the Roman imperial system. Immediately, perhaps the most important institutional effect of the religious change was the social promotion of a large number of 'service Christians', who had made their administrative careers by their loyalty to the new faith, to the ranks of the enlarged 'clarissimate' of the 4th century.[57] Most of these were recruited from the East, where they came to throng the second Senate developed in Constantinople by Constantius II. Their integration into the capacious machinery of the Dominate, with its proliferation of new bureaucratic positions, both reflected and reinforced its steady augmentation of the total dimensions of the State in late Roman society. Moreover, the establishment of Christianity as the official Church of the Empire was henceforward to add a huge clerical bureaucracy – where none had previously existed – to the already ominous weight of the secular State apparatus. Within the Church itself, a similar process of expanded mobility probably occurred, as the ecclesiastical hierarchy was recruited mainly from the curial class. The salaries and perquisites of these religious dignitaries, from the immense rents yielded by the corporate wealth of the Church, were soon greater than those of equivalent ranks in the secular bureaucracy. Constantine and his successors presided over their new dispensation with lavish palatine extravagance; indictions and taxes climbed inexorably upwards. Meanwhile, and above all, the size of the army itself was further expanded by Constantine, who created new cavalry and infantry units and built up its strategic reserves: in the course of the 4th century it was to reach nearly 650,000 – nearly four times the troop-levels of the early Principate. The Roman Empire

57. For this phenomenon, see Jones, 'The Social Background of the Struggle between Paganism and Christianity' in A. Momigliano (ed.), *The Conflict Between Paganism and Christianity in the Fourth Century*, Oxford 1963, pp. 35–7.

of the 4th and 5th centuries was thus loaded with a vast, superadded increase in its military, political and ideological superstructures.

On the other hand, the swelling of the State was accompanied by a shrinkage of the economy. The demographic losses of the 3rd century were never made good again: although the statistical decline in population cannot be calculated, the continued abandonment of once cultivated lands (the *agri deserti* of the later Empire) is unmistakeable evidence of a general downward trend. In the 4th century, the political renovation of the imperial system produced a certain temporary upswing in urban construction, and a restoration of monetary stability with the issue of the gold *solidus*. But both recoveries were limited and precarious. Urban growth was largely concentrated in new military and administrative centres under the direct patronage of the Emperors: Milan, Trier or Sardica – above all, Constantinople. It was not a spontaneous economic phenomenon, and could not offset the long-term dwindling of the cities. The municipal oligarchies which had once presided over proud and vital towns were subjected to increasing supervision and interference in the early Principate, when special imperial 'curators' from Rome were appointed to watch over the provincial cities. But from the crisis of the 3rd century onwards, the relationship between the centre and the periphery was curiously reversed; henceforward, Emperors constantly strove to persuade or coerce the decurion class entrusted with municipal administration to fulfill their hereditary duties in the urban councils, while these local landowners shunned their civic responsibilities (and the consequent expenses) and towns decayed for lack of public funds or private investment. The typical 'flight of the decurions' was into the higher ranks of the clarissimate or central bureaucracy, where they were exempt from municipal obligations. Lower down socially, meanwhile, small artisans and craftsmen were drifting out of the towns, seeking security and employment on the estates of country magnates, despite official decrees banning such migrations.[58] The great network of roads that linked together the cities of the Empire – always primarily strategic rather

58. Weber rightly commented that this exodus was the exact opposite of the typical mediaeval pattern of peasant flights from the land into the towns, to gain urban freedom and employment. 'Die Sozialen Gründe des Untergangs der Antiken Kultur', pp. 306–7.

than commercial constructs – may in the end have in some cases actually become negative for the economies of the regions which they traversed, mere conduits for billeting and tax-collection, rather than routes of trade or investment. In these conditions, the stabilization of currency and reconversion of taxes into cash in the 4th century did not represent any genuine revival of the urban economy. Rather, the new coinage inaugurated by Constantine combined an elite gold standard for the use of the State and the rich, with constantly depreciated copper units for the needs of the poor, without any intervening scale of denominations between the two, so that virtually two separate monetary systems were created – a faithful tally of the social polarization of the later Empire.[59] Throughout most provinces, urban trade and industry progressively declined: there was a gradual but unmistakeable ruralization of the Empire.

It was in the countryside itself, of course, that the final crisis of Antiquity originated; and while the towns stagnated or dwindled, it was in the rural economy that far-reaching changes now occurred, presaging the transition to another mode of production altogether. The inexorable limits to the slave mode of production, once the imperial frontiers had ceased to advance, have been indicated: it was they which preceded and underlay the political and economic derangement of the 3rd century. Now, in the recessive conditions of the later Empire, slave labour – always linked to a system of political and military expansion – became increasingly scarce and cumbersome; it was therefore widely converted by landowners into dependent adscription to the soil. A critical turning-point occurred when the price-curve of slaves – which, as we have seen, sloped steeply upwards in the first two hundred years of the Principate, because of supply shortages – started to flatten out and fall in the 3rd century, a sure sign of contracting demand.[60] Owners henceforward increasingly ceased to provide for the upkeep of many of

59. There is a good analysis of the currency situation in André Piganiol, *L'Empire Chrétien (325–395)*, Paris 1947, pp. 294–300. See also Jones, 'Inflation under the Roman Empire', *Economic History Review*, V, No. 3, 1953, pp. 301–14.

60. Jones, 'Slavery in the Ancient World', p. 197; Weber, 'Agrarverhältnisse im Altertum', pp. 271–2. Weber overstates the ultimate fall of slave prices during the later Empire; as Jones shows, these declined to about half the levels of the 2nd century, slaves remaining a relatively expensive commodity except in the border provinces.

their slaves directly, but established them on small plots to look after themselves, from which they collected the surplus produce.[61] Estates tended to become divided into nuclear home-farms, still worked by slave-labour, and a mass of peasant tenancies, tilled by dependants, surrounding them. Productivity may have marginally increased with this shift, although – given a decreased total labour-force in the countryside – not output. At the same time, villages of small-holders and free tenants – which had always existed side by side with slaves in the Empire – fell under the 'patronage' of great agrarian magnates in their search for protection against fiscal exactions and conscription by the State, and came to occupy economic positions very similar to those of ex-slaves.

The result was the emergence and eventual dominance, in most provinces, of the *colonus* – the dependent peasant tenant, tied to his landlord's estate, and paying him rents either in kind or cash for his plot, or tilling it on a share-cropping basis (labour services proper were abnormal). The *coloni* generally retained about half the yield of their plots. The cost advantages for the exploiting class of this new labour system eventually became brutally clear when landowners were willing to pay more than the market price of a slave to keep a *colonus* from induction into the Army.[62] Diocletian had decreed that tenants were to be regarded as bound to their villages for the purposes of tax-collection; the juridical powers of landowners over *coloni* thereafter steadily increased throughout the 4th and 5th centuries, with successive decrees by Constantine, Valens and Arcadius. Meanwhile, agricultural slaves gradually ceased to become conventional commodities, until Valentinian I – the last great praetorian Emperor of the West – formally banned their sale apart from the lands they worked.[63] Thus by a convergent process, a class of dependent rural producers – juridically and economically distinct both from slaves and from free tenants or small-holders – was formed by the later Empire. The emergence of this colonate did not mean a diminution in the wealth or power of the land-owning class: on the contrary, precisely because it absorbed formerly

61. The best account of this process is Marc Bloch's posthumous essay, 'Comment et Pourquoi Finit l'Esclavage Antique?', *Annales E.S.C.*, 2, 1947, pp. 30–44, 161–70.

62. Jones, *The Later Roman Empire*, II, p. 1042.

63. Jones, op. cit., p. 795.

independent small peasants, and yet alleviated problems of large-scale management and supervision, it signified a major overall increase in the size of the estates owned by the Roman aristocracy. The aggregate possessions of rural magnates – often dispersed over many provinces – reached their peak by the 5th century.

Naturally, slavery itself by no means disappeared altogether. The imperial system, indeed, could never dispense with it. For the State apparatus still rested on slave-manned provisioning and communications systems, which were kept up to near traditional strength down to the very end of the Empire in the West. Slaves everywhere provided lavish household service for the possessing classes, if their role in urban artisanal production notably declined. Moreover, at least in Italy and Spain, and probably to a greater extent than is often supposed in Gaul as well, they remained relatively thick on the ground in the countryside, working the latifundia of provincial landowners. The noblewoman Melania, turning to religion in the early 5th century, may have owned 25,000 slaves in 62 villages on her local estates near Rome alone.[64] The slave sector of the rural economy, the slave service population and the slave industries run by the State, were together amply sufficient to ensure that labour continued to be marked with social degradation and invention to be precluded from the domain of work. 'Dying slavery left behind its poisonous sting by branding as ignoble the work of the free' wrote Engels, 'This was the blind alley in which the Roman world was caught'.[65] The isolated technical finds of the Principate, ignored at the height of the slave mode of production, lay equally hidden in the epoch of its disintegration. Technology received no impetus from the conversion of slaves into *coloni*. The forces of production of Antiquity remained blocked at their traditional levels.

But with the formation of the colonate, the central thread of the whole economic system now passed elsewhere: it ran essentially along the relationship between the dependent rural producer, the landlord and the State. For the increased military and bureaucratic machine of

64. In all, she possesed lands in Campania, Apulia, Sicily, Tunisia, Numidia, Mauretania, Spain and Britain; and yet her income was for contemporaries merely that of a senatorial family of medium wealth. See Jones, *The Later Roman Empire* II, pp. 793, 782, 554.

65. Marx-Engels, *Selected Works*, London 1968, p. 570.

the later Empire exacted a terrific price from a society whose own economic resources had actually decreased. The advent of urban fiscal levies enfeebled trade and artisanal production in the towns. But above all a crushing incubus of taxation fell unremittingly and unbearably on the peasantry. Annual budget estimates or 'indictions' doubled from 324 to 364. By the end of the Empire, the rates of taxation on the land were probably over three times those of the later Republic, and the State was absorbing between a quarter and a third of gross agrarian output.[66] Moreover, the cost of tax-collection was born by the subject, who could pay up to some 30 per cent on top of official rates for the placation and maintenance of the functionaries who extorted them.[67] Often, indeed, taxes were collected by landlords themselves, who were able to evade their own fiscal liabilities while enforcing those of their *coloni*. The established Church – an institutional complex unknown to classical Antiquity, by contrast with the Near Eastern civilizations which had preceded it – added a further parasitic burden to the plight of agriculture, from which 90 per cent of its rents were drawn. The ostentatious ease of the Church and the ruthless avarice of the State were accompanied by a drastic concentration of private rural property, as great noble magnates acquired estates from lesser landlords and appropriated the lands of formerly independent peasants.

The Empire was thus riven by mounting economic difficulties and social polarization as the last years of the 4th century unfolded. But it was in the West alone that these processes achieved their climactic end, with the collapse of the whole imperial system before barbarian invaders. The conventional analysis of this final disaster resorts to the concentration of Germanic pressure on the Western provinces, and their generally greater strategic vulnerability than the Eastern provinces. In Piganiol's famous epitaph: *L'Empire Romaine n'est pas mort de sa belle mort; elle a été assassinée.*[68] This account has the merit of starkly emphasizing the irreducibly *catastrophic* character of the fall in the West, against numerous erudite attempts to present it as a peaceable and imperceptible mutation, scarcely noticeable by those who lived

66. A. H. M. Jones, 'Over-Taxation and the Decline of the Roman Empire', *Antiquity*, XXXIII, 1959, pp. 39–40.

67. Jones, *The Later Roman Empire*, I, p. 468.

68. 'The Roman Empire did not die a natural death; it was assassinated': *L'Empire Chrétien*, p. 422.

through it.[69] But the belief that 'the internal weaknesses of the empire cannot have been a major factor in its decline' is clearly untenable.[70] It provides no structural explanation of the reasons why the Empire in West succumbed to the primitive bands of invaders who wandered across it in the 5th century, while the Empire in the East – against whom their attacks had initially been much more perilous – escaped and survived. The answer to the question lies in the whole prior historical development of the two zones of the Roman imperial system. Orthodox discussions nearly always situate its ultimate crisis against much too brief a temporal background; in fact, the roots of the separate fates of the Eastern and Western Mediterranean in the 5th century A.D. descend to the origins of their respective integrations into Roman rule at the outset of Republican expansion. The West, as we have seen, was the true proving-ground of Roman imperial expansion, the theatre of its authentic and decisive enlargement of the whole universe of classical Antiquity. It was there that the Republican slave economy perfected in Italy was successfully transported and implanted on virtually virgin social terrain. It was there that Roman cities were overwhelmingly founded. It was there that the bulk of the later provincial ruling class which rose to power with the Principate always resided. It was there that the Latin language became the basic – first official, eventually popular – spoken idiom. In the East, on the other hand, Roman conquest merely overlaid and coordinated an advanced Hellenistic civilization, which had already established the fundamental social 'ecology' of the region – Greek cities, peasant/gentry hinterlands, oriental royalism. The developed slave mode of production which powered the Roman imperial system was thus from its birth naturalized mainly

69. The polar view was expressed by Sundwall: *das weströmische Reich ist ohne Erschütterung eingeschlafen* – 'The Western Empire fell asleep without convulsions': J. Sundwall, *Weströmische Studien*, Berlin 1915, p. 19; a dictum much quoted thereafter, particularly by Dopsch, and recently endorsed again in K. F. Stroheker, *Germanentum und Spätantike*, Zurich 1965, pp. 89–90. These contrasting judgments have not been exempt from intermingled national sentiment.

70. This is the last sentence of Jones's work: *The Later Roman Empire*, II, 1068. It is contradicted by the burden of his own evidence. The greatness, and narrowness, of Jones as a historian are summed up in the short, superb notice by Momigliano, *Quarto Contribuito alla Storia degli Studi Classici e del Mondo Antico*, Rome 1969, pp. 645–7, who justly criticizes this conclusion.

in the West. It was therefore logical and predictable that the endogenous contradictions of that mode of production should have worked
themselves out to their uttermost conclusion in the West, where they
were not buffered or checked by any antecedent or alternative historical forms. Where the environment was purest, the symptoms were
most extreme.

Thus, to begin with, the decline in population of the Empire from
the 3rd century onwards must have affected the much less densely
inhabited West more gravely than the East. Exact estimates are
impossible, although it can be reckoned that the population of Egypt
in the later Empire may have numbered some 7,500,000, compared to
perhaps 2,500,000 for Gaul.[71] The towns of the East were much more
numerous, of course, and preserved their commercial vitality to a far
greater extent: the glittering ascent of Constantinople, as the second
capital of the Empire, was the great urban success of the 4th and 5th
centuries. Conversely, it was no accident that, as we have seen, slave
latifundia remained most concentrated in Italy, Spain and Gaul to the
very end, where they had first been pioneered. More strikingly, the
geographical pattern of the new colonate system followed the same
basic division. The institution of the colonate derived from the East,
especially Egypt, where it initially appeared: it is thus all the more
notable that its extension into a major rural system came in the West,
where it eventually predominated to a much greater extent than in the
Hellenistic countryside of the Eastern Mediterranean.[72] Similarly, the
patrocinium was in origin a phenomenon common to Syria and Egypt,
where it usually betokened the granting of a military official's protection to villages against abuses by petty agents of the State. But it was
in Italy, Gaul and Spain that it came to mean the surrender by the
peasant of his lands to a landlord patron, who then granted them back
as a temporary tenancy (the so-called *precario*).[73] This type of patronage
never became so widespread in the East, where free villages often
retained their own autonomous councils and their independence as
rural communities longer than did the municipal cities themselves;[74]

71. Jones, *The Later Roman Empire*, II, pp. 1040–1.

72. Joseph Vogt, *The Decline of Rome*, London 1965, pp. 21–2.

73. M. T. W. Arnheim, *The Senatorial Aristocracy in the Later Roman Empire*,
Oxford 1972, pp. 149–52; Vogt, *The Decline of Rome*, p. 197.

74. Jones, *The Greek City from Alexander to Justinian*, pp. 272–4.

and where therefore small peasant property subsisted to a much greater degree – combined with adscriptive and dependent tenancies – than in the West. The imperial tax burden, too, seems to have been comparatively lighter in the East: it appears that in Italy at least, fiscal exactions on the land in the 5th century ran at perhaps double the rate in Egypt. Moreover, the officially sanctioned rates of extortion by tax-collectors in the shape of 'fees' for their services appear to have been up to sixty times greater in the West than in the East.[75]

Finally, and crucially, the two regions were dominated by significantly different possessing classes. In the East, rural proprietors formed a medium gentry, based in the towns, which was accustomed both to exclusion from central political power and obedience to royal and bureaucratic command: it was the one wing of the provincial landowning class that had never produced an imperial dynasty. With the increased upper mobility of the later Empire, and the creation of the second capital at Constantinople, this stratum provided the bulk of the state administration of the East. It was they who formed the great bulk of the 'service Christians' and thronged the new Constantinople Senate—enlarged to some 2,000 by Constantius II, and solidly composed of parvenu officials and dignitaries of the Greek-speaking provinces. Their wealth was more limited than that of their older and more senior peers in Rome, their local power less oppressive, and their loyalty to the State correspondingly greater.[76] There were virtually no civil wars in the East, from Diocletian to Maurice, while the West was racked by repeated usurpations and internecine strife within the magnate class. This was partly a matter of the political tradition of Hellenistic veneration for sacred royal rulers, still strong in the region: but it was also a reflection of the different social balance between the State and the gentry. No Western Emperor ever attempted to check the spread of the *patrocinium*, despite the fact that it subtracted whole territorial areas from the surveillance of the agents of the State: but

75. Jones, *The Later Roman Empire*, I, pp. 205–7, 468; III, p. 129. The Italian tax-rate might have taken up to ⅔ of the peasant's harvest. Landlords, of course, did not pay a proportionate share of the fiscal burden. Their obligations were particularly widely evaded in the West. For Sundwall, the inability of the imperial State to tax the landed aristocracy adequately was the cause of its final collapse in the West; *Weströmische Studien*, p. 101.

76. Peter Brown, *The World of Late Antiquity*, London 1971, pp. 43–4.

successive Eastern Emperors legislated against it, repeatedly, in the 4th century.[77]

The senatorial aristocracy of the West represented quite another force. It no longer comprised the same network of families as in the early Principate: the very low birth-rates within the Roman aristocracy and the political turbulence of the post-Antonine age had raised new lineages to prominence throughout the West. The provincial landowners of Gaul and Spain lost political importance at the capital in the middle Empire;[78] on the other hand, it is notable that the only zone to produce a separatist 'dynasty' in this epoch was Gaul, where a series of regional usurpers – Postumus, Victorinus and Tetricus – maintained a relatively stable regime for over a decade, whose power extended into Spain. The Italian nobility had naturally remained closer to the centre of imperial politics. The advent of the Tetrarchy, however, drastically curtailed the traditional prerogatives of the landed aristocracy throughout the West; but it did not reduce their economic strength. The senatorial class had lost its military commands and much of its direct political influence in the course of the 3rd century. But it had never been deprived of its lands, and it had not forgotten its traditions: estates which had always been the largest in the Empire, and memories of an anti-imperial past. Diocletian, himself of extremely humble origins and rough barracks outlook, had deprived the senatorial order of nearly all provincial governorships, and systematically excluded it from the top administrative positions in the Tetrarchy. His successor Constantine, however, reversed his anti-aristocratic policies and amply reopened the upper reaches of the imperial bureaucratic apparatus in the West to the senatorial class, now fused with the equestrian order, to form the single nobility of the clarissimate. Senatorial *praesides* and *vicarii* multiplied once more in Italy, Spain, North Africa and elsewhere in the West under his rule.[79] The motivation for Constan-

77. Jones, *The Later Roman Empire*, II, pp. 777–8.

78. For analyses of role of the Spanish and Gallic nobilities in the later Empire, see K. F. Stroheker, 'Spanische Senatoren der spätromischen und westgotischen Zeit', *Germanentum und Spätantike*, pp. 54–87; and *Der Senatorische Adel im Spätantiken Gallien*, Tübingen 1948, pp. 13–42. Stroheker emphasises the later political come-back achieved by each after their eclipse in the 3rd century, in the epoch of Gratian and Theodosius.

79. Arnheim, *The Senatorial Aristocracy in the Later Roman Empire*, pp. 216–219, provides statistical computations.

tine's rapprochement with the Western aristocracy can be inferred from the other great change of his reign, his conversion to Christianity. The senatorial order in the West was not only economically and politically the most powerful segment of the landed nobility in the Empire: it was also ideologically the stronghold of traditional paganism, and potentially most hostile to Constantine's religious innovations. The reintegration of this class into the imperial administrative elite was thus probably inspired in the short-run by the need to conciliate it, amidst the hazards of establishing the Christianity as the official religion of the Empire.[80] But in the longer-run, it was the fortunes and connections of the great patrician families of the West – the intermarried clans of the Anicii, Betitii, Scipiones, Ceionii, Acilii and others – which secured their political come-back.

For the senatorial aristocracy of the West, side-tracked politically under the Tetrarchy, had recouped economically on an enormous scale. High rates of engrossment and low rates of birth had led to ever greater concentrations of landed property in the hands of fewer and fewer magnates, until the average income of the Western aristocracy in the 4th century was something like 5 times that of its predecessors in the 1st century.[81] The Emperors who followed Constantine were frequently military officers of low social extraction, from Jovian onwards increasingly often recruited from the *scholae palatinae* or palace guards themselves;[82] but every one of them, even the acridly anti-senatorial Valentinian I, ended by entrusting the clarissimate with the key civilian posts of the Western administration, from the praetorian prefecture downwards. The contrast with the East is arresting: there

80. Arnheim, op. cit., 5–6, 49–51, 72–3. It should be noted, however, that whatever resistances the Western senatorial class might evince towards imperial Christianization, within their own ranks they were informally tolerant of religious diversity in mores and marriage patterns. See Peter Brown, *Religion and Society in the Age of St Augustine*, London 1972, pp. 161–82.

81. Brown, *The World of Late Antiquity*, p. 34. During the later Empire, the landed aristocracy probably annexed a larger share of the agrarian surplus in rents than the imperial state in taxes – at a time of unprecedented fiscal exactions: see Jones, 'Rome', *Troisieme Conference Internationale d'Histoire Economique*, p. 101.

82. Jovian, Valentinian I, Valens and Majorian were all *scholae* officers. For a perceptive discussion of the role of the late imperial military elite, see R. I. Frank, *Scholae Palatinae. The Palace Guards of the Later Roman Empire*, Rome 1969, especially pp. 167–94.

the same bureaucratic functions were filled with non-nobles, and those few aristocrats who gained appointments were often – even more strikingly – themselves Westerners.[83] The military machinery of the Western Empire remained outside the centre of the aristocratic network of the West. But with the death of Valentinian in 375, the senatorial plutocracy increasingly recaptured the imperial office itself from the army, and with blind patrician egoism progressively ran down the whole defense apparatus which had been the special care of the military rulers of the Empire since Diocletian. Tax evasion and withholding of conscripts had long been endemic among the Western landowning class. Its now indurated civilianism was given a new lever with the passing of army commands in the West to Germanic generals who were ethnically unable to assume the imperial dignity themselves, as their Pannonian predecessors had done, and were exposed to popular xenophobia among the soldiery they led, as the Balkan generals had never been. Arbogast or Stilicho, a Frank and a Vandal, could thus never cash their military authority into stable political power. Successive weak Emperors, Gratian, Valentinian II and Honorius, could be manipulated by aristocratic cliques in Rome against these isolated and alien generals, whose responsibilities for defense no longer ensured them domestic dominance or security. The landed nobility of the West thus finally, and fatally, regained central influence in the imperial State.

Within a few years, this gathering aristocratic coup from above was followed by mass insurrections from below. Ever since the late 3rd century, there had been sporadic peasant revolts in Gaul and Spain: runaway slaves, army deserters, depressed *coloni* and the rural poor had periodically joined into marauding bands, designated Bacaudae, which for years on end had waged guerilla wars against army garrisons and provincial notables, sometimes necessitating direct intervention by the Emperor to subdue them. These risings, which had no equivalent anywhere in the East, combined rebellions against both slavery and the colonate – the initial and final labour systems of the agrarian West. At the turn of the 5th century, amidst the unendurable fiscal and rental pressures and the dilapidation and insecurity of the frontiers after the senatorial restoration, the Bacaudae insurrections exploded with a new scale and intensity, in 407–17, 435–7 and 442–3. In the central rebel

83. Arnheim, *The Senatorial Aristocracy in the Later Roman Empire*, pp. 167–8.

zone of Armorica, stretching north from the Loire valley, peasant insurgents created virtually an independent state, expelling officers, expropriating landlords, punishing slave-owners with slavery, and creating their own judiciary and army.[84] The social polarization of the West thus ended in a sombre double finale, in which the Empire was rent from above and below by forces within it, before forces from without delivered their quietus.

84. For the Bacaudae, see V. Sirago, *Gallia Placidia e La Trasformazione Politica dell'Occidente*, Louvain 1961, pp. 376–90; E. A. Thompson, 'Peasant Revolts in Late Roman Gaul and Spain', *Past and Present*, November 1952, pp. 11–23 – much the best synoptic account. The importance of Gallic slavery is evident from the reports of the time. Thompson comments: 'Our sources seem to suggest that these revolts were primarily due to the agricultural slaves, or at any rate that slaves played a prominent role in them.' (p. 11). The other main category of agrarian poor – dependent *coloni* – also undoubtedly participated in the insurrections in Gaul and Spain. The roving *circumcelliones* in North Africa, by contrast, were free rural labourers of higher condition, inspired by Donatism; the social and religious character of this movement made it a phenomenon apart, which was never so massive or menacing as the Bacaudae. See B. H. Warmington, *The North African Provinces from Diocletian to the Vandals*, Cambridge 1954, pp. 87–8, 100.

II. The Transition

The Germanic Background

It was into this darkening world of sybaritic oligarchs, dismantled defences and desperate rural masses that the Germanic barbarians entered when they crossed the frozen Rhine on the last day of 406. What was the social order of these invaders? When the Roman legions had first encountered the Germanic tribes in the time of Caesar, they were settled agriculturalists, with a predominantly pastoral economy. A primitive communal mode of production prevailed among them. Private ownership of land was unknown: each year the leading men of a tribe would determine which part of the common soil was to be ploughed and would allocate sections of it to respective clans, who would till and appropriate the fields collectively: the periodic redistributions prevented great disparities of wealth between clans and households, although herds were privately owned and provided the wealth of the leading tribal warriors.[1] There were no peacetime chieftains with authority over a whole people: exceptional military chiefs were elected in time of war. Many of the clans were still matrilineal. This rudimentary social structure was soon modified by the arrival of the Romans at the Rhine, and their temporary occupation of Germany up to the Elbe in the first century A.D. Trade in luxury commodities across the frontier rapidly produced a growing internal stratification within the Germanic tribes: to buy Roman goods, leading tribal warriors sold cattle, or raided other tribes to capture slaves for export

1. This description follows E. A. Thompson, *The Early Germans*, Oxford 1965, pp. 1–28: a Marxist study of the Germanic social formations from Caesar to Tacitus that is a model of clarity and elegance. Thompson's works form an invaluable cycle that in effect covers the whole evolution of Germanic society in Antiquity from this epoch down to the fall of the Visigothic kingdom of Spain, some seven centuries later.

to Roman markets. By the time of Tacitus, land had ceased to be allocated by clans and was distributed directly to individuals, while the frequency of reallocations declined. Cultivation was still often shifting, amidst empty forest terrain, so that tribes had no great territorial fixity: the agrarian system encouraged seasonal warfare and permitted frequent large-scale migrations.[2] A hereditary aristocracy with accumulated wealth composed a permanent council which exercised strategic power in the tribe, although a general assembly of free warriors could still reject its proposals. Dynastic quasi-royal lineages were emerging, which provided elective chiefs above the council. Above all, the leading men in each tribe had gathered about them 'retinues' of warriors for raiding parties, which cut across clan units of kinship. These retinues were recruited from the nobility, maintained by the produce of lands allocated to them, and divorced from participation in agricultural production. They formed the nucleus for permanent class division and institutionalized coercive authority within these primitive social formations.[3] Struggles between common warriors and ambitious noble leaders seeking to usurp dictatorial power within the tribes on the strength of their loyal retinues, increasingly broke out; Arminius himself, victor of the Teutoburg Forest, was aspirant and victim of one of them. Roman diplomacy actively fanned these internecine disputes, by means of subventions and alliances, in order to neutralize barbarian pressures on the frontier and to crystallize a stratum of aristocratic rulers willing to cooperate with Rome.

Thus both economically and politically, by trading exchange and diplomatic intervention, Roman pressure accelerated social differentia-

2. M. Bloch, 'Une Mise au Point: Les Invasions', *Mélanges Historiques*, I, Paris 1963, pp. 117–18.

3. Thompson, *The Early Germans*, pp. 48–60. The formation of a retinue system is everywhere a decisive preliminary step in the gradual transition from a tribal towards a feudal order. For it constitutes the critical break with a social system governed by kinship relations: the retinue is always definable as an elite that cuts across kin solidarity, substituting conventional for biological bonds of loyalty. It signals an approaching demise of the clan system. A fully formed feudal aristocracy, of course, will have its own (new) kinship system, which historians are only just starting to study: but these will never be its dominant structure. There is a good discussion of this central point in Owen Lattimore's stimulating article, 'Feudalism in History', *Past and Present*, No. 12, November 1957 p. 52.

tion and the disintegration of communal modes of production in the German forests. The peoples most closely in contact with the Empire of all, inevitably revealed the most 'advanced' social and economic structures, and the greatest departures from the traditional way of life of the tribes. The Alamanni in the Black Forest and, above all, the Marcomanni and Quadi in Bohemia had Roman-style villas, with estates tilled by the slave-labour of war captives. The Marcomanni, moreover, had subjected other Germanic peoples, and created an organized State with royal rule in the Central Danubian region, by the 2nd century. Their Empire was soon overthrown, but it was a symptom of the shape of things to come. A hundred and fifty years later, the Visigoths who had occupied Dacia after Aurelian evacuated the legions from it, exhibited yet further signs of the same social process, in the early 4th century. Their agricultural techniques were more advanced, and they were mostly ploughmen raising crops, with village crafts (use of the potters' wheel) and a rudimentary alphabet. The Visigothic economy in this once Roman province, with its residual towns and forts, was now so dependent on Trans-danubian trade with the Empire, that the Romans could successfully resort to commercial blockade as a decisive war measure against it. The general assembly of warriors had entirely disappeared. A confederate council of optimates exercised central political authority over obedient villages. The optimates were a possessing class with estates, retinues and slaves, clearly demarcated from the rest of their people.[4] The longer, in effect, the Roman imperial system subsisted, the more its power of influence and example tended to draw the Germanic tribes along its borders towards greater social differentiation and higher levels of political and military organization. The successive increases in barbarian pressure on the Empire from the epoch of Marcus Aurelius onwards were thus not random strokes of ill-fortune for Rome – they were to a large extent structural consequences of its own existence and success. The slow changes induced in its external environment, by imitation and intervention, were to become cumulative: the danger from the Germanic borderlands grew as Roman civilization gradually altered them.

Meanwhile, within the Roman Empire itself, increasing numbers of

4. E. A. Thompson, *The Visigoths in the Time of Ulfila*, Oxford 1966, esp. pp. 40–51; another pellucid study that forms the sequel to his earlier work.

Germanic warriors were used in the ranks of the imperial armies. Roman diplomacy had traditionally tried wherever possible to ring the frontiers of the Empire with an external glacis of *foederati*, allied or client chiefs who kept their independence beyond the Roman borders, but defended Roman interests within the barbarian world in exchange for financial subventions, political support and military protection. In the later Empire, however, the imperial government took to regular recruitment of soldiers for its own units from these tribes. At the same time, barbarian refugees or captives were settled on vacant lands as *laeti*, owing military service to the army in return for their holdings. Moreover, many free Germanic warriors volunteered for enlistment in Roman regiments, attracted by the prospects of pay and promotion within the imperial military establishment.[5] By the mid 4th century, a relatively high percentage of crack palatine troops, officers and generals were of Germanic origin, culturally and politically integrated into the Roman social universe: Frankish generals like Silvanus or Arbogast, who achieved the rank of *magister militum* or commander-in-chief in the West, were a common occurrence. There was thus a certain inter-weaving of Roman and Germanic elements within the imperial State apparatus itself. The social and ideological effects of the integration of large numbers of Teutonic soldiers and officers into the Roman world, on the Germanic world which they had permanently or provisionally left behind, are not difficult to reconstruct: they represented a powerful reinforcement of the differentiating and stratifying trends already at work within the tribal societies beyond the frontiers. Political auto-cracy, social rank, military discipline and monetary remuneration were all lessons learnt abroad and readily assimilable by local chiefs and optimates at home. Thus, by the time of the *Völkerwanderungen* of the 5th century, when the whole of Germany was thrown into commotion by the pressure of the Hunnic nomad invaders from Central Asia, and the tribes started to stream across the Roman frontiers, both internal and external pressures had taken Germanic society a considerable distance from its forms in the days of Caesar. By now, a solidified retinue nobility and individual wealth in land had nearly everywhere succeeded the rough original clan equality. The long symbiosis of

5. Frank, *Scholae Palatinae*, pp. 63–72; Jones, *The Later Roman Empire*, II, pp. 619–22.

Roman and Germanic social formations in the boundary regions had gradually narrowed the gap between the two, although it still remained in most important respects an immense one.[6] It was from their final, cataclysmic collision and fusion that feudalism was ultimately to be born.

6. In this century, there has sometimes been a tendency among historians to exaggerate the degree of prior symbiosis of the two worlds, in reaction against traditional conceptions. An extreme example is Porshnev's argument that the whole Roman infrastructure rested throughout on captured barbarian slave-labour, and therefore the two social systems were structurally interlocked from the outset: the warrior assemblies of the early Germanic peoples becoming simply defensive responses to the slaving expeditions of the Romans. According to this conception, the Empire always formed a 'complex and antagonistic unity' with its barbarian periphery. See B. F. Porshnev, *Feodalizm i Narodny Massye*, Moscow 1964, pp. 510–12. This view greatly overstates the role of captive slave-labour in the Later Empire, and the proportion of slaves drawn from the Germanic *limes* even in the early Empire.

2

The Invasions

The Germanic invasions which overran the Western Empire unfolded in two successive phases, each with a separate pattern and thrust. The first great wave started with the momentous march across the ice-bound Rhine on the winter's night of 31 December 405, by a loose confederation of Suevi, Vandals and Alans. Within a few years, the Visigoths under Alaric had sacked Rome, in 410. Two decades later, the Vandals had taken Carthage, in 439. By 480, the first crude system of barbarian states had been established on former Roman soil: the Burgundians in Savoy, the Visigoths in Aquitaine, the Vandals in North Africa and the Ostrogoths in North Italy. The character of this awesome initial irruption – which provided later epochs with their archetypal images of the onset of the Dark Ages – was, in fact, very complex and contradictory: for it was at one and the same time both the most radically destructive assault of the Germanic peoples on the Roman West, and the most markedly conservative in its respect for the Latin legacy. The military, political and economic unity of the Western Empire was irretrievably shattered. A few of the Roman field armies of *comitatenses* survived for some decades after the *limitanei* frontier defenses had been swept away; but encircled and isolated by barbarian-dominated territory, autonomous military pockets like Northern Gaul only emphasised the complete disruption of the imperial system as such. Provinces relapsed into endemic disorder and confusion, their traditional administration submerged or adrift; social rebellion and banditry were rife over large areas; archaic and buried local cultures surfaced, as the Roman patina cracked in remoter regions. In the first half of the 5th century, the imperial order was laid waste by the inrush of barbarians throughout the West.

Yet the Germanic tribes which broke apart the Western Empire were not themselves capable of substituting a new or coherent political universe for it. The difference in 'water-levels' between the two civilizations was still too great: an artificial series of locks was necessary to join them. For the barbarian peoples of the first series of tribal invasions, despite their progressive social differentiation, remained extremely inchoate and primitive communities when they burst into the Roman West. None had ever known a durable territorial State; all were ancestrally pagan in religion; most were devoid of literacy; few possessed any articulated or stabilized property system. The haphazard conquest of vast blocks of former Roman provinces naturally presented them with intractable problems of immediate appropriation and administration. These intrinsic difficulties were intensified by the geographical pattern of the first wave of invasions. For in these *Völkerwanderungen* proper – often immense peregrinations across the whole continent – the final settlement of each barbarian people was very distant from its starting-point. The Visigoths travelled from the Balkans to Spain; the Ostrogoths from the Ukraine to Italy; the Vandals from Silesia to Tunisia; the Burgundians from Pomerania to Savoy. There was no case of a barbarian community simply occupying the Roman lands directly contiguous with its own original region of domicile. The result was that the clusters of Germanic settlers in Southern France, Spain, Italy and North Africa were from the outset necessarily limited in number, because of the long itinerary behind them, and were largely cut off from further reinforcements by natural migration.[1] The improvised arrangements of the first barbarian states reflected this basic situation, of relative weakness and isolation. They therefore lent heavily on preexistent imperial structures, which were paradoxically preserved whenever subjectively possible in combination

---

1. The only reliable figure for the size of the first invasions is that of the Vandal community, which was counted by its chiefs before crossing to North Africa, and numbered 80,000 – making an army of perhaps 20–25,000: see C. Courtois, *Les Vandales et l'Afrique*, Paris 1955, pp. 215—21. Most of the Germanic peoples who broke across the imperial frontiers in this epoch were probably of similar size, rarely fielding armies of more than 20,000. Russell estimates that by A.D. 500, the maximum possible barbarian population within the former Western Empire was no more than 1,000,000 out of 16,000,000. J. C. Russell, *Population in Europe 500–1500*, London 1969, p. 21.

with Germanic analogues, to form a systematic institutional dualism.

Thus the first and most fundamental issue to be decided for the invading communites, after their victories in the field, was the economic disposal of the land. The solution normally adopted was at once a close model of earlier Roman practices particularly familiar to Germanic soldiers, and a critical rupture away from the tribal past towards a sharply differentiated social future. The regime of *hospitalitas* was imposed on local Roman landowners by the Visigoths, Burgundians and Ostrogoths. Derived from the old imperial billeting system, in which many German mercenaries had participated, this ultimately accorded ⅔ of the sown acreage of large estates to the barbarian 'guests' in Burgundy and Aquitaine; and ⅓ in Italy, whose larger overall size permitted a smaller share of individual *villae* to be allocated to them, and where undivided estates paid a special tax to equalize the system. The Burgundian *hospes* also received ⅓ of Roman slaves and ½ of forest lands.[2] In Spain, the Visigoths were later to take ⅓ of the home-farm and ⅔ of the tenancies in any given estate. In North Africa alone, the Vandals simply expropriated the bulk of the local nobility and the church outright, without any compromise or concessions whatever – an option that was to cost them dearly in the long run. The distribution of lands under the 'hospitality' system probably affected the structure of local Roman society relatively little: given the small number of barbarian conquerors involved, the *sortes* – or lots allocated to them – never covered more than a proportion of the territories under their rule. This was usually further concentrated by their fear of military dispersal after occupation: the clustered settlements of the Ostrogoths in the Po valley were a typical pattern. There is no sign that the division of large estates met with violent resistance on the part of the Latin proprietors. On the other hand, its effect on the Germanic communities could not be other than drastic. For the *sortes* were not allocated wholesale to the incoming Germanic warriors. On the contrary, all surviving pacts between Romans and barbarians, governing the divisions of land, involve two persons only – the provincial landowner

2. The fullest account of the various *hospitalitas* arrangements is F. Lot, 'Du Regime de l'Hospitalité', *Recueil des Travaux Historiques de Ferdinand Lot*, Geneva 1970, pp. 63–99; see also Jones, *The Later Roman Empire*, II, pp. 249–53, III, 46.

and one Germanic partner; while subsequently the *sortes* were actually tilled by a number of Germans. It therefore seems probable that the lands were appropriated by clan optimates, who then settled rank-and-file tribesmen on them as their tenants, or possibly as poor small-holders.[3] The former became at one stroke the social equals of the provincial aristocracy, while the latter fell directly or indirectly into economic dependence on them. This process – only obliquely visible from the documents of the time – was undoubtedly mitigated by fresh recollections of forest egalitarianism and by the armed nature of the whole invader community, which ensured the ordinary warrior his free condition. Initially, the *sortes* were not full or hereditary property, and the common soldiers who cultivated them probably retained most of their customary rights. But the logic of the system was evident: within a generation or so, a Germanic aristocracy was consolidated on the land, with a dependent peasantry beneath it: indeed, in some cases with ethnic slaves as well.[4] Class stratification crystallized rapidly, once wandering tribal federations became territorially fixed within the former imperial boundaries.

The political development of the Germanic peoples after the invasions confirmed and reflected these economic changes. State formation was now ineluctable, and with it coercive central authority over the free warrior community. The passage from one to the other was in some cases achieved only after lengthy and tortuous internal convulsions; the political evolution of the Visigoths as they wound their way across Europe from Adrianople to Toulouse, between 375 and 417, is a sequence of such graphic episodes, in which authoritarian royal power – actively assisted and promoted by Roman influences – gradually asserted its sway over a turbulent tribal soldiery, until with arrival in the temporary resting-place of Aquitaine an institutionalized dynastic

3. This is Thompson's reconstruction: 'The Visigoths from Fritigern to Euric', *Historia*, Bd XII, 1963, pp. 120–1 – the most acute recent discussion of the social implications of these settlements. Bloch believed that the *sortes* were distributed unequally, within the tribal community, by rank, from a fund composed of all the confiscated land, thereby initially creating Germanic large landowners and small peasants, rather than dependent tenants; but the eventual outcome would probably not have been very different, if this hypothesis were correct: *Mélanges Historiques*, I, pp. 134–5.

4. E. A. Thompson, 'The Barbarian Kingdoms in Gaul and Spain', *Nottingham Mediaeval Studies*, VII, 1963, p. 11.

State within the imperial framework was at last fastened down.[5] The royal 'Book of Constitutions' promulgated by the new Burgundian realm shortly afterwards, was consecrated by a small group of 31 leading nobles, whose authority had now manifestly eliminated any popular say in the laws of the tribal community. The Vandal State in Africa became the most ruthless autocracy of all, weakened only by an exceptionally wayward and eccentric succession system.[6] Just as the economic design of the first German settlements was based on a formal partition of Roman lands, so the political and juridical shape of the new Germanic States was founded on an official dualism, separating the realm administratively and legally into two distinct orders – plainest evidence of the inability of the invaders to master the old society and organize a coherent new polity coextensive with it. The typical Germanic kingdoms of this phase were still rudimentary monarchies, with uncertain rules of succession, resting on bodies of royal guards or household retinues[7] half-way between the personal followers of the

5. Thompson, 'The Visigoths from Fritigern to Euric', pp. 105–26, provides an admirable account of this complicated geo-political itinerary.

6. For the Vandal passage from a conciliar tribalism to a royal autocracy, hindered by a 'tanistry' succession system, see Courtois, *Les Vandales et l'Afrique*, pp. 234–48.

7. Traditional credence in the generalized existence of Germanic retinues up to and during the Dark Ages has been sharply attacked by Hans Kuhn, 'Die Grenzen der germanischen Gefolgschaft', *Zeitschrift der Savigny-Stiftung für Rechstgeschichte (Germanistische Abteilung)*, LXXXVI, 1956, pp. 1–83, who argues largely from philological evidence that free retinues proper were a comparatively rare phenomenon, initially confined to Southern Germany, which should not be confused with unfree military servitors or *Dienstmänner*, whom he thinks were much more widespread. However, Kuhn himself vacillates over the question of whether tribal retinues existed during the *Völkerwanderungen* themselves, eventually appearing to concede their presence (compare pp. 15–16, 19–20, 79, 83). In fact, the problem of the *Gefolgschaft* cannot really be solved by recourse to philology: the very term itself is a modern coinage. The impurity of its forms was inherent in the instability of the tribal social formations issuing from Germany, both before and after the invasions: unfree servitors, whose later descendants were the mediaeval *ministeriales*, might give way to free retainers with shifts in mobile social relations, and vice-versa. The circumstances of the epoch often permitted little etymological or juridical precision in the definition of the armed groups surrounding successive tribal leaders. Naturally, political territorialization after the invasions in turn produced further mixed and transitional bodies of the type outlined above. For a vigorous rebuttal of Kuhn's revisions, see Walter Schlesinger, 'Randbemerkungen zu drei Aufsätzen über Sippe, Gefolgschaft und

tribal past and the landed nobles of the feudal future. Below these were the rank-and-file warriors and peasants, wherever possible – especially in the towns – residentially segregated from the rest of the population.

The Roman community, on the other hand, characteristically kept its own administrative structure, with comital units and functionaries, and its own judicial system, both manned by the provincial landowning class. This dualism was most developed in Ostrogothic Italy, where a Germanic military apparatus and Roman civilian bureaucracy were effectively juxtaposed within Theodoric's government, which preserved most of the legacy of the imperial administration. Two separate legal codes normally subsisted, applicable to each population respectively – a Germanic law derived from customary traditions (tariffed penalties, jurors, kin bonds, oaths), and a Roman law that survived virtually unaltered from the Empire. The Germanic legal systems themselves often revealed pronounced Latin influences, inevitable once oral customs became written codices: numerous elements of Theodosius II's imperial code were borrowed by Burgundian and Visigothic law in the 5th century.[8] Moreover, the spirit of these loans was generally hostile to the kin and clan principles embedded in earlier barbarian traditions: the authority of the new royal states had to be built up against the tenacious influence of these older kindred patterns.[9] At the same time, there was little or no attempt to tamper with the strictly Latin legality governing the life of the Roman population. Thus in many ways, Roman juridical and political structures were left intact within these early barbarian realms: bastardized Germanic counterparts were merely added side by side to them. The ideological pattern was similar. All the major Germanic invaders were still pagan on the eve of their irruption into the Empire.[10] Tribal social organization was inseparable

---

Treue', *Beiträge zur Deutschen Verfassungsgeschichte des Mittelalters*, Bd. 1, Göttingen 1963, pp. 296–316.

8. J. M. Wallace-Hadrill, *The Barbarian West 400–1000*, London 1967, p. 32.

9. Thompson, 'The Barbarian Kingdoms in Gaul and Spain', pp. 15–16, 20.

10. This is contested by Vogt, *The Decline of Rome*, pp. 218–20. But the evidence marshalled by Thompson in his essay 'Christianity and the Northern Brabarians', in A. Momigliano (ed.) *The Conflict between Paganism and Christianity in the Fourth Century*, Oxford 1963, pp. 56–78, seems persuasive. The only exception in this epoch seems to have been the minor contingent of Rugi, converted in Lower Austria prior to 482.

from tribal religion. The political passage to a territorial State system was equally invariably accompanied by ideological conversion to Christianity – which in every case seems to have occurred within a generation of the initial crossing of the frontiers. This was not the fruit of missionary endeavours by the Catholic Church, which ignored or disdained the newcomers to the Empire.[11] It was the objective work of the remoulding process of transplantation itself, of which a change of faith was the interior sign. The Christian religion consecrated the abandonment of the subjective world of the clannic community: a wider divine order was the spiritual complement of a firmer terrestrial authority. Here too, the first wave of Germanic invaders reproduced the same combination of respect and distance for the institutions of the Empire. They unanimously adopted Arianism, rather than Catholic Orthodoxy, and thereby assured their separate religious identity within the common universe of Christianity. The consequence was a Germanic Church 'in parallel' to the Roman Church in all the early barbarian kingdoms. There was no Arian persecution of the majority Catholic population, except in Vandal Africa, where the former aristocracy had been expropriated and the Church was rigorously repressed with it. Elsewhere, the two faiths peacefully coexisted, and proselytism between the two communities was generally minimal in the 5th century. Indeed, the Ostrogoths in Italy and the Visigoths in Spain actually made it legally difficult for Romans to adopt their own Arian creed, to ensure the separations of the two populations.[12] Germanic Arianism was neither fortuitous nor aggressive: it was a badge of apartness, within a certain accepted unity.

The economic, political and ideological impact of the first wave of barbarian invasions was thus comparatively limited in its positive scope, once its original and irreversible demolition of the imperial defences had been accomplished. Aware of the disparity between what they had

11. Momigliano's claim that one of the reasons for the ascendancy of Christianity in the later Roman Empire was that it had a programme for integrating the barbarians by conversion, where classical paganism offered only exclusion, seems fanciful: *The Conflict between Paganism and Christianity in the Fourth Century*, pp. 14–15. In fact, the Catholic Church did virtually no official proselytizing work among the Germanic peoples at this date.

12. E. A. Thompson, 'The Conversion of the Visigoths to Catholicism', *Nottingham Mediaeval Studies*, IV, 1960, pp. 30–1; Jones, *The Later Roman Empire*, II, p. 263.

destroyed and what they could build, most of the Germanic rulers strove to restore as much as possible of the Roman edifices they had initially scattered: the greatest of them, the Ostrogoth Theodoric, created a meticulous administrative condominium in Italy, decorated its capital, patronized post-classical art and philosophy, and conducted foreign relations in traditional imperial style. In general, these barbarian kingdoms modified the social, economic and cultural structures of the later Roman world to a relatively limited extent, and more by fission than fusion. Significantly, large-scale agrarian slavery was preserved in them, along with the other basic rural institutions of Western Empire, including the colonate. The new Germanic nobles showed no sympathy whatever for the Bacaudae, understandably, and were on occasion used by the Roman landowners who were now their social partners to put them down. It was only the last Ostrogothic leader Totila, confronted with victorious Byzantine armies, who resorted *in extremis* to emancipation of slaves in Italy – itself a testimony of their importance – to rally popular support in a final, desperate throw before his destruction.[13] Apart from this solitary instance, Vandals, Burgundians, Ostrogoths and Visigoths alike conserved slave-gangs on the large estates where they found them. In the Mediterranean West, rural slavery continued to be a major economic phenomenon. Visigothic Spain, in particular, seems to have contained exceptionally large numbers of such slaves, to judge from the punitive legal provisions concerned with their control, and the fact they appear to have supplied most of the forced drafts for the standing army.[14] Thus while towns

13. Santo Mazzarino, 'Si può Parlare di Rivoluzione Sociale alla Fine del Mondo Antico?', *Centro Italiano di Studi Sull'Alto Medioevo, Settimani di Spoleto*, IX, 6–12 April 1961, pp. 415–16, 422. Mazzarino believes that insurgent Pannonian peasants participated in the Vandal-Alan invasions of Gaul in 406, which would represent a unique case of a barbarian-peasant alliance against the imperial State. But the evidence suggests that the 5th century source reference is in fact to Ostrogothic ex-federates temporarily settled in Pannonia, amid the local population. See Laszlo Varady, *Das Letzte Jahrhundert Pannoniens (376–476)*, Amsterdam 1969, p. 218 ff. On the other hand, Thompson's suggestion that the Visigoths and Burgundians may actually have been to some extent planted by Roman authorities in Aquitaine and Savoy to hold down the danger of local Bacaudae outbreaks, may be unduly contrived: 'The Settlement of the Barbarians in Southern Gaul'. *The Journal of Roman Studies*, XLVI, 1956, pp. 65–75.

14. Thompson, 'The Barbarian Kingdoms in Gaul and Spain', pp. 25–7; Robert Boutruche, *Seigneurie et Féodalité*, Paris 1959, I, p. 235. The legal and

continued to decline, the countryside was left largely untouched by the first wave of invasions, apart from the disarray of war and civil war, and the introduction of German estates and peasants side by side with their Roman prototypes. The most telling index of the limits of barbarian penetration in this phase was that it nowhere altered the linguistic boundary between the Latin and Teutonic world: no region of the Roman West was Germanized in speech by any of these initial conquerors. At most, their arrival merely disrupted Roman dominance in remoter provincial corners sufficiently to allow local pre-Roman languages and cultures to emerge: Basque and Celtic registered advances more than German, in the early 5th century.

The life-span of the founder barbarian states was not long. Frankish expansion subjugated the Burgundians and expelled the Visigoths from Gaul. Byzantine expeditions crushed the Vandals in Africa and after a long war of attrition exterminated the Ostrogoths in Italy. Finally, Islamic invaders rolled up Visigothic rule in Spain. Little trace of their respective settlements were left behind, except in the northernmost redoubts of Cantabria. It was the next wave of Germanic migrations which determined the later map of Western feudalism profoundly and permanently. The three main episodes of this second phase of barbarian expansion were, of course, the Frankish conquest of Gaul, the Anglo-Saxon occupation of England and – a century later, in its own way – the Lombard descent on Italy. The character of these migrations differed from those of the first wave, and probably therefore their scale too.[15] For in each case, they represented a comparatively modest and straightforward extension from an adjacent geographical starting-base. The Franks inhabited contemporary Belgium before they infiltrated southwards into Northern Gaul. The Angles and Saxons were located on the North Sea coasts of Germany opposite England; the Lombards were congregated in Lower Austria prior to their invasion of Italy. Lines of communication between the newly conquered regions and the

---

military aspects of Visigothic slavery are documented by Thompson, *The Goths in Spain*, Oxford 1969, pp. 267–74, 318–19, and at greater length by Charles Verlinden, *L'Esclavage dans l'Europe Medievale*, I, Bruges 1955, pp. 61–102.

15. For a comparison of the two waves of migration, see Lucien Musset, *Les Invasions. Les Vagues Germaniques*, Paris 1965, pp. 116–17, ff. Musset's book is much the most illuminating work of synthesis on the whole of the period.

recently inhabited homelands were consequently short, so that further contingents of identical or allied tribes could constantly arrive to reinforce the initial migrants. The result was a slow, piece-meal advance in Gaul, an obscure plethora of landings in England, and a gradual series of shifts southwards into Italy, which peopled these ex-Roman provinces much more densely than had the first military breakthroughs in the epoch of the Huns. Only the initial Lombard invasions retained the epic character of a military *Völkerwanderung* proper. But even these were slowed down and sifted, as they extended further and deeper than the Ostrogothic occupation before them. Although Lombard power was to be centred in the Northern plains, as that of their predecessors had been, Lombard settlements pushed barbarian penetration for the first time into the deep South of Italy. Frankish and Anglo-Saxon migrations were steady movements of armed colonization into regions where there was effectively a prior political vacuum. Northern Gaul was the outpost of the last forlorn Roman field army, sixty years after the imperial system had collapsed elsewhere in the West. Roman rule in Britain had never even been challenged in battle; it had expired quietly once its life-line to the continent had gone, the country relapsing into molecular Celtic chieftainries once more. The depth of these second-wave migrations can be judged from the linguistic shifts to which they led. England was Germanized *en bloc*, as far as Anglo-Saxon settlement extended – the Celtic margins of the island providing not even an admixture of vocabulary to the speech of the conquerors: a token of the tenuous Romanization of the most northerly province of the Empire, which manifestly never affected the mass of the population. On the Continent, the Romance frontier was pushed back a band of territory some 50–100 miles deep from Dunkirk to Basle, and some 100–200 miles to the south of the Upper Danube.[16] Frankish, moreover, bequeathed some 500 words to French vocabulary, and Lombard 300 to Italian (where Visigothic left a mere 60 to Spanish, Suevic 4 to Portuguese). The cultural sedimentation of the second wave of conquests was much deeper and more lasting than the first.

One of the main reasons for this, of course, was that the initial wave had cleared the ground so thoroughly of actual organized resistance by the imperial system in the West. Its own creations proved singularly

16. Musset, *Les Invasions. Les Vagues Germaniques*, pp. 172–81.

imitative and fragile, and mostly did not even claim to occupy the whole terrain thus levelled. The successor migrations had both the weight and space to construct more inclusive and durable social forms in the West. The rigid and brittle dualism of the 5th century progressively disappeared in the 6th (except in the last fortress of the first generation states – Visigothic Spain, where it died away in the 7th). A slow process of fusion, integrating both Germanic and Roman elements into a new synthesis that was to supersede both of them, gradually started to occur. The most important of these developments – the emergence of a new agrarian system – is unfortunately the most dimly-lit for subsequent historiography. The rural economy of Merovingian Gaul and Lombard Italy remains one of the most opaque chapters in the history of Western agriculture. But certain facts are evident about this period. There was no further resort to the *hospitalitas* system. Neither Franks nor Lombards (nor *a fortiori* Anglo-Saxons, of course) proceeded to any similar regulated partition of Roman landed estates. Instead, a more amorphous two-fold pattern of settlement appears to have occurred. On the one hand, both Frankish and Lombard rulers simply confiscated local latifundia on a large scale, annexing them to the royal treasury or distributing them to their noble retinues. The senatorial aristocracy which survived in Northern Gaul had mostly fallen back south of the Loire even before Clovis had defeated Syagrius's army in 476 and taken possession of the provincial spoils of his victory. In Italy, the Lombard kings made no attempt to conciliate Roman landowners, who were crushed and eliminated wherever they posed an obstacle to appropriation of the land; some were reduced to the condition of slaves themselves.[17] The turnover of large agrarian property was thus probably much greater in the second than in the first wave of invasions. On the other hand, however, since the demographic mass of the later migrations was considerably greater than those of the earlier, and the pace of its advance often slower and steadier, the popular and peasant component of the new rural order was also more marked. It was in this period especially that the village communities that were so prominent a subsequent feature of mediaeval feudalism seem to have first become widely entrenched in France and elsewhere.

17. L. M. Hartmann, *Geschichte Italiens im Mittelalter*, II/ii, Gotha 1903, pp. 2–3.

Villages multiplied, while *villae* as organized units of production declined, amidst the uncertainty and anarchy of the times.

In Gaul, at least, this phenomenon can be attributed to two convergent processes. The break-up of Roman rule undermined the stability of the basic instrument of Latin rural colonization, the *villa* system; there now reemerged from beneath it an older Celtic landscape, revealing primitive hamlets of huts and peasant dwellings that had been overlaid by the Romanization of Gaul. At the same time, the migrations of local Germanic communities southwards and westwards – not necessarily in warrior array any longer – brought with them many of the agrarian traditions of their tribal homelands, less eroded by time and travel than in the epoch of the first epic *Völkerwanderungen*. Thus both allodial peasant plots and communal village lands – direct legacies of the Northern forests – reappeared in the new migrant settlements. On the other hand, the subsequent warfare of the Merovingian epoch led to new enslavements, drawn especially from the borderlands of Central Europe. The proportions of the final combination of Germanic noble estates, dependent tenures, small peasant holdings, communal lands, surviving Roman *villae* and rural slavery, are impossible to estimate in the confusion and obscurity of this epoch. But it is clear that in England, France and Italy alike, a free ethnic peasantry was initially one of the elements of Anglo-Saxon, Frankish and Lombard migrations – although its extent cannot be determined. In Italy, Lombard peasant communities were organized in military colonies, with their own autonomous administration. In Gaul, the Frankish nobility received lands and offices across the country in a pattern notably variant from that of Frankish rural settlement, clearly indicating that commoner migrants were by no means necessarily dependent tenants of the former optimate stratum.[18] In England, the Anglo-Saxon invasions led to an early and total collapse of the *villa* system – anyway far more precarious than on the continent because of the limited extent of Romanization. There too, however, barbarian lords and free peasants coexisted in different combinations after the migrations, with a general tendency towards an increase of rural dependency as more stable political units emerged. In England, the more abrupt chasm between the Roman and Germanic orders perhaps led to a sharper

18. Musset, *Les Invasions. Les Vagues Germaniques*, p. 209.

change in methods of agrarian cultivation themselves. At all events, the pattern of Anglo-Saxon rural settlements contrasted notably with that of the Roman farming which had preceded it, and prefigured some of the most important changes of the later feudal agriculture. Whereas Roman estates were usually sited on hilly ground with lighter soils, which approximated to Mediterranean terrain and could be cultivated with scratch ards, Anglo-Saxon farms were typically located in valleys with heavy, moist soils, on which the inhabitants used iron ploughs; where Roman agriculture had a larger pastoral element, the Anglo-Saxon invaders tended to clear wide tracts of forest and marsh for arable farming.[19] Scattered Celtic hamlets gave way to nucleated villages, in which the individual property of peasant households was combined with collective co-aration of open fields. Above these settlements, local chiefs and lords consolidated their personal powers: by the turn of the 7th century, a legally defined and hereditary aristocracy was consolidated in Anglo-Saxon England.[20] Thus while the second wave of invasions everywhere produced both a Germanic aristocracy endowed with larger estates than ever before, it also populated the countryside with durable village communities and clumps of small peasant property. At the same time, it often replenished agricultural slavery too, from the war-captives of the time.[21] It could not yet organize these disparate elements of the rural economy of the Dark Ages into a new and coherent mode of production.

Politically, the second wave of invasions marked or presaged the end of dualist administrations and laws, with a withering away of Roman juridical legacies. The Lombards made no effort to repeat Ostrogothic parallelism in Italy. They recast the civil and juridical system of the country in the regions which they occupied, promulgating a new legal code based on traditional Germanic norms, but drafted in Latin, which soon predominated over Roman law. The Merovingian kings retained a double legal system, but with the growing anarchy of their rule, Latin memories and norms progressively faded. Germanic law became progressively dominant, while the land taxes inherited

19. H. R. Loyn, *Anglo-Saxon England and the Norman Conquest*, London 1962 pp. 19–22.

20. Loyn, *Anglo-Saxon England and the Norman Conquest*, pp. 199 ff.

21. For the continuing importance of slaves in the later Dark Ages, see Georges Duby, *Guerriers et Paysans*, Paris 1973, pp. 41–3.

from Rome broke down amidst the resistance of the population and Church to a fiscality which no longer corresponded to any public services or integrated State. Taxation progressively lapsed altogether in the Frankish kingdoms. In England, Roman law and administration had anyway disappeared virtually completely before the Anglo-Saxons arrived, so the issue never arose. Even in Visigothic Spain, the one barbarian State whose ancestry now went back to the first wave of invasions, dualist law and administration came to an end in the later 7th century, when the monarchy of Toledo abolished the Roman legacies altogether and subjected the whole population to a modified Gothic system.[22] On the other hand, Germanic religious separatism now conversely ebbed away. The Franks adopted Catholicism directly with the baptism of Clovis in the last years of the 5th century, after his victory over the Alamanni. The Anglo-Saxons were gradually converted from paganism by Roman missions in the 7th century. The Visigoths in Spain relinquished their Arianism, with the conversion of Reccared in 587. The Lombard realm accepted Catholicism in 653. *Pari passu* with these changes, there was a steady intermarriage and assimilation of the two landed classes, where they coexisted, Roman and Germanic. This process was limited in Italy by Lombard exclusiveness and Byzantine revanchism, which together prevented any lasting pacification of the peninsula and whose conflict laid the foundation for the secular division of north and south in later epochs. But in Gaul it proceeded steadily under Merovingian rule; by the early 7th century it was substantially completed, with the consolidation of a single rural aristocracy, no longer senatorial or retainer in its outlook. The comparable blending of Roman and Germanic strands in the Church took considerably longer: bishops in Gaul continued to be Roman virtually to a man throughout most of the 6th century, and no complete ethnic fusion occurred in the ecclesiastical hierarchy until the 8th century.[23]

The supersession of simple dualist accommodations to Roman imperial forms did not, however, itself yield any cogent or permanent new political formula in the later Dark Ages. If anything, the abandonment of the advanced traditions of classical Antiquity led to a regression

22. For the possible social background to this process, see Thompson, *The Goths in Spain*, pp. 216–17.

23. Musset, *Les Invasions. Les Vagues Germaniques*, p. 190.

in the level of sophistication and performance of the successor
States, aggravated by the consequences of Islamic expansion in the
Mediterranean from the early 7th century onwards, which further
stoppered trade and blockaded Western Europe in rural isolation. It is
possible that climatic improvements in the 7th century, ushering in a
somewhat warmer and dryer cycle of weather in Europe, and a pick-up
of demographic growth, may have started to benefit the rural
economy.[24] But little incidence of such progress was discernible in the
political confusion of the time. Gold coinage disappeared after 650, the
consequence of endemic trade deficits with the Byzantine East as much
as of Arab conquests. The Merovingian monarchy proved incapable of
keeping control of minting, which became degraded and dispersed.
Public taxation in Gaul lapsed into oblivion; diplomacy stiffened and
narrowed; administration was blunted and parochialized. The Lombard
States in Italy, splintered and weakened by Byzantine enclaves, remained primitive and defensive. In these conditions, it was fitting that
perhaps the major positive achievement of the barbarian states was the
conquest of Germany itself, accomplished by the Merovingian campaigns up to the Weser in the 6th century.[25] These acquisitions for the
first time integrated the homelands of the migrations into the same
political universe as the former imperial provinces, and thereby unified
the two zones whose original conflict had unleashed the Dark Ages,
into a single territorial and cultural order. The lowering down of the
institutional levels of urban civilization in Frankish Gaul accompanied
and permitted their relative elevation in Bavarian and Alamannic
Germany. However, even in this field, Merovingian administration was
singularly crude and poor: neither literacy, currency nor Christianity
were introduced by the counts dispatched to rule beyond the Rhine. In
its economic, social and political structures, Western Europe had left
behind the precarious dualism of the first decades after Antiquity; a

24. This hypothesis is advanced by Duby: *Guerriers et Paysans*, pp. 17–19,
84–5. But the evidence is too sparse for any confident conclusions. Duby
generally tends to present a more optimistic interpretation of this epoch than
other historians. Thus the disappearance of gold currency he regards as a sign of
revived trade, the smaller silver coins of the time as an index of more supple and
frequent commercial transactions – the reverse of the usual view of the Merovingian monetary record.

25. Musset, *Les Invasions. Les Vagues Germaniques*, pp. 130–2.

rough mixing process had occurred, but the results still remained unformed and heteroclite. Neither simple juxtaposition nor crude mixture could release a new general mode of production, capable of surmounting the impasse of slavery and colonate, and with it a new and internally coherent social order. In other words, only a genuine *synthesis* could achieve this. A few premonitory signs alone presaged the advent of such an ultimate outcome. The most notable was the emergence, already evident in the 6th century, of completely novel anthroponymic and toponymic systems – combining Germanic and Roman linguistic elements into organized units foreign to both – in the borderlands between Gaul and Germany.[26] Spoken language, far from always following material changes, may sometimes anticipate them.

26. Musset, *Les Invasions. Les Vagues Germaniques*, p. 197.

3

Towards Synthesis

The historical synthesis which finally occurred was, of course, feudalism. The precise term – *Synthese* – is Marx's, along with that of other historians of his time.[1] The catastrophic collision of two dissolving anterior modes of production – primitive and ancient – eventually produced the feudal order which spread throughout mediaeval Europe. That Western feudalism was the specific result of a fusion of Roman and Germanic legacies was already evident to thinkers of the Renaissance, when its genesis was first debated.[2] Modern controversy over the question dates essentially from Montesquieu, who pronounced the origins of feudalism to be Germanic in the Enlightenment. Ever since, the problem of the exact 'proportions' of the mixture of Romano-Germanic elements which eventually generated feudalism has aroused the passions of successive nationalist historians. Indeed, the very timbre of the end of Antiquity itself frequently altered according to the patriotism of the chronicler. For Dopsch, writing in Austria after the First World War, the collapse of the Roman Empire was merely the culmination of centuries of pacific absorption by the Germanic peoples: it was lived as a calm liberation by the inhabitants of the West. 'The Roman world was gradually won from within by the Germans, who had penetrated it peacefully for centuries and assimilated its culture,

1. In his major statement of historical method, Marx spoke of the results of the Germanic conquests as a process of 'interaction' (*Wechselwirkung*) and 'fusion' (*Verschmelzung*) which generated a new 'mode of production' (*Produktionsweise*) that was a 'synthesis' (*Synthese*) of its two predecessors: *Grundrisse der Kritik der Politischen Okonomie (Einleitung)*, Berlin 1953, p. 18.

2. For the Renaissance debate, see D. R. Kelley, 'De Origine Feudorum: The Beginnings of a Historical Problem', *Speculum*, XXXIX, April 1964, No. 2, pp. 207–28; Montesquieu's discussion is in *De L'Esprit des Lois*, Books XXX and XXXI.

indeed frequently taken over its administration, so that the removal of its political dominion was merely the final consequence of a lengthy process of change, like the rectification of the nomenclature of an enterprise whose old name has long since ceased to correspond to the real directors of the concern . . . The Germans were not enemies to destroy or wipe out Roman culture, on the contrary they preserved and developed it.'[3] For Lot, writing in France at about the same time, the end of Antiquity was an unimaginable disaster, the holocaust of civilization itself: Germanic law was responsible for the 'perpetual, unbridled, frenzied violence' and 'insecurity of property' of the succeeding epoch, whose 'frightful corruption' made it 'a truly accursed period of history.'[4] In England, where there was no confrontation, but merely a caesura, between the Roman and the Germanic orders, the controversy was shifted to the inverse invasion of the Norman Conquest, and Freeman and Round successively polemicized over the relative merits of the 'Anglo-Saxon' or 'Latin' contributions to the local feudalism.[5] The embers of these disputes still glow today; Soviet historians traded sharp exchanges over them at a recent conference in Russia.[6] In fact, of course, the precise admixture of once Roman or Germanic elements

3. Alfons Dopsch, *Wirtschaftliche und Soziale Grundlagen der europäischen Kulturentwicklung aus der Zeit von Caesar bis auf Karl den Grossen*, Vienna 1920–1923, Vol. I, p. 413.

4. Ferdinand Lot, *La Fin du Monde Antique et le Début du Moyen Age*, Paris 1952 (reedition), pp. 462, 469 and 463. Lot finished his book in late 1921.

5. For Freeman; 'the Norman conquest was the temporary overthrow of our national being. But it was only a temporary overthrow. To a superficial observer the English people might seem for a while to be wiped out of the roll-call of nations, or to exist only as the bondmen of foreign rulers in their own land. But in a few generations, we led captive our conquerors; England was England once again.' Edward A. Freeman, *The History of the Norman Conquest of England, Its Causes and Results*, Oxford 1867, Vol. I, p. 2. Freeman's panegyric of the Anglo-Saxon heritage was countered by Round's scarcely less vehement exaltation of the Norman arrival. In 1066, 'the long, long canker of peace had done its work. The land was ripe for the invader, and a Saviour of Society was at hand.'; the Norman Conquest at last brought England 'something better than the arid entries in our jejune native chronicle'. J. H. Round, *Feudal England*, London 1964 (reedition), pp. 304–5, 247.

6. See the lengthy discussion in *Srednie Veka*, Fasc 31, 1968, of the report by A. D. Liublinskaya, 'Tipologiya Rannevo Feodalizma v Zapadnoi Evrope i Problema Romano-Germanskovo Sinteza', pp. 17–44. Participants were O. L. Vainshtein, M. Ya. Siuziumov, Ya. L. Bessmertny, A. P. Kazhdan, M. D. Lordkipanidze, E. V. Gutnova, S. M. Stam, M. L. Abramson, T. I. Desnitskaya,

in the pure feudal mode of production as such is of much less importance than their respective distribution in the variant social formations
which emerged in mediaeval Europe. In other words, as we shall see,
a *typology* of European feudalism is necessary – rather than a mere
pedigree.

The original derivation of specific feudal institutions often appears
in any case inextricable, given the ambiguity of the sources and the
parallelism of developments within the two antecedent social systems.
Thus vassalage may have its main roots in either the German *comitatus*
or the Gallo-Roman *clientela*: two forms of aristocratic retinue that
existed on either side of the Rhine well before the end of the Empire,
and both of which undoubtedly contributed to the ultimate emergence
of the vassal system.[7] The benefice, with which it eventually fused to
form the fief, can equally be traced both to the late Roman ecclesiastical
practices and to German tribal distributions of land.[8] The manor, on
the other hand, certainly derives from the Gallo-Roman *fundus* or *villa*,
which had no barbarian counterpart: huge, self-contained estates tilled
by dependent peasant *coloni*, delivering produce in kind to their
magnate landowners, in an obvious adumbration of a domain economy.[9]
The communal enclaves of the mediaeval village, by contrast, were
basically a Germanic inheritance, survival of the original rural systems

---

M. M. Friedenberg and V. T. Sirotenko. Note in particular the tone of the interventions of Vainstein and Siuziumov, champions respectively of the Barbarian
and Imperial contributions to feudalism, the latter – a Byzantine historian –
unmistakably striking an anti-German national note. In general, Soviet
Byzantinists appear occupationally prone to privilege the weight of Antiquity in
the feudal synthesis. Liublinskaya's reply to the discussion is serene and sensible.

7. Compare Dopsch, *Wirtschaftliche und Soziale Grundlagen*, II, pp. 300–2,
with Bloch, *Feudal Society*, Vol. I, 147–51. Intermediate forms were the Gallo-
Roman *bucellarii* or bodyguards, and the Frankish *antrustiones* (palace guards) or
leudes (military retainers). For the latter, see Carl Stephenson, *Mediaeval
Institutions*, Ithaca 1954, pp. 225–7, who deems the *leudes* the direct ancestors of
the Carolingian *vassi*.

8. Dopsch, *Wirtschaftliche und Soziale Grundlagen*, II, pp. 332–6.

9. Dopsch, *Wirtschaftliche und Soziale Grundlagen*, I, pp. 332–9. The etymology
of the key terms of European feudalism may throw a shadowy light on their
varied origin. 'Fief' is derived from the Old German *vieh*, the word for herds.
'Vassal' comes from the Celtic *kwas*, originally meaning a slave. On the other
hand, 'village' derives from the Roman *villa*, 'serf' from *servus*, and 'manor'
from *mansus*.

of the forest after the general evolution of the barbarian peasantry through allodial to dependent tenures. Serfdom itself probably descends both from the classical statute of the *colonus* and from the slow degradation of free Germanic peasants by quasi-coercive 'commendation' to clan warriors. The legal and constitutional system which developed in the Middle Ages was equally hybrid. Folk justice of a popular character and a tradition of formally reciprocal obligation between rulers and ruled within a common tribal community left a widespread mark on the juridical structures of feudalism, even where folk-courts proper did not survive, as in France. The estates system which later emerged within the feudal monarchies owed much to the latter, in particular. On the other hand, the Roman legacy of a codified and written law was also of central importance for the specific jural synthesis of the Middle Ages; while the conciliar heritage of the classical Christian Church was likewise doubtless critical for the development of the estates system.[10] At the peak of the mediaeval polity, the institution of the feudal monarchy itself initially represented a mutable amalgam of the Germanic war leader, semi-elective and with rudimentary secular functions, and the Roman imperial ruler, sacred autocrat of unlimited powers and responsibilities.

The infrastructural and superstructural complex that was to make up the general structure of a feudal totality in Europe thus had a deep double derivation, after the collapse and confusion of the Dark Ages. One single institution, however, spanned the whole transition from Antiquity to the Middle Ages in essential continuity: the Christian Church. It was, indeed, the main, frail aqueduct across which the cultural reservoirs of the Classical World now passed to the new universe of feudal Europe, where literacy had become clerical. Strange historical object *par excellence*, whose peculiar temporality has never coincided with that of a simple sequence from one economy or polity to another, but has overlapped and outlived several in a rhythm of its own, the Church has never received theorization within historical materialism.[11] No attempt can be made to remedy this lack here. But

10. Hintze emphasized this filiation in his essay 'Weltgeschichtliche Bedingungen der Repräsentativverfassung', in Otto Hintze, *Gesammelte Abhandlungen*, Vol. I, Leipzig 1941, pp. 134–5.

11. Issued from a post-tribal ethnic minority, triumphant in late Antiquity, dominant in feudalism, decadent and renascent under capitalism, the Roman

some brief comments are necessary on the significance of its role in the transition from antiquity to feudalism, since this has been alternatively exaggerated or neglected in much historical discussion of the epoch. In late Antiquity, the Christian Church – as has been seen – indubitably contributed to the weakening of the powers of resistance of the Roman imperial system. It did so, not by demoralizing doctrines or extra-mundane values, as Enlightenment historians believed, but by its sheer worldly bulk. For the vast clerical apparatus which it spawned in the later Empire was one of the main reasons for the parasitic overweight which exhausted Roman economy and society. For a second, super-added bureaucracy was thus conjoined to the already oppressive onus of the secular State. By the 6th century, the bishops and clergy within the remaining empire were actually both much more numerous than the administrative officers and functionaries of the State, and received con-siderably higher salaries.[12] The intolerable burden of this top-heavy edifice was a central determinant of the collapse of the Empire. Gibbon's limpid thesis that Christianity was one of the two fundamental causes of the fall of the Roman Empire – expressive summation of En-lightenment idealism – thus permits a materialist reformulation today.

Yet the same Church was also the moving site of the first symptoms of liberation of technique and culture from the limits of a world built on slavery. The extraordinary achievements of Graeco-Roman civilization had been the property of a small ruling stratum, entirely divorced from production. Manual labour was identified with servi-tude, and was *eo ipso* degrading. Economically, the slave mode of production led to technical stagnation: there was no impulse to labour-

---

Church has survived every other institution – cultural, political, juridical or linguistic – historically coeval with it. Engels reflected briefly on its long odyssey in *Ludwig Feuerbach and the End of German Classical Philosophy* (Marx-Engels, *Selected Works*, London 1968, pp. 628–31); but limited himself to registering the dependence of its mutations on those of the general history of modes of produc-tion. Its own regional autonomy and adaptability – extraordinary by any com-parative standards – have yet to be seriously explored. Lukács believed it to lie in a relative permanence of man's relation to nature, unseen substratum of the religious cosmos. But he never ventured more than asides on the question. See G. Lukács, *History and Class Consciousness*, London 1971, pp. 235–6.

12. Jones, *The Later Roman Empire*, Vol. II, pp. 933–4, 1046.

saving improvements within it. Thus Alexandrine technology, as we have seen, on the whole persisted throughout the Roman Empire: few significant inventions were made, none was ever widely applied. On the other hand, culturally slavery rendered possible the elusive harmony of man and the natural universe that marked the art and philosophy of much of classical Antiquity: unquestioned exemption from labour was one of the preconditions of its serene absence of tension with nature. The toil of material transformation or even its managerial supervision was a substratum substantially excluded from its sphere. Yet the grandeur of the intellectual and cultural heritage of the Roman Empire was not only accompanied by a technical immobility: it was by its very preconditions restricted to the thinnest layer of the metropolitan and provincial ruling classes. The most telling index of its vertical limitation was the fact that the great mass of the population in the pagan Empire knew no Latin. The language of government and letters itself was the monopoly of a small elite. It was the ascent of the Christian Church which first signalled a subversion and alteration of this pattern. For Christianity ruptured the union between man and nature, the spirit and the world of the flesh, potentially twisting the relationship between the two in opposite, tormented directions: asceticism and activism.[13] Immediately, the Church's victory in the later Empire did nothing to alter traditional attitudes to either technology or slavery. Ambrose of Milan expressed the new official opinion when he condemned even the purely theoretical sciences of astronomy and geometry as impious: 'We do not know the secrets of the Emperor and yet we claim to know those of God.'[14] Likewise, Church Fathers from Paul to Jerome unanimously accepted slavery, merely advising slaves to be obedient to their masters and masters to be just to their slaves –

13. The rupture was not, of course, peculiar to the new religion, but extended into traditional paganism as well. Brown evokes it characteristically: 'After generations of apparently satisfying public activity, it was as if a current that passed smoothly from man's inner experience into the outside world had been cut. The warmth drained from the familiar environment . . . The classical mask no longer fitted over the looming and inscrutable core of the universe.' *The World of Late Antiquity*, pp. 51–2. But as he shows, the most intense pagan response to it was Neo-Platonism, last doctrine of inner reconciliation between man and nature, first theory of sensuous *beauty*, rediscovered and appropriated in another epoch by the Renaissance.

14. E. A. Thompson, *A Roman Reformer and Inventor*, Oxford 1952, pp. 44–5.

true liberty, after all, was not to be found in this world anyway.[15] In practice, the Church of these centuries was often a large institutional slave-owner, and its bishops could on occasion pursue their legal rights over runaway property with more than ordinary punitive zeal.[16]

However, on the margins of the ecclesiastical apparatus itself, the growth of monasticism pointed in a different possible direction. The Egyptian peasantry had a tradition of solitary desert hermitage or *anachoresis*, as a form of protest against tax-collection and other social evils; this was adapted by Anthony into an ascetic religious anchoritism in the late 3rd century A.D. It was then developed by Pachomius in the early 4th century into communal coenobitism in the cultivated areas near the Nile, where agricultural work and literacy were enjoined as well as prayer and fasting;[17] and in the 370's, Basil linked asceticism, manual labour and intellectual instruction into a coherent monastic rule, for the first time. However, although this evolution can retrospectively be seen as one of the first signs of a slow sea-change in social attitudes to labour, the growth of monasticism in the later Roman Empire itself probably merely aggravated the economic parasitism of the Church, by withdrawing further manpower from production. Nor did it thereafter play any specially tonic role in the Byzantine economy, where Eastern monasticism soon became at best merely contemplative and at worst otiose and obscurantist. On the other hand, transplanted to the West and reformulated by Benedict of Nursia during the sombre

15. Engels scornfully remarked that: 'Christianity is perfectly innocent of this gradual dying out of slavery. It had partaken of the fruits of slavery in the Roman Empire for centuries, and later did nothing to prevent the slave-trade of Christians.' Marx-Engels, *Selected Works*, p. 570. This judgment was a shade too peremptory, as can be seen from Bloch's nuanced analysis of the Church's attitude to slavery in 'Comment et Pourquoi Finit l'Esclavage Antique?' (esp. pp. 37–41). But Bloch's substantive conclusions do not diverge very much from those of Engels, despite the necessary qualifications he adds to them. For more recent and confirmatory discussions of early Christian attitudes towards slavery, see Westermann, *The Slave Systems of Greek and Roman Antiquity*, pp. 149–62; A. Hadjinicolaou-Marava, *Recherches sur la Vie des Esclaves dans le Monde Byzantin*, Athens 1950, pp. 13–18.

16. For example, see Thompson, *The Goths in Spain*, pp. 305–8.

17. D. J. Chitty, *The Desert a City*, Oxford 1966, pp. 20–1, 27. It is regrettable that what appears to be the only full-length recent study of early monasticism should be so single-mindedly devotional in approach. Jones's comments on the mixed record of monasticism in the late Antiquity are sharp and pertinent: *The Later Roman Empire*, II, pp. 930–3.

depths of the 6th century, monastic principles proved organizationally efficacious and ideologically influential from the later Dark Ages onwards. For in the Western monastic orders, intellectual and manual labour were provisionally united in the service of God. Agrarian toil acquired the dignity of divine worship, and was performed by literate monks: *laborare est orare*. With this, one of the cultural barriers to technical invention and progression undoubtedly fell. It would be an error to attribute this change to any self-sufficient power within the Church[18] – the different course of events in East and West alone should be enough to make it clear that it was the total complex of social relations, not the religious institution itself, which ultimately allocated the economic and cultural roles of monasticism. Its productive career could only start once the disintegration of classical slavery had released the elements for another dynamic, to be achieved with the formation of feudalism. It is the ductility of the Church in this difficult passage that is striking, rather than any rigorism.

At the same time, however, the Church was without doubt more directly responsible for another formidable, silent transformation in the last centuries of the Empire. The very vulgarization and corruption of classical culture, which Gibbon was to denounce, was in fact part of a gigantic process of assimilation and adaptation of it to a wider population – which was both to ruin and rescue it amid the collapse of its traditional infrastructure. The most striking manifestation, once again, of this transmission was that of language. Up to the 3rd century, the peasants of Gaul or Spain had spoken their own Celtic tongues, impermeable to the culture of the classical ruling class: any Germanic conquest of these provinces at this date would have had incalculable

18. This is the main defect of Lynn White's essay, 'What Accelerated Technological Progress in the Western Middle Ages?', in A. C. Crombie (ed.), *Scientific Change*, London 1963, pp. 272–91 – a bold exploration of the consequences of monasticism, in certain respects superior to his *Mediaeval Technology and Social Change* in that technique is not fetichized into a historical first cause, but at least linked to social institutions. White's assertion of the importance of the ideological de-animation of nature by Christianity as a precondition of its subsequent technological transformation appears seductive, but overlooks the fact that Islam was responsible for an even more thorough *Entzauberung der Welt* shortly afterwards, with no noticeable impact on Muslim technology. The significance of monasticism as a premonitory solvent of the classical labour system should not be exaggerated.

consequences for later European history. With the Christianization of the Empire, however, the bishops and clergy of the Western provinces, by undertaking the conversion of the mass of the rural population, durably Latinized their speech in the course of the 4th and 5th centuries.[19] The Romance languages were the outcome of this popularization, one of the essential social bonds of continuity between Antiquity and the Middle Ages. The consequences of a Germanic conquest of these Western provinces without their prior Latinization have only to be envisaged for the momentous importance of this achievement to be evident.

This central achievement of the early Church indicates its true place and function in the transition to feudalism. Its autonomous efficacy was not to be found in the realm of economic relations or social structures, where it has sometimes mistakenly been sought, but in the cultural sphere above them – in all its limitation and immensity. The civilization of classical Antiquity was defined by the development of superstructures of unexampled sophistication and complexity, over material infrastructures of comparatively invariant crudity and simplicity: there was always a dramatic disproportion in the Graeco-Roman world between the vaulting intellectual and political sky and the cramped economic earth beneath it. When its final collapse came, nothing was less obvious than that its superstructural heritage – now impossibly distant from immediate social realities – should survive it, in however compromised a form. A specific vessel was necessary for this, sufficiently apart from the classical institutions of Antiquity and yet moulded within them, and so capable of escaping the general wreckage to transmit the mysterious messages of the past to the less advanced

19. Brown, *The World of Late Antiquity*, p. 130. This work is in some ways the most brilliant meditation for many years on the end of the classical epoch. One of its central themes is the vital creativity of the adulterated transmission of classical culture by Christianity, which produced the typical art of Late Antiquity, to lower orders and later ages. Social and intellectual debasement was the salutary ordeal which saved it. The similarity of this conception, much more powerfully expressed by Brown than by any other writer, to Gramsci's typical notion of the relationship between the Renaissance and Reformation, is noticeable. Gramsci believed that the cultural splendour of the Renaissance, refinement of an aristocratic elite, had to be coarsened and dimmed in the obscurantism of the Reformation, to pass across to the masses and so ultimately reemerge on a wider and freer foundation. *Il Materialismo Storico*, Turin 1966, p. 85.

future. The Church objectively performed this role. In certain key respects, the superstructural civilization of Antiquity remained superior to that of feudalism for a millennium – right down to the epoch that was consciously to call itself its Renaissance, to mark the intervening regression. The condition of its praetermitted power, through the chaotic and primitive centuries of the Dark Ages, was the endurance of the Church. No other dynamic transition from one mode of production to another reveals the same splay in superstructural development: equally, none other contains a comparable spanning institution.

The Church was thus the indispensable bridge between two epochs, in a 'catastrophic', not 'cumulative' passage between two modes of production (whose structure thus necessarily diverged *in toto* from the transition between feudalism and capitalism). Significantly, it was the official mentor of the first systematic attempt to 'renovate' the Empire in the West, the Carolingian Monarchy. With the Carolingian State, the history of feudalism proper begins. For this massive ideological and adminstrative effort to 'recreate' the Imperial System of the old world, in fact, by a typical inversion, contained and dissembled the involuntary laying of the foundations of the new. It was in the Carolingian era that the decisive steps in the formation of feudalism were taken.

The imposing expansion of the new Frankish dynasty gave little immediate hint, however, of its ultimate legacy to Europe. Its dominating overt theme was the political and military unification of the West. Charles Martel's defeat of the Arabs at Poitiers in 753 halted the advance of Islam, which had just absorbed the Visigothic State in Spain. Thereafter, in thirty rapid years, Charlemagne annexed Lombard Italy, conquered Saxony and Friesland, and incorporated Catalonia. He thereby became the sole ruler of the Christian continent beyond the frontiers of Byzantium, with the exception of the inaccessible Asturian littoral. In 800, he assumed the long defunct title of Emperor of the West. Carolingian expansion was not merely territorial aggrandizement. Its imperial claims corresponded to a real administrative and cultural revival throughout the boundaries of the continental West. The coinage system was reformed and standardized, and central control of minting resumed. In close coordination with the Church, the Carolingian monarchy sponsored a renovation of literature, philosophy, art and education. Religious missions were dispatched to pagan lands beyond the Empire. The great new frontier-zone of Germany, enlarged by the subjugation of the Saxon tribes, was for the first time carefully tended and systematically converted – a programme facilitated by the shift of the Carolingian court eastwards to Aachen, mid-way between the Loire and the Elbe. Moreover, an elaborate and centralized administrative grid was laid down over the whole land-mass from Catalonia to Schleswig and Normandy to Styria. Its basic unit was the county, derived from the old Roman *civitatis*. Trusted nobles were appointed as counts with military and judicial powers to govern these regions in a clear and firm delegation of public authority, revocable by the Emperor. There were perhaps 250–350 of these officials throughout the Empire; they were paid no salaries but received a proportion of the local royal revenues and landed endowments in the county.[20] Comital careers were not confined to any one district: a competent noble could successively be transferred to different regions, although in practice revocations or shifts of countship were infrequent. Intermarriage and migration of landed families from the various regions of the Empire created a certain social basis for a 'supra-ethnic' aristocracy imbued with imperial ideology.[21] At the same time, the regional system of counties was superimposed by a smaller central group of clerical and secular magnates, mainly recruited from Lorraine and Alsace, often closer to the personal entourage of the Emperor himself. These provided the *missi dominici*, a mobile reserve of direct imperial agents sent out as plenipotentiaries to deal with especially difficult or demanding problems in outlying provinces. The *missi* became a regular institution of Charlemagne's rule from 802 onwards; typically dispatched in pairs, they were increasingly recruited from bishops and abbots, to insulate them from local pressures on their missions. It was they who in principle ensured the effective integration of the far-flung comital network. An increasing use was made of written documents, in efforts to improve the traditions of unadorned illiteracy inherited from the Merovingians.[22] But in practice, there were many gaps and delays in this machinery, whose functioning was always extremely slow and

20. F. L. Ganshof, *The Carolingians and the Frankish Monarchy*, London 1971, p. 91.

21. H. Fichtenau, *The Carolingian Empire*, Oxford 1957, pp. 110–13.

22. Ganshof, *The Carolingians and the Frankish Monarchy*, pp. 125–35.

cumbersome, in the absence of any serious palatine bureaucracy to provide an impersonal integration of the system. Nevertheless, given the conditions of the age, the scope and scale of Carolingian administrative ideals were a formidable achievement.

The real and germinal innovations of this epoch, however, lay elsewhere – in the gradual emergence of the fundamental institutions of feudalism below the apparatus of imperial government. Merovingian Gaul had known both the oath of personal fealty to the reigning monarch, and the grant of royal lands to noble servitors. But these were never combined into a single or significant system. The Merovingian rulers had usually distributed estates outright to loyal retainers, borrowing the ecclesiastical term 'beneficium' for such gifts. Later, many of the estates allocated in this fashion had been confiscated from the Church by the Arnulfing line, to raise additional troops for their armies;[23] while the Church was compensated with the introduction of tithes by Peppin III, henceforward the only approximation to a general tax in the Frankish realm. But it was the epoch of Charlemagne himself which ushered in the critical synthesis between donations of land and bonds of service. In the course of the later 8th century, 'vassalage' (personal homage) and 'benefice' (grant of land) slowly fused, while in the course of the 9th century 'benefice' in its turn became increasingly assimilated to 'honour' (public office and jurisdiction).[24] Grants of land by rulers thereby ceased to be gifts, to become conditional tenures, held in exchange for sworn services; and lower administrative positions tended to approximate legally to them. A class of *vassi dominici*, direct vassals of the Emperor, who held their benefices from Charlemagne himself, now developed in the countryside, forming a local landowning class interspersed among the comital authorities of the Empire. It was these royal *vassi* who provided the nucleus of the Carolingian army, called up year after year for service in Charlemagne's constant foreign campaigns. But the system extended well beyond direct fealty to the Emperor. Other vassals were benefice-holders of princes who were themselves vassals of the supreme ruler. At the same time, legal 'immunities' initially peculiar to the Church – juridical exemptions

23. D. Bullough, *The Age of Charlemagne*, London 1965, pp. 35–6.
24. L. Halphen, *Charlemagne et l'Empire Carolingien*, Paris 1949, pp. 198–206, 486–93; Boutruche, *Seigneurie et Féodalité*, I, pp. 150–9.

granted from inimical Germanic codes earlier in the Dark Ages –
started to spread to secular warriors. Henceforward, those vassals
equipped with such immunities were proof against comital interference
in their properties. The eventual result of this convergent evolution
was the emergence of the 'fief', as a delegated grant of land, vested
with juridical and political powers, in exchange for military service.
The military development, at about the same time, of heavy armoured
cavalry contributed to the consolidation of the new institutional nexus,
although it was not responsible for its appearance. It took a century for
the full fief system to become moulded and rooted in the West; but its
first unmistakable nucleus was visible under Charlemagne.

Meanwhile, the constant wars of the reign increasingly tended to
depress the bulk of the rural population. The preconditions of the free
warrior peasantry of traditional Germanic society had been shifting
cultivation, and warfare that was local and seasonal. Once agrarian
settlement was stabilized, and military campaigns became longer-range
and lengthier, the material basis for a social unity of fighting and tilling
was inevitably broken. War became the distant prerogative of a
mounted nobility, while a sedentary peasantry laboured at home to
maintain a permanent rhythm of cultivation, disarmed and burdened
with provision of supplies for the royal armies.[25] The result was a
general deterioration in the position of the mass of the agrarian population. Thus it was in this period too that the characteristic feudal unit of
production, tilled by a dependent peasantry, took shape. The Carolingian Empire was in practice a largely landlocked area, with minimal
foreign trade despite its Mediterranean and North Sea frontiers, and
sluggish monetary circulation: its economic response to isolation was
the development of a manorial system. The *villa* of Charlemagne's
reign already anticipated the structure of the manor of the early Middle
Ages – a large autarchic estate composed of a demesne and a multitude
of small peasant plots. The size of these noble or clerical domains was
often very considerable – 2,000 to 4,000 acres in extent. Agrarian yields
remained extremely low; even ratios of 1 : 1 were by no means unknown,
so primitive were farming methods.[26] The seigneurial reserve itself,

25. See the perceptive remarks by Duby: *Guerriers et Paysans*, p. 55.
26. J. Boussard, *The Civilization of Charlemagne*, London 1968, pp. 57–60;
Duby, *Guerriers et Paysans*, p. 38.

the *mansus indominicatus*, might cover perhaps a quarter of the total area; the rest was typically cultivated by *servi* or *mancipia* settled on small 'manses'. These formed the great bulk of the dependent rural labour force; although their legal appellation was still that of the Roman word for 'slave', their condition was in fact now nearer that of the future mediaeval 'serf', a change registered by a semantic shift in the use of the term *servus* in the 8th century. The *ergastulum* had disappeared. The Carolingian *mancipia* were generally peasant families bound to the soil, owing dues in kind and labour services to their masters: exactions which were in fact probably larger than those of the old Gallo-Roman colonate. The large Carolingian estates could also contain free peasant tenants (on *r .nses ingenuiles*), owing dues and services, but without servile dependence; but these were much less common.[27] More frequently, the *mancipia* would be supplemented for work on the demesne itself by hired labour and genuine chattel slaves, which had by no means yet disappeared. Given the ambiguous terminology of the time, it is impossible to fix with any precision the size of the real slave-labour force in Carolingian Europe: but it has been estimated at some 10–20 per cent of the rural population.[28] The *villa* system did not, of course, mean that landed property had become exclusively aristocratic. Small allodial holdings owned and tilled by free peasants – *pagenses* or *mediocres* – still subsisted, between the great tracts of domainial estates. Their relative quantity has yet to be determined, although it is clear that in the early years of Charlemagne himself, a significant part of the peasant population remained above the condition of serfdom. But the basic rural relations of production of a new age were henceforward increasingly in place.

By the death of Charlemagne, the central institutions of feudalism were thus already present, beneath the canopy of a pseudo-Roman centralized Empire. In fact, it soon became clear that the rapid spread of benefices, and their increasing heritability, tended to undermine the whole unwieldy Carolingian State apparatus – whose ambitious

27. R.-H. Bautier, *The Economic Development of Mediaeval Europe*, London 1971, pp. 44–5.

28. Boutruche, *Seigneurie et Féodalité*, I, pp. 130–1; see also Duby's discussion, *Guerriers et Paysans*, pp. 100–3. There is a good analysis of the general shift in Carolingian France from slavery and serfdom as a legal status in C. Verlinden, *L'Esclavage dans l'Europe Médiévale*, I, pp. 733–47.

expanse had never corresponded to its real capacities of administrative integration, given the extremely low level of the forces of production in the 8th and 9th centuries. The internal unity of the Empire soon foundered, amidst dynastic civil wars and growing regionalization of the magnate class that once held it together. A precarious tripartite division of the West succeeded. Savage and unexpected external attacks from all points of the compass, on sea and land, by Viking, Saracen and Magyar invaders then pulverized the whole para-imperial system of comital rule that remained. No permanent army or navy existed to resist these onslaughts; the Frankish cavalry was slow and clumsy to mobilize; the ideological flower of the Carolingian aristocracy had perished in the civil wars. The centralized political structure bequeathed by Charlemagne crumbled away. By 850, benefices were virtually everywhere inheritable; by 870 the last *missi dominici* had vanished; by the 880's the *vassi dominici* were mediatized to local potentates; by the 890's counts had effectively become hereditary regional lords.[29] It was in the last decades of the 9th century, as Viking and Magyar bands ravaged the West European mainland, that the term *feudum* first started to come into use – the full mediaeval word for 'fief'. It was then too that the countryside of France, in particular, became criss-crossed with private castles and fortifications, erected by rural seigneurs without any imperial permission, to withstand the new barbarian attacks, and dig in their local power. The new castellar landscape was both a protection, and a prison, for the rural population. The peasantry, already falling into increasing subjection in the last deflationary, war-torn years of Charlemagne's rule, were now finally thrust downwards to generalized serfdom. The entrenchment of local counts and landowners in the provinces, through the nascent fief system, and the consolidation of their manorial estates and lordships over the peasantry, proved to be the bedrock of the feudalism that slowly solidified across Europe in the next two centuries.

29. Boussard, *The Civilization of Charlemagne*, pp. 227–9; L. Musset, *Les Invasions. Le Second Assaut contre l'Europe Chrétienne*, Paris 1965, pp. 158–65.

Part Two

I. Western Europe

The Feudal Mode of Production

The feudal mode of production that emerged in Western Europe was characterized by a complex unity. Traditional definitions of it have often rendered this partially, with the result that it has become difficult to construct any account of the dynamic of feudal development It was a mode of production dominated by the land and a natural economy, in which neither labour nor the products of labour were commodities. The immediate producer – the peasant – was united to the means of production – the soil – by a specific social relationship. The literal formula of this relationship was provided by the legal definition of serfdom – *glebae adscripti* or bound to the earth: serfs had juridically restricted mobility.[1] The peasants who occupied and tilled the land were not its owners. Agrarian property was privately controlled by a class of feudal lords, who extracted a surplus from the peasants by politico-legal relations of compulsion. This extra-economic coercion, taking the form of labour services, rents in kind or customary dues owed to the individual lord by the peasant, was exercised both on the manorial demesne attached directly to the person of the lord, and on the strip tenancies or virgates cultivated by the peasant. Its necessary result was a juridical amalgamation of economic exploitation with political authority. The peasant was subject to the jurisdiction of his lord. At the same time, the property rights of the lord over his land were typically of degree only: he was invested in them by a superior

1. Chronologically, this legal definition emerged much later than the factual phenomenon it designated. It was a definition invented by Roman-law jurists in the 11–12th centuries, and popularized in the 14th century. See Marc Bloch, *Les Caractères Originaux de l'Histoire Rurale Française*, Paris 1952, pp. 89–90. We shall repeatedly encounter examples of this lag in the juridical codification of economic and social relationships.

noble (or nobles), to whom he would owe knight-service – provision of a military effective in time of war. His estates were, in other words, held as a fief. The liege lord in his turn would often be the vassal of a feudal superior,[2] and the chain of such dependent tenures linked to military service would extend upwards to the highest peak of the system – in most cases, a monarch – of whom all land could in the ultimate instance be in principle the eminent domain. Typical intermediary links of such a feudal hierarchy in the early mediaeval epoch, between simple lordship and suzerain monarchy, were the castellany, barony, county or principality. The consequence of such a system was that political sovereignty was never focused in a single centre. The functions of the State were disintegrated in a vertical allocation downwards, at each level of which political and economic relations were, on the other hand, integrated. This parcellization of sovereignty was constitutive of the whole feudal mode of production.

Three structural specificities of Western feudalism followed, all of fundamental importance for its dynamic. Firstly, the survival of communal village lands and peasant allods from pre-feudal modes of production, although not generated by the latter, was not incompatible with it either. For the feudal division of sovereignties into particularist zones with overlapping boundaries, and no universal centre of competence, always permitted the existence of 'allogenous' corporate entities in its interstices. Thus although the feudal class tried on occasion to enforce the rule of *nulle terre sans seigneur*, in practice this was never achieved in any feudal social formation: communal lands – pastures, meadows and forests – and scattered allods always remained a significant sector of peasant autonomy and resistance, with important consequences for total agrarian productivity.[3] Moreover,

2. Liegeancy was technically a form of homage taking precedence over all other homages, in cases where a vassal owed loyalty to multiple lords. In practice, however, liege lords soon became synonymous with any feudal superior, and liegeancy lost its original and specific distinction. Marc Bloch, *Feudal Society*, London 1962, pp. 214–18.

3. Engels always justly emphasized the social consequences of village communities, integrated by common lands and the three-field system, for the condition of the mediaeval peasantry. It was they, he remarked in *The Origin of the Family, Private Property and the State*, that gave 'to the oppressed class, the peasants, even under the harshest conditions of mediaeval serfdom, local cohesion and the means of resistance which neither the slaves of antiquity nor the modern

even within the manorial system itself, the scalar structure of property was expressed in the characteristic division of estates into the lord's demesne, directly organized by his stewards and tilled by his villeins, and the peasant virgates, from which he received a complementary surplus but in which the organization and control of production was in the hands of the villeins themselves.[4] There was thus no simple, horizontal concentration of the two basic classes of the rural economy within a single, homogeneous property form. Relations of production were mediated through a dual agrarian statute within the manor. Moreover, there was often a further disjuncture between the justice to which serfs were subject in the manorial courts of their lord, and the seigneurial jurisdictions of territorial lordship. Manors did not normally coincide with single hamlets, but were distributed across a number of them; hence conversely in any given village a multiplicity of manorial holdings of different lords would be interwoven. Above this tangled juridical maze would typically lie the *haute justice* of territorial seigneuries, whose area of competence was geographical, not domainial.[5] The peasant class from which the surplus was extracted in this system thus inhabited a social world of overlapping claims and powers, the very plurality of whose 'instances' of exploitation created latent interstices and discrepancies impossible in a more unified juridical

---

proletarians found ready to hand.' Marx-Engels, *Selected Works*, London 1968, p. 575. Basing himself on the work of the German historian Maurer, Engels wrongly believed these communities, which dated back to the earliest Dark Ages, to be 'mark associations'; in fact, the latter were an innovation of the late Middle Ages, which first appeared in the 14th century. But this error does not affect his essential argument.

4. Mediaeval manors varied in structure according to the relative balance between these two components within it. At one extreme, there were (a few) estates entirely devoted to demesne-farming, such as the Cistercian 'granges' tilled by lay brethren; while at the other, there were some estates entirely leased out to peasant tenants. But the modal type was always a combination of home-farm and tenancies, in varying proportions: 'this bilateral composition of the manor and of its revenues was the true hallmark of the typical manor.' M. M. Postan, *The Mediaeval Economy and Society*, London 1972, pp. 89–94.

5. There is an excellent account of the basic traits of this system in B. H. Slicher Van Bath, *The Agrarian History of Western Europe*, London 1963, pp. 46–51. Where territorial lordships were absent, as in most of England, plural manors within a single village gave the peasant community considerable leeway for self-regulation: see Postan, *The Mediaeval Economy and Society*, p. 117.

and economic system. The coexistence of communal lands, allods and virgates with the demesne itself was constitutive of the feudal mode of production in Western Europe, and had critical implications for its development.

Secondly, however, and even more importantly, the feudal parcellization of sovereignties produced the phenomenon of the mediaeval town in Western Europe. Here again, the genesis of urban commodity production is not to be located within feudalism as such: it of course predates it. But the feudal mode of production nevertheless was the *first* to permit it an *autonomous development* within a natural-agrarian economy. The fact that the largest mediaeval towns never rivalled in scale those of either Antiquity or Asian Empires has often obscured the truth that their function within the social formation was a much more advanced one. In the Roman Empire, with its highly sophisticated urban civilization, the towns were subordinated to the rule of noble landowners who lived in them, but not from them; in China, vast provincial agglomerations were controlled by mandarin bureaucrats resident in a special district segregated from all commercial activity. By contrast, the paradigmatic mediaeval towns of Europe which practised trade and manufactures were self-governing communes, enjoying corporate political and military autonomy from the nobility and the Church. Marx saw this difference very clearly, and gave memorable expression to it: 'Ancient classical history is the history of cities, but cities based on landownership and agriculture; Asian history is a kind of undifferentiated unity of town and country (the large city, properly speaking, must be regarded merely as a princely camp, superimposed on the real economic structure); the Middle Ages (germanic period) starts with the countryside as the locus of history, whose further development then proceeds through the opposition of town and country; modern history is the urbanization of the countryside, not, as among the ancients, the ruralization of the city.'[6] Thus a *dynamic opposition* of town and country was alone possible in the feudal mode of production: opposition between an urban economy of increasing commodity exchange, controlled by merchants and organized in guilds and corporations, and a rural economy of natural exchange, controlled by nobles and organized in manors and strips, with communal and

6. Karl Marx, *Pre-Capitalist Formations*, London 1964, pp. 77–78.

individual peasant enclaves. It goes without saying that the preponderance of the latter was enormous: the feudal mode of production was overwhelmingly agrarian. But its laws of motion, as will be seen, were governed by the complex unity of its different regions, not by any simple predominance of the manor.

Thirdly, there was an inherent ambiguity or oscillation at the vertex of the whole hierarchy of feudal dependencies. The 'summit' of the chain was in certain important respects its weakest link. In principle, the highest superordinate level of the feudal hierarchy in any given territory of Western Europe was necessarily different not in kind, but only in degree, from the subordinate levels of lordship beneath it. The monarch, in other words, was a feudal suzerain of his vassals, to whom he was bound by reciprocal ties of fealty, not a supreme sovereign set above his subjects. His economic resources would lie virtually exclusively in his personal domains as a lord, while his calls on his vassals would be essentially military in nature. He would have no direct political access to the population as a whole, for jurisdiction over it would be mediatized through innumerable layers of subinfeudation. He would, in effect, be master only on his own estates, otherwise to great extent a ceremonial figurehead. The pure model of such a polity, in which political power was stratified downwards in such a way that its apex retained no qualitatively separate or plenipotentiary authority at all, never existed anywhere within mediaeval Europe.[7] For the lack of any real integrating mechanism at the top of a feudal system implied by this type of polity posed a permanent threat to its stability and survival. A complete fragmentation of sovereignty was incompatible with the class unity of the nobility itself, for the potential

7. The Crusader State in the Levant has often been considered the closest approximation to a perfect feudal constitution. The overseas constructs of European feudalism were created *ex nihilo* in an alien environment, and thus assumed an exceptionally systematic juridical form. Engels, among others, remarked on this singularity: 'Did feudalism ever correspond to its concept? Founded in the kingdom of the West Franks, further developed in Normandy by the Norwegian conquerors, its formation continued by the French Norsemen in England and Southern Italy, it came nearest to its concept – in the ephemeral kingdom of Jerusalem, which in the *Assize of Jerusalem* left behind it the most classic expression of the feudal order.' Marx-Engels, *Selected Correspondence*, Moscow, 1965, p. 484. But the practical realities of even the Crusader realm never corresponded to the legal codification of its baronial jurists.

anarchy implied by it was necessarily disruptive of the whole mode of production on which their privileges rested. There was thus an inbuilt contradiction within feudalism, between its own rigorous tendency to a decomposition of sovereignty and the absolute exigencies of a final centre of authority in which a practical recomposition could occur. Feudal *monarchy*, therefore, was never wholly reducible to a royal suzerainty: it always existed to some extent in an ideological and juridical realm beyond that of those vassal relationships whose summit could otherwise be ducal or comital potentates, and possessed rights to which the latter could not aspire. At the same time, actual royal power always had to be asserted and extended against the spontaneous grain of the feudal polity as a whole, in a constant struggle to establish a 'public' authority outside the compact web of private jurisdictions. The feudal mode of production in the West thus originally specified in its very structure a dynamic tension and contradiction within the centrifugal State which it organically produced and reproduced.

Such a political system necessarily precluded any extensive bureaucracy, and functionally divided class rule in a novel fashion. For on the one hand, the parcellization of sovereignty in early mediaeval Europe led to the constitution of a separate ideological order altogether. The Church, which in Late Antiquity had always been directly integrated into the machinery of the imperial State, and subordinated to it, now became an eminently autonomous institution within the feudal polity. Sole source of religious authority, its command over the beliefs and values of the masses was immense; but its ecclesiastical organization was distinct from that of any secular nobility or monarchy. Because of the dispersal of coercion inherent in emergent Western feudalism, the Church could defend its own corporate interests, if necessary, from a territorial redoubt and by armed force. Institutional conflicts between lay and religious lordship were thus endemic in the mediaeval epoch: their result was a scission in the structure of feudal legitimacy, whose cultural consequences for later intellectual development were to be considerable. On the other hand, secular government itself was characteristically narrowed into a new mould. It became essentially the exercise of 'justice', which under feudalism occupied a functional position wholly distinct from that under capitalism today. Justice was the *central* modality of political power – specified as such by the very nature of the feudal polity. For the pure feudal hierarchy, as we have seen, excluded any 'executive' at all, in the modern sense of a permanent administrative apparatus of the State for the enforcement of the law: the parcellization of sovereignty rendered one unnecessary and impossible. At the same time, there was no room for an orthodox 'legislature' of the later type either, since the feudal order possessed no general concept of political innovation by the creation of *new* laws. Royal rulers fulfilled their station by preserving traditional laws, not by inventing novel ones. Thus political power came for a period to be virtually identified with the single 'judiciary' function of interpreting and applying the existing laws. Moreover, in the absence of any public bureaucracy, local coercion and administration – policing, fining, tolling and enforcing powers – inevitably accrued to it. It is thus necessary always to remember that mediaeval 'justice' factually included a much wider range of activities than modern justice, because it structurally occupied a far more pivotal position within the total political system. It was the ordinary name of power.

2

Typology of Social Formations

We have so far discussed the genesis of feudalism in Western Europe as a synthesis of elements released by the concurrent dissolution of primitive-communal and slave modes of production; and then outlined the constitutive structure of the developed feudal mode of production in the West as such. It now remains to show briefly how the inherent nature of this synthesis produced a variegated typology of social formations in the mediaeval epoch. For the mode of production just sketched never existed in a 'pure state' anywhere in Europe, any more than the capitalist mode of production was to do later. The concrete *social formations* of mediaeval Europe were always composite systems, in which other modes of production survived and intertwined with feudalism proper: slaves, for example, existed throughout the Middle Ages, and free peasants were never wholly wiped out anywhere by the Dark Ages. It is thus essential to survey, however rapidly, the diversity of the map of Western feudalism as it emerged from the 9th century onwards. TheSoviet historians Liublinskaya, Gutnova and Udaltsova have correctly advanced a three-fold classification.[1] In effect, the core region of European feudalism was that in which a 'balanced synthesis' of Roman and Germanic elements occurred: essentially, Northern

1. A. D. Liublinskaya, 'Tipologiya Rannevo Feodalizma v Zapadnoi Evrope i Problema Romano-Germanskovo Sinteza', *Srednie Veka*, Fasc. 31, 1968, pp. 9–17; Z. V. Udaltsova and E. V. Gutnova, 'Genezis Feodalizma v Stranakh Evropy', *13th World Congress of Historical Sciences*, Moscow 1970. The problem of a typology was earlier briefly raised by Porshnev in his *Feodaliẓm i Narodni Massy*, cited above, pp. 507–18. The paper by Udaltsova and Gutnova is careful and thoughtful, even where its particular conclusions cannot always be accepted. The authors regard the Byzantine State of the early Middle Ages as one of the variants of feudalism, with a confidence it is difficult to share.

France and zones contiguous to it, the homeland of the Carolingian Empire.[2] To the South of this area, in Provence, Italy or Spain, the dissolution and recombination of barbarian and ancient modes of production occurred under the dominant legacy of Antiquity. To the North and East of it, in Germany, Scandinavia and England, where Roman rule had either never reached or had taken only shallow root, there was conversely a slow transition towards feudalism, under the indigenous dominance of the barbarian heritage. The 'balanced' synthesis generated feudalism most rapidly and completely, and provided its classic form – which in turn had a great impact on outlying zones with a less articulated feudal system.[3] It was here that serfdom first emerged; a manorial system was developed; seigneurial justice was most pronounced; and hierarchical subinfeudation became thickest. The Northern and Southern sub-types were, for their part, symmetrically distinguished by the presence of powerful survivals from their respective anterior modes of production. In Scandinavia, Germany and Anglo-Saxon England, an allodial peasantry with strong communal institutions persisted well after the onset of stable hierarchical differentiation in rural society, the growth of ties of dependence, and the consolidation of clan warriors into a landed aristocracy. Serfdom was not introduced into Saxony until the 12th or 13th centuries; it was never properly established in Sweden at all. On the other hand, in Italy and adjacent regions, the urban civilization of late Antiquity never wholly foundered, and municipal political organization – blended with ecclesiastical power, where the Church had inherited the position of the old senatorial patriciate – flourished from the 10th century onwards; while the Roman legal conceptions of property as free, heritable and alienable, qualified feudal landed norms from the start.[4] The map of

2. For a recent attempt to identify five regional sub-types within the feudalism that emerged in post-barbarian Gaul, see A. Ya. Shevelenko, 'K Tipologii Genezisa Feodalizma', *Voprosy Istorii*, January 1971, pp. 97–107.

3. Throughout Europe, the spread of feudal relations was always topographically uneven within each major region. For mountainous zones everywhere resisted manorial organization, which was inherently difficult to impose, and unprofitable to maintain, in rocky and infertile uplands. Hence mountains tended to conserve pockets of poor but independent peasant communities, economically and culturally more backward than the seigneurialized plains below them, but often militarily capable of defending their gaunt fastnesses.

4. Germanic allods were always distinct from Roman property, since is a

early European feudalism thus essentially comprised three zones running from North to South, roughly demarcated by the respective
density of allods, fiefs, and towns.

Against this background, it is possible to sketch some of the main
differences between the major social formations of Western Europe in
this epoch, which were often to have important ulterior repercussions.
In each case, our main concern will be the pattern of rural relations
of production, the extent of urban enclaves, and – especially – the
type of political state that emerged in the early Middle Ages. This
latter focus will inevitably be dominated by discussion of the origins
and vicissitudes of monarchy in the various Western European
countries.

France, as the central homeland of European feudalism, can be dealt
with relatively briefly. Northern France, in effect, always conformed
more closely to the archetypal feudal system than any other region of
the continent. The collapse of the Carolingian Empire in the 9th century
was followed by a welter of internecine warfare and Norse invasions.
Amidst generalized anarchy and insecurity, there occurred a universal
fragmentation and localization of noble power, which became concentrated into selected strong-points and castles across the country,
in conditions which accelerated the dependence of a peasantry exposed
to constant threat of Viking or Muslim rapine.[5] Feudal power was thus
pressed singularly close to the soil in this bleak epoch. Harsh seigneurial jurisdictions over an enserfed rural mass, which had lost any
popular courts of its own, prevailed virtually everywhere; although the
South, where the impress of Antiquity was greater, was somewhat less
feudalized, with a greater proportion of noble estates held outright
rather than in fief, and a larger non-dependent peasant population.[6]

---

transitional form between communal and individual landownership in the village,
they were a type of private property still typically subject to customary obligations and cycles within the community and were not freely alienable.

5. Bloch's description of this time, in the first part of *Feudal Society*, is justly
famous. For the spread of castles, see Boutruche, *Seigneurie et Féodalité*, II,
Paris 1970, pp. 31–9.

6. This configuration was accompanied by the greater survival of slavery in
Southern France throughout the Middle Ages: for the renewed traffic of the
13th century onwards, see Verlinden, *L'Esclavage Médiéval*, I, pp. 748–833. As

The more organic character of Northern feudalism ensured it the economic and political initiative throughout the Middle Ages. However, by the late 10th and early 11th centuries, the general French pattern was a uniquely comprehensive feudal hierarchy, built from the ground upwards, often in multiple tiers of subinfeudation. The complement of this vertical system was extreme territorial disunity. By the late 10th century, there were over 50 distinct political divisions in the country as a whole. Six major potentates exercised autonomous provincial power – the Dukes or Counts of Flanders, Normandy, France, Burgundy, Acquitaine and Toulouse. It was eventually the Duchy of France which provided the nucleus for the construction of a new French monarchy.

Initially confined to a feeble enclave in the Laon-Paris region, the Capetian royal house slowly consolidated its base and asserted increasing suzerain rights over the great duchies, by dint of military aggression, clerical aid and matrimonial alliances. The first great architects of its power were Louis VI and Suger, who pacified and unified the Duchy of France itself. The rise of the Capetian monarchy in the 12th and 13th centuries was accompanied by marked economic progress, with extensive land reclamations both in the royal demesne and those of its ducal and comital vassals, and the emergence of flourishing urban communes, particularly in the far North. The reign of Philippe Auguste in the early 13th century was decisive for the establishment of monarchical power into an effective kingship above the duchies: Normandy, Anjou, Maine, Touraine, and Artois were annexed to the royal demesne, which was trebled in size. Adroit rallying of the Northern towns further strengthened Capetian military power: it was their troops and transport that ensured the signal French victory over Anglo-Flemish forces at Bouvines in 1212, a turning-point in the international political struggles of the age. Philippe Auguste's successor, Louis VIII, successfully seized much of Languedoc, and therewith extended Capetian rule down to the Mediterranean. A relatively large and loyal officialdom of *baillis* and *sénéschaux* was created to administer the lands directly under royal control. However, the size of this bureaucracy was an index, not so much of the intrinsic

we shall see later, there is a repeated correlation between the presence of slaves and the incompletion of serfdom in different regions of feudal Europe.

power of the French kings, as of the problems confronting any unitary administration of the country.[7] The dangerous devolution of newly acquired regions into appanages controlled by lesser Capetian princes, was only another sign of the inherent difficulty of the task. For the independent power of provincial rulers meanwhile subsisted, and an analogous fortification of their administrative apparatuses occurred. The basic process in France thus remained a slow 'concentric centralization', in which the degree of royal control exercised from Paris was still very precarious. After the victories of Louis IX and Philippe Le Bel, this inner instability was to become all too evident. In the prolonged civil wars of the next three centuries (Hundred Years' War, Religious Wars), the fabric of French feudal unity was to be repeatedly and menacingly rent, without ever finally coming apart.

In England, by contrast, a centralized feudalism was imported from the outside by the Norman conquerors, and systematically implanted from above, in a compact land that was only a quarter the size of France. The Anglo-Saxon social formation that succumbed to the Norman invasion had been the most highly developed example in Europe of a potentially 'spontaneous' transition of a Germanic society to a feudal social formation, unaffected by any direct Roman impact. England had, of course, on the other hand been heavily affected by Scandinavian invasions from the 9th century onwards. The local Anglo-Saxon societies had slowly evolved towards consolidated social hierarchies, with a subordinated peasantry, in the 7th and 8th centuries, but without either political unification of the island or much urban development. Increasing Norwegian and Danish attacks from 793 onwards gradually modified the tempo and direction of this development. Scandinavian occupation, first of half England in the 9th century, and then its complete conquest and integration into a North Sea Empire in the early 11th century, had dual effects on Anglo-Saxon society. Norse settlements generally promoted towns and planted free peasant communities, in the regions of their densest immigration. At the same time, Viking military pressure led to social processes within the island as a whole similar to those which were occurring on the continent, in the epoch of the long ships: constant rural insecurity led to a growth of

7. For the Capetian administrative system, see Charles Petit-Dutaillis, *Feudal Monarchy in England and France*, London 1936, pp. 233–58.

commendation and an increasing degradation of the peasantry. In England, the economic charge of local lords on the rural population was combined with royal defense taxes levied for the purposes of Anglo-Saxon resistance, or placation, of Danish aggression, the *geld* moneys which became the first regular tax to be collected in Western Europe in the later Dark Ages.[8] By the mid 11th century, Scandinavian rule had been shaken off, and a recently unified Anglo-Saxon kingdom restored. The peasantry were by this time generally semi-dependent tenants, except in the North-Eastern areas of former Danish settlement, where allodial plots of 'sokemen' were more numerous. Slaves still existed, comprising some 10 per cent or so of the labour force; they were economically most important in the remoter Western regions, where Celtic resistance to Anglo-Saxon conquest had been longest, and in which slaves made up a fifth or more of the population. A local aristocracy of thegns dominated the rural social structure, exploiting estates of a proto-manorial type.[9] The monarchy possessed a relatively advanced and coordinated administrative system, with royal taxation, currency and justice effective throughout the country. On the other hand, no secure system of dynastic succession had been established. The critical external weakness of this island kingdom, however, was the lack of that structural bond between landownership and military service which formed the foundation of the continental fief system.[10] The thegns were a noble infantry, who rode to battle yet fought

8. Loyn, *Anglo-Saxon England and the Norman Conquest*, pp. 139, 195–7, 305, 309–14.

9. The political powers of this nobility are stressed, perhaps somewhat too heavily, by E. John, 'English Feudalism and the Structure of Anglo-Saxon Society', *Bulletin of the John Rylands Library*, 1963–4, pp. 14–41.

10. Henry Loyn, *The Norman Conquest*, London 1965, pp. 76–7 and G. O. Sayles, *The Mediaeval Foundations of England*, London 1964, pp. 210, 225, both of which generally tend to minimize the political distance between the Anglo-Saxon and Anglo-Norman social formations. It is a curiosity that Sayles should pay homage to the legacy of Freeman, as an inspiration for contemporary scholarship. Freeman's extreme racism is, of course, a matter of record; Africans were 'hideous apes', Jews and Chinese 'filthy strangers', while Normans were Teutonic kinsmen of the Saxons 'who had gone into Gaul to get covered with a French varnish, and who came into England to be washed clean again' (sic): for documentation, see M. E. Bratchel, *Edward Augustus Freeman and the Victorian Interpretation of the Norman Conquest*, Ilfracombe 1969. But it can be tacitly ignored, because his central message, the mystically 'unbroken drama' of English history, by contrast with that of the European continent with its revolutionary

archaically on foot. The Anglo-Saxon Army was thus a combination of housecarls (royal military retainers) and fyrd (folk-militia). It was no match for the steeled Norman cavalry, military spearhead of a much more fully developed feudal society on the rim of the French mainland, where the linkage of estate tenure and equestrian service had long been the lynchpin of the social order. The Normans themselves, of course, were Norse invaders who had only settled and fused in Northern France a century earlier. The Norman Conquest, outcome of the uneven development of two barbarian communities facing each other across the Channel, one of which had undergone a 'Romano-Germanic' fusion, thus generated a 'belated' synthesis in England of two comparatively advanced social formations. The result was the peculiar combination of a highly centralized State and a resilient popular justice that distinguished mediaeval England thereafter.

Immediately after his victory, William I proceeded to a planned and systematic distribution of some 5,000 fiefs to occupy and hold down the country. Contrary to continental usages, sub-vassals had to swear allegiance not only to their immediate lords, but also to the monarch himself – ultimate donor of all land. The Norman kings further exploited pre-feudal survivals from the Anglo-Saxon social formation to strengthen their State: the fyrd militia was on occasion added to the conventional feudal host and the household troops;[11] more important, the traditional defence tax of the *danegeld*, a phenomenon outside the orthodox revenue system of a mediaeval monarchy, continued to be collected, in addition to the incomes yielded from the very large royal demesne and the exaction of feudal incidences. The Anglo-Norman State thus represented the most unified and solidified institutional system in Western Europe at this date. The most developed manorial-

---

ruptures, is still widely and fervently believed. The cherished ideological motifs of England's inviolate 'continuity', from the tenth to the twentieth century, recur with oneiric insistence in much of the local historiography. Loyn ends his serious and useful book with the typical credo: 'In the field of institutions continuity is the essential theme of English history', *The Norman Conquest*, p. 195.

11. For discussions of the post-conquest military system, see J. O. Prestwich, 'Anglo-Norman Feudalism and the Problem of Continuity', *Past and Present*, No. 26, November 1963, pp. 35–57 – a salutary criticism of the parochial and chauvinist myths of continuity; and Warren Hollister, '1066: the Feudal Revolution', *American Historical Review*, Vol. LXXIII, No. 3, February 1968, pp. 708–

ism was established mainly in the South and South-Centre of the country, where the efficacy of seigneurial exploitation notably increased, with an intensification of labour services and a marked degradation of the local peasantry. Elsewhere, considerable areas were left with small holdings only lightly burdened with feudal obligations, and a rural population that escaped immediate servile status. The trend towards a general enserfment was, however, unmistakeable. In the next hundred years, there was a progressive levelling downwards of the juridical condition of the English peasantry under the Norman and Angevin dynasties, until by the 12th century *villani* and *nativi* formed a single serf class. On the other hand, given the complete disappearance of Roman law in England and the absence of any neo-imperial experience of the Carolingian type, the shire and hundred courts of the Anglo-Saxon social formation – originally sites of popular communal justice – survived into the new order. Now, of course, dominated by royal appointees from the baronial class, they nevertheless formed a system of 'public' justice relatively less implacable to the poor than the private seigneurial franchises which were the normal pattern elsewhere.[12] The presiding office of sheriff never became hereditary, after a thorough purge to avert this danger by Henry II in the 12th century; while royal justice proper was extended by the assize courts of the same sovereign. Towns of any size were few and enjoyed no substantive independence. The result was to create a feudal polity with limited subinfeudation, and a great degree of administrative flexibility and unity.

Germany presents a polar opposite to this experience. There, the East Frankish lands were in the main recent conquests of the Carolingian Empire, and lay outside the frontiers of classical Antiquity altogether. The Roman element in the final feudal synthesis was correspondingly far weaker, mediated at a remove through the novel hold of the Carolingian State itself on these frontier regions. Thus whereas in France the comital administrative structure coincided with the old Roman *civitatus*, and presided over an increasingly articulated vassalage system with a servile peasantry beneath it, the primitive-communal character of Germanic rural society – still legally organized

---

723, which provides a brief historical survey of the controversy on the question.
12. Manorial courts, of course, flourished, and the real economic power of the

on a quasi-tribal basis – precluded any direct replica of this. The counts who ruled in the Emperor's name possessed uncertain jurisdictions over hazily defined regions, without much real power over the local popular courts or firm backing in large royal domains.[13] In Franconia and Lorraine, adjoining Northern France and already part of the Merovingian realm, a proto-feudal aristocracy and a serf agriculture had developed. But in much the greater part of Germany – Bavaria, Thuringia, Swabia and Saxony – there was still a free allodial peasantry and a federative clan nobility, unorganized in any network of vassalage. German lordship was traditionally a 'continuous medium'[14] in which gradations of rank had little formal sanction; monarchy was not itself vested with any special superordinate value. Carolingian imperial administration was imposed on a social formation which lacked the complex hierarchies of dependence that were emerging in France: its memory therefore survived much longer, in this more primitive milieu. Moreover, Germany was not scourged to the same extent as France by the new wave of barbarian attacks in the 9th and 10th centuries: where the latter was ravaged by all three invaders – Vikings, Magyars and Saracens – the former confronted only the Magyars. These nomads were finally defeated at Lechfeld in the East, while Normandy was being ceded to the Vikings in the West. Germany thus escaped the worst of the tribulations of this epoch, as the comparatively rapid Ottonian recovery was to demonstrate. But the Carolingian political heritage, less effaced here, provided no durable substitute for a compact seigneurial hierarchy. Thus with the collapse of the dynasty itself, there was initially something like a political vacuum in Germany during the 10th century. Into it soon emerged usurper 'stem' duchies of a tribal character which established loose control over the five main regions of the country, Bavaria, Thuringia, Swabia, Franconia and Saxony. The danger of Magyar invasions induced these rival ducal

English lords in the Middle Ages was certainly no less than that of their continental opposites, as Hilton underlines. R. H. Hilton, *A Mediaeval Society: The West Midlands at the End of the Twelfth Century*, London 1964, pp. 227–41.

13. Sidney Painter, *The Rise of the Feudal Monarchies*, Ithaca 1954, p. 85.

14. *Die Herrschaftsformen gehen kontinuierlich ineinander über*: this apt phrase is the coinage of Walter Schlesinger, 'Herrschaft und Gefolgschaft in der germanisch-deutschen Verfassungsgeschichte', *Beiträge zur deutschen Verfassungsgeschichte des Mittelalters*, Bd. I, Gottingen 1963, p. 32.

magnates to elect a formal royal suzerain. The history of the German monarchy was thereafter to be largely that of abortive attempts to create an organic pyramid of feudal allegiances on this unsatisfactory foundation. The most powerful (and non-feudal) of the stem duchies, Saxony, provided the first dynasty to try to unify the country. Mobilizing the aid of the Church, the Ottonian rulers of Saxony progressively subordinated their clerical rivals and established royal authority throughout Germany. To safeguard his western flank, Otto I also assumed the imperial mantle that had devolved from the Carolingians to the decrepit 'middle kingdom' of Lotharingia, that included Burgundy and Northern Italy. In the East, he expanded German frontiers into Slav territory, and established suzerainty over Bohemia and Poland. The Ottonian 'Renovation' was both ideologically and adminstratively the last successor of the Carolingian Empire; it too witnessed a classicist revival culturally, and laid claim to a universal dominion. But its life-span was to be even briefer.

For Ottonian successes created new difficulties and dangers for a unitary German state in their turn. The subjugation of the ducal magnates by the Saxon line in practice merely freed a stratum of nobles below them, thereby simply shifting the problem of regional anarchy downwards. The Salian dynasty which followed in the 11th century attempted to deal with widespread aristocratic resistance and turbulence by creating a special class of unfree royal *ministeriales*, who formed a corps of loyal castellans and administrators planted across the country. This resort to servile functionaries, vested with powerful political posts yet no equivalent social position, often loaded with estates yet without vassal privileges, and hence exterior to any noble hierarchy, was the mark of the continuing weakness of the monarchical function, in a social formation which still had no comprehensive system of feudal social relations at village level. On the surface, the Salian rulers registered considerable progress towards a centralized imperial rule: dissident aristocratic rebellions in Saxony were suppressed, a permanent capital was founded at Goslar and the royal domain greatly enlarged. However, at this point the Investiture dispute with the Papacy crippled any further consolidation of royal power. Gregory VII's struggle with Henry IV over control of episcopal appointments unleashed generalized civil war in Germany, as the local nobility seized the opportunity to rise against the Emperor, with Papal blessing. During fifty years of constant strife, a great social change now occurred in Germany: in the conditions of ruthless depredations, anarchy and social violence, the German aristocracy destroyed the allodial basis of the non-noble free population that had always predominated in Saxony and Thuringia and been a pervasive presence in Bavaria and Swabia. The peasantry was reduced to serfdom, as public and folk justice lapsed, feudal dues were exacted, and military obligations were intensified and codified between the members of the noble class itself, to whose ranks the *ministeriales* were now added, amidst the turmoil of the times and the high turnover of traditional families.[15]

A full feudalism, delayed so long in Germany, now finally arrived in the 12th century. But it was constructed *against* monarchical integration of the country, by contrast with England where the feudal social hierarchy was itself installed by the Norman monarchy, or France, where it preceded the emergence of the monarchy and was thereafter slowly reoriented round it in the process of concentric centralization. Once this had happened, the political effects proved irreversible. The Hohenstaufen dynasty, which emerged after the new social structure had crystallized, sought to build a renovated imperial power on its basis, accepting the mediatization of jurisdictions and the ramifications of vassalage that had now developed in Germany. Frederick I, in fact, himself took the lead in organizing a new feudal hierarchy of un-exampled complexity and rigidity – the *Heerschildordnung* – and creating a princely class from his tenants-in-chief by raising them above the rest of the nobility, to the rank of *Reichsfürsten*.[16] The logic of this policy was to convert the monarchy to feudal suzerainty proper, abandoning the whole tradition of Carolingian regalian administration. However, its necessary complement was the carving out of an ade-quately large royal domain to provide the Emperor with an autono-mous financial base from which to render his suzerainty effective. Since the Hohenstaufen family estates in Swabia were wholly in-sufficient for this, and direct aggression against fellow German princes was inadvisable, Frederick tried to convert Northern Italy – which had

15. Geoffrey Barraclough, *The Origins of Modern Germany*, Oxford 1962, pp. 136–40: the classic account.

16. Barraclough, *The Origins of Modern Germany*, pp. 175–7, 189–90.

always nominally been an Imperial fief – into a solid external bastion of royal power across the Alps. For the Papacy, this activation of the interlocking of German and Italian sovereignties threatened a fatal blow to its own power in the peninsula, especially after Sicily, in its rear, was added to the Imperial possessions by Henry VI. The consequent renewal of war between the Empire and the Papacy finally cancelled any chance of a stable imperial monarchy in Germany itself. With Frederick II, the Hohenstaufen dynasty became essentially Italianized in character and orientation, while Germany was left to its own baronial devices. After another hundred years of war, the final outcome was the neutralization of any hereditary monarchy in the 13th century, when the Empire became definitively elective, and the conversion of Germany into a confused archipelago of principalities.

If the establishment of German feudalism was marked and impeded by the persistence of tribal institutions dating back to the time of Tacitus, the evolution of feudalism in Italy was correspondingly abbreviated and inflected by the survival of classical traditions. The Byzantine reconquest of most of the peninsula from the Lombards in the 6th century had, despite the material destruction it wrought, helped to preserve these through a critical phase of the Dark Ages. Barbarian settlement had anyway been relatively thin. The result was that Italy never lost the municipal urban life which it had possessed in the Roman Empire. The major towns soon acted again as trading centres for commercial traffic across the Mediterranean, flourishing as ports and entrepots well in advance of any other cities in Europe. The Church inherited much of the social and political position of the old senatorial aristocracy; bishops were the typical administrative rulers of the Italian towns up to the 11th century. Because of the predominance of the Roman components in the feudal synthesis of this zone, where the legal heritage of Augustus and Justinian inevitably had a great weight, property relations were never aligned unilaterally with mainstream feudal patterns. Rural society was always very heterogeneous from the Dark Ages onwards, combining fiefs, free-hold peasants, latifundia and urban landowners in different regions. Manors proper were predominantly to be found in Lombardy and the North, while landed property on the other hand was most concentrated in the South, where classical latifundia worked by slaves survived under Byzantine rule right into the early Middle Ages.[17] Small peasant holdings were probably most numerous in the mountainous Centre of the country. The manorial system was consequently always much weaker in Italy than north of the Alps, and the rise of urban communes was earlier and more important than elsewhere.

Initially, the cities were dominated by small feudal nobles under their episcopal rulers. But by the end of the 11th century, seigneurial jurisdictions were already dwindling in the countryside, while the Investiture Contest gave the merchant communities inside the towns the opportunity of throwing off ecclesiastical overlordship and instituting communal self-government proper, initially in the form of an elective 'consular' system and later by the hiring of professional external administrators, the *podestà* of the 13th century. From 1100 or so onwards, these communes dominated the whole of Northern Italy and systematically set out to conquer the surrounding countryside, attacking baronial fiefs and abolishing feudal immunities, razing castles and forcing neighbouring lords into submission. The aim of this aggressive urban expansion was to conquer a territorial *contado* from which the town could thereafter raise taxes, troops and grain to increase its own power and prosperity *vis-à-vis* its rivals.[18] Rural relations were radically altered by the spread of the *contado*, for the towns tended to introduce new forms of semi-commercialized dependence for the peasantry that were a considerable remove from serfdom: *mezzadria* or contractual share-cropping became customary over much of North and Central Italy by the 13th century. The development of manufactures within the communes then led to increasing social tensions between the merchants and magnates (a ruling stratum with both rural and urban property), and the artisanal and professional groups organized in guilds and excluded from city government. In the 13th century, the political ascent of the latter found a curious expression in the institution of the *Capitano del Popolo*, who often enjoyed an uneasy condominium with the *Podestà* inside the same precincts: the office itself a striking memento of the classical Roman tribune.[19] This fragile

17. Philip Jones, 'The Agrarian Development of Mediaeval Italy', *Second International Conference of Economic History*, Paris 1965, p. 79.

18. For this whole evolution, see Daniel Waley, *The Italian City-Republics*, London 1969, pp. 12–21, 56–92.

19. Max Weber, *Economy and Society*, New York 1968, Vol. III, pp. 1308–9;

equilibrium did not last long. In the next century, the Lombard communes fell one after the other under the sway of hereditary personal tyrannies, the *signorie*; power was henceforward concentrated in the hands of autocratic adventurers, most of them ex-feudatories or *condottieri*. Tuscany followed in the same direction in the next hundred years. The most advanced regions of Italy thus became a chequerboard of competing city-states, in which the intervening countryside, unlike any other part of Europe, was annexed to the towns: no rural feudal pyramid ever arose. The presence of the Papacy athwart the peninsula, vigilant against the threat of any over-mighty secular State, was an important additional obstacle to the emergence of any peninsular monarchy, of course.

In two regions of Italy alone, was a full-scale feudal politico-economic system implanted. It is no accident that both were essentially 'extensions' of the most organic and powerful feudalism in Europe, that centred in France. Piedmont, abutting onto Savoy, was a frontier territory across the Alps: a seigneurial hierarchy and a dependent peasantry did develop in these uplands, beyond the influence of the communes on the plains. But in this epoch, the extreme North-East corner of the peninsula was too small and poor to be of any general importance in Italy. Much more formidable was the Southern kingdom of Naples and Sicily, which the Normans had created after their conquests from the Byzantines and the Arabs in the 11th century. There, fiefs were distributed and a true baronial system emerged, complete with appanages and serfdom; the monarchy which ruled over this southern simulacrum of the French synthesis was, if anything, strengthened by orientalized conceptions of royal paramountcy due to lingering Arab and Byzantine influences. It was this authentically feudal state which provided Frederick II with the base for his attempt to conquer and organize the whole of Italy in a unified mediaeval monarchy. For reasons which will be considered later, this project failed. The division of the peninsula into two distinct social systems was to persist for centuries afterwards.

In Spain, only two centuries separated the Visigothic occupation

Daniel Waley, *The Italian City-Republics*, pp. 182–97. A central reason for the emergence of the institutions of the *popolo* were the fiscal extortions of the patriciates; see J. Lestocquoy, *Aux Origines de la Bourgeoisie*, Paris 1952, pp. 189–93.

from the Muslim conquest. In this span of time, only the most shadowy combinations of Germanic and Roman elements could emerge: indeed, there was for most of the period – as we have seen – a complete legal and administrative separation of the two communities, after the barbarian settlement. In these conditions, no developed synthesis was possible. Christian Spain fell a century before Charlemagne created the Empire which acted as the real incubator for European feudalism. The Visigothic heritage was thus virtually wiped out by the Islamic conquest, and the residual Christian society in the Asturias had to restart from something like zero. Henceforward, the specific historical struggle of the Reconquest was the fundamental determinant of the forms of Spanish feudalism, rather than the original collision and fusion of barbarian and imperial societies. This basic fact set Spain apart from the other West European countries early on, producing an array of characteristics which are not homologous with those of the main types of European feudalism. The matrix of Spanish mediaeval society was in this respect always a unique one. The exception to the general pattern was to be Catalonia, which was incorporated into the Carolingian realm in the 9th century and consequently underwent the standard experience of *vassi dominici*, the benefice system and comital administration. In the early Middle Ages, the condition of the peasantry underwent a progressive degradation similar to that of contemporary France, with especially heavy personal dues and a developed seigneurial system. Catalan serfdom was established by the local lords over a course of two hundred years, from the mid-11th century onwards.[20] To the West, on the other hand, the peculiar conditions of the long struggle against Moorish power gave rise to a dual development. On the one hand, the initial 'slow reconquest' from the extreme north downwards created wide no man's lands – *presuras* – between Christian and Muslim States which were colonized by free peasants, in general conditions of labour shortage. These *presuras* also weakened seigneurial jurisdiction in the Christian territories proper, since the vacant lands provided potential refuge for fugitives.[21] Free peasant com-

20. J. Vicens Vives, *Historia de los Remensas en el Siglo XV*, Barcelona 1945, pp. 26–37.

21. J. Vicens Vives, *Manual de Historia Economica de España*, Barcelona 1959, pp. 120–3.

munities often collectively commended themselves to lords for protection, the so-called *behetrías*. In loose, fluctuating social formations of this kind, with constant unsettling raids by both sides across the shifting lines of religious demarcation, there was little possibility for a fully fixed feudal hierarchy to take shape. The religious character of the border wars, moreover, meant that enslavement of captives lasted as a regular social practice in Spain much longer than anywhere else in Western Europe. The availability of Muslim slave-labour thus generally delayed the consolidation of a Christian serf-class in the Iberian peninsula (an inverse correlation between the two labour systems is a general rule in the mediaeval epoch, as we shall see). From the turn of the 11th century onwards, there was a considerable extension of seigneurial estates and large domains in Castile and Leon.[22] Castilian *solariegos* or villeins were by no means negligible from this time onwards, but they never constituted a majority of the rural population. Aragonese frontier expansion was relatively less important, and serfdom was correspondingly more pronounced in its interior highlands.

The monarchs of the Christian kingdoms in the 10th and 11th centuries owed their exceptional authority to their supreme military functions in the permanent crusade towards the South and to the small size of their States, rather than to any very articulated feudal suzerainty or consolidated royal demesne.[23] Personal vassalage, landed benefices and seigneurial jurisdictions existed, but they remained dissociated elements which had not yet merged to form a fief system proper. An indigenous class of *caballeros villanos* – commoner knights – paradoxically resided in the towns, and provided cavalry service for the advance southwards in exchange for municipal and fiscal privileges.[24] After 1100, French feudal influences on the Castilian court and church led to the multiplication of *senorios* or territorial lordships, although these did not acquire the autonomy of their models across the Pyrenees. Cistercian initiatives were likewise responsible for

22. Luis De Valdeavellano, *Historia de España*, Madrid 1955, I/II, pp. 293–304.

23. C. Sanchez-Albornoz, *Estudios sobre Las Instituciones Medievales Españoles*, Mexico 1965, pp. 797–9.

24. Elena Lourie, 'A Society Organized for War: Medieval Spain', *Past and Present* No. 35, December 1966, pp. 55–66. This article provides a competent summary of some of the main lines of Spanish mediaeval historiography.

the creation of the three large military-monastic orders – Santiago, Calatrava and Alcantara – which henceforward played a key role in Castile.

This anomalous complex of institutions lasted down to the late 12th century, by which time the Reconquest had gradually inched forward to the line of the Tagus. Then in the 13th century, virtually the whole of the South fell, swiftly and suddenly, to the 'quick Reconquest'. Andalusia was absorbed in 30 years. With this enormous territorial windfall, the whole process of colonization was now inverted, and an agrarian order the very opposite of that which had grown up in the North was created in the South. The victorious campaigns had been to a considerable extent organized and led by the great military orders of Castile – whose characteristic structure had been copied from the Islamic enemy for the prosecution of the faith. These warrior confraternities now seized vast estates and appropriated seigneurial jurisdictions over them; it was from the military captains of this century that emerged most of the class of grandees which was to dominate Spanish feudalism thereafter. The Muslim artisanate was rapidly ejected from the towns to the remaining Islamic emirate of Granada – a blow which simultaneously hit the Muslim small-holder agriculture that had traditionally been linked to the Andalusian urban economy. The subsequent crushing of the Moorish peasant rebellions then depopulated the land. There was thus an acute labour shortage which could only be solved by the reduction of the rural labour force to serfdom – a condition the more easily imposed, with the arrival of noble armies at the Mediterranean. The construction of vast latifundia in Andalusia was further promoted by the widespread conversion of sown acreage to extensive pasturage for wool. In these barren conditions, most of the foot-soldiers who had gained small farms in the South sold up to the large landowners and went back North.[25] The new Southern pattern now reacted back on Castile: to prevent a drainage of labour from their estates by the wealthier Andalusian aristocracy, the Northern *hidalgo* class fastened increasing ties of dependence on its peasantry, until by the 14th century an increasingly similar villein class had emerged throughout most of Spain. The Castilian and Aragonese monarchies, neither of them yet wholly

25. G. Jackson, *The Making of Mediaeval Spain*, London 1972, pp. 86–8.

consolidated institutions, nevertheless reaped substantial benefits from this feudalization of their warrior aristocracies. The traditions of military fealty to the royal commander were reinforced, a powerful yet loyal nobility was created, and a servile peasant class stabilized on the land.

Portugal, on the far Atlantic edge of the Iberian peninsula, was the last important feudal monarchy to emerge in Western Europe. The North-Western region of Roman Hispania had been the recipient of the Suevi, the only Germanic people of the initial confederation that crossed the Rhine in 406 to settle in the lands they first conquered. The Suevi left behind them the densest cluster of Germanic toponyms in the peninsula, the heavy northern plough and the fleeting memory of the first Catholic barbarian ruler in Europe, before they were conquered and absorbed by the Visigothic kingdom in the 6th century. Thereafter the Western borderlands of Iberia had little separate history from the rest of the peninsula, experiencing Muslim conquest and a mountainous Christian redoubt beyond it like Spain itself. Its independent history reemerged when Portugal – then a modest tract of land between the Minho and the Douro – was granted as an appanage of Castile-Leon to a scion of the Duke of Burgundy in 1095. Fifty years later, his grandson founded the Portuguese monarchy. In this distant frontier region, much of the general pattern of Spanish development was to be repeated, and exaggerated. Reconquest of the South was much briefer than in Spain, and consequently led to even more pronounced royal power. The country was cleared of Muslim occupation with the capture of the Algarve in 1249, two centuries before the fall of Granada. Largely as a result, no formalized intra-seigneurial hierarchy emerged, and noble separatism was weak. Sub-vassalage was confined to a few powerful magnates like the Bragança house. A restricted group of *cavaleiros-vilãos* formed a relatively prosperous village elite with emphyteutic leases. Small peasant property was minimal, except in the far North, because there was no 'slow' phase of reconquest comparable to that in Castile and Leon. The great mass of the rural population were tenants paying feudal rents on large estates, with comparatively few demesnes. Predial and fiscal dues together could take up to 70 per cent of the direct producer's output; additional labour services might be 1–3 days a week, although these were not universal.[26] On the other hand, glebe serfdom was disappearing as early as the 13th century, at least in part because of the abundance of Muslim captives in the South; while maritime trade with England and France was already growing significantly. At the same time, the importance of the military religious orders for the social pattern of mediaeval Portugal was even greater than in Spain. The distribution of landed property within the ruling class was probably unique in Western Europe: down to the Avis revolution of 1383, the annual income of the monarchy was approximately equal to that of the church, and the two combined were between four and eight times larger than the total revenues of the nobility.[27] This extreme centralization of feudal property was a vivid indicator of the singularity of the Portuguese social formation. Combined with the absence of adscriptive serfdom and the ascent of sea-board commerce from the 13th century onwards, it early marked Portugal off for a separate future.

26. A. H. de Oliveira Marques, *A Sociedade Medieval Portuguesa*, Lisbon 1964, pp. 143–4.
27. Armando Castro, *Portugal na Europa do seu Tempo*, Lisbon 1970, pp. 135–8.

The Far North

The differential character and trajectory of the Scandinavian social formations, from the Dark Ages onwards, form a fascinating problem for historical materialism, and a necessary *control* for any general Marxist typology of European regional development, that is all too often neglected.[1] There is little space to explore this complex and under-documented question here. But a brief sketch of the early development of the area is essential for an understanding of the hinge-role later played by Sweden in the history of early modern Europe.

It will suffice to say at the outset that the *fundamental* historical determinant of Scandinavian 'specificity' was the peculiar nature of Viking social structure, which originally separated the whole zone from the rest of the continent. Scandinavia, of course, had lain wholly outside the Roman world. No contiguity with the legionaries and traders of the *limes* had disrupted or quickened the life of its tribal populations in the centuries of the *pax romana*. Although the great

1. In a famous remark, Hecksher once commented that 'countries of second rank' had no right to expect their history to be generally studied. Arguing that 'every historical study should lead either to the discovery of general laws or to the discernment of mechanisms of a major evolution', he concluded that the development of such lands as Sweden was only of significance in so far as it adumbrated or conformed to a wider international pattern. The residue could effectively be neglected: 'let us not complicate the tasks of science unnecessarily.' (E. Hecksher, 'Un Grand Chapitre de l'Histoire du Fer: Le Monopole Suédois', *Annales* No. 14, March 1932, p. 127). In fact, the tasks of historical science cannot be considered discharged if a region that controverts many of its accepted categories is ignored by it. Scandinavian development is not merely a catalogue of particularities, to be optionally added to an indefinite inventory of social forms. Its very deviations, on the contrary, have certain general lessons for any integral theory of European feudalism, both in the mediaeval and early modern epochs.

wave of barbarian invasions in the 4th and 5th centuries had included many originally Scandinavian peoples among them, notably the Goths and Burgundians,[2] these had long since settled amidst the rest of the Germanic populations on the other side of the Baltic, before their plunge into the Empire. Scandinavia proper was thus itself virtually untouched by the great drama of the collapse of Antiquity. Thus by the later Dark Ages, after three centuries of Frankish or Lombard rule over the former provinces of the Roman West, and the corresponding social evolution and synthesis that had produced the foundations of a fully-developed feudalism, the social formations of the Far North preserved virtually intact the primitive internal pattern of Germanic tribal communities of the time of Tacitus: an arms-bearing peasantry (*bondi*), a free council of farmer-warriors (*thing*), a leading class of clan optimates (led by *jarls*), a retinue system for raiding expeditions (*hirdh*) and a precarious, semi-elective kingship.[3] By the 8th century, these rudimentary Scandinavian societies, in their turn, became one of the barbarian frontiers of the 'restored' Carolingian Empire, as it expanded across North Germany into Saxony, along a line adjacent to contemporary Denmark. Contact was succeeded by a sudden and devastating reproduction of the barbarian invasions which had swept south to attack the Roman Empire. From the 8th to the 11th centuries, Viking bands ravaged Ireland, England, the Netherlands and France, marauding as far as Spain, Italy and Byzantium. Viking settlers colonized Iceland and Greenland; and Viking soldiers and traders created the first territorial State in Russia.

These invasions have often appeared to be a 'second assault' against Christian Europe. In fact, their structure was *decisively* different from that of the Germanic barbarians which brought Antiquity in the West to an end. For firstly, they were not *Völkerwanderungen* proper, because whole peoples did not migrate across land in them: they were *maritime* expeditions, necessarily far more limited in numbers. Recent scholarship has drastically reduced the exaggerated estimates of the

2. Probably from Götland and Bornholm, respectively.

3. A crisp recent account in a non-Scandinavian language is Gwyn Jones, *A History of the Vikings*, Oxford 1968, pp. 145–55. Kuhn contends that the *hirdh* was a later Anglo-Danish innovation of the 10th and 11th centuries, subsequently reimported back to Scandinavia – an isolated view: 'Die Grenzen der germanischen Gefolgschaft', pp. 43–7.

panic-stricken victims of the Viking raiding parties. Most of the marauding bands were no more than 300–400 strong: the largest group ever to attack England in the 9th century numbered less than 1,000.[4] Secondly, and essentially, Viking expansion was markedly *commercial* in character: the objects of their seaborne expeditions included not merely land for settlement, but also currency and commodities. They sacked some towns in their path, but they also founded and built far more – in diametric contrast to their predecessors. For towns were the ganglia of their trade. Moreover, the central traffic of this trade was slaves, who were captured and transported from all over Europe, but above all from the Celtic West and Slav East. It is necessary, of course, to distinguish the respective pattern of Norwegian, Danish and Swedish expansion in this epoch: the differences between them were much more than mere regional nuances.[5] The Norwegian Vikings on the extreme Western flank of the overseas drive seem to have been impelled by land shortages in their mountainous homeland; they typically sought, beyond simple booty, soil for settlement, no matter how inhospitable the environment: besides raiding Ireland and Scotland, it was they who peopled the bleak Faroes, and discovered and colonized Iceland. The Danish expeditions in the Centre, which conquered and planted North-Eastern England and Normandy, were much more organized assaults, under disciplined quasi-royal command, and created compacter and more hierarchical overseas societies, in which extorted treasure and protection money (such as *danegeld*) was spent locally on building up stable territorial occupation. Swedish piratical expansion on the extreme Eastern flank, on the other hand, was overwhelmingly commercial in orientation: Varangian penetration of Russia was not concerned with land-settlement, but with control of the riverine trade-routes to Byzantium and the Muslim East. Whereas the typical Viking States founded in the Atlantic (Orkneys, Iceland or Greenland) were settled agrarian communities, the Varangian realm in Russia was a commercial empire built fundamentally on the sale of

4. P. H. Sawyer, *The Age of Vikings*, London 1962, p. 125. This is the most sober and stringent study of the whole topic, although it is also the tersest on Scandinavian social structure at home.

5. See Lucien Musset, *Les Invasions: Le Second Assaut contre l'Europe Chrétienne* (*VIIe – XIe Siècles*), Paris 1965, pp. 115–18; Johannes Bronsted, *The Vikings*, London 1967, pp. 31–6, has a similar, if less adequate discussion.

slaves to the Islamic world, initially via the Khazar and Bulgar Khanates, and later directly from the central emporium of Kiev itself.

The Varangian trade in the Slav East was on such a scale that, as we have seen, it created the new and permanent word for slavery throughout Western Europe. Its importance was especially great for Sweden, because of the latter's marked specialization in this form of Scandinavian plunder. But the Russian traffic was itself no more than a regional concentrate of a general and fundamental characteristic of Viking expansion. In Iceland itself, distant antipode of Kiev, the estates of the *godar* priest-nobility were from the outset tilled by Celtic slaves, seized and transported from Ireland. The full scale and pattern of Viking slave-raids throughout Europe have yet to receive adequate historical study.[6] But for our purposes here what most needs to be, and is least often, emphasized is the critical impact of the generalized use of slave-labour *within* the Scandinavian homelands themselves. For the result of this predatory commerce abroad was, paradoxically, to *preserve* much of the primitive structure of Viking society at home. For the Scandinavian social formations were the last in Europe to make widespread and normal use of slave-labour. 'The slave himself was the foundation-stone of Viking life at home.'[7] The typical pattern of tribal communities in the initial phase of social differentiation, as we have seen, was the dominance of a warrior aristocracy whose lands are tilled by captured slaves. It was precisely the presence of this *external* forced labour that permitted the coexistence of a nobility with an indigenous free peasantry, organized in agnatic clans. The surplus labour necessary for the emergence of a landed nobility did not yet have to be extracted from impoverished kinsmen: slavery is thus normally at this stage a 'safeguard' against serfdom. The Viking social formations, in which there was a constant import and replenishment of foreign slaves (thralls), thus did not undergo any real slide towards

6. E. I. Bromberg, 'Wales and the Mediaeval Slave Trade', *Speculum*, Vol. XVII, No. 2, April 1942, pp. 263–9, considers Viking operations in the Irish Sea area, and passes some emphatic judgements on the attitude of the Christian Church to the trade in the early Middle Ages.

7. Jones, *A History of the Vikings*, p. 148. The fullest account of Scandinavian slavery is provided by P. Foote and D. M. Wilson, *The Viking Achievement*, London 1970, pp. 65–78. This work rightly underlines the critical importance of slave-labour for the economic and cultural achievements of Viking society: p. 78.

feudal dependence and tied labour: they remained extremely vigorous, primitive clan communities, of which Iceland furnishes the heroic example, on the remote hyperborean rim of mediaeval Europe. Up to the 12th century, Scandinavian peasant villages retained a social pattern extremely close to that of the Germanic peoples of the 1st century. There was collective allocation of strips of land each year to each household, according to conventional norms, within a juridical community which was governed by its own customs.[8] Common lands of an orthodox type – forests, meadows and pastures – were shared by village or neighbourhood communities. Full individual property was acknowledged only after 4 or 6 generations, or more, of possession, and was generally restricted to notables. An ordinary *bondi* farmer might have a work-force of three slaves, a noble perhaps thirty thralls.[9] Both alike attended the free clan assemblies of *thingar*, which were organized in successive tiers, from the 'hundred' level upwards: factually dominated by the local optimates, these nevertheless represented the whole rural community, and could, as in the time of Tacitus, veto the initiatives of the nobles. A naval levy or *leding* for the maintenance of warships was borne by all free men. Royal dynasties, weakened by hazardous and unstable mechanisms of succession, supplied kings who had to be 'elected' by a provincial *thing* for their accession to be confirmed. Viking rapine and enslavement overseas thus conserved relative clan liberty and jural equality at home.

After three centuries of overseas raids and settlements, the dynamic of Viking expansion eventually came to an end with the last great Norwegian attack on England in 1066, in which Harald Hardrada, once a Varangian commander for Byzantium, was defeated and killed

8. Lucien Musset, *Les Peuples Scandinaves au Moyen Age*, Paris 1951, pp. 87–91: for those confined to other Western languages, this excellent work is far the best account of mediaeval Scandinavia. Musset adds that even in Norway and Iceland, where there was dispersed settlement and transhumant pastoral agriculture, an extended 'neighbourhood' community redistributed arable soil and shared prairie lands. There is an extremely interesting discussion of Scandinavian *odal* land tenure, and its multiple social connotations, in A. Gurevich, 'Représentations et Attitudes à l'Egard de la Propriété pendant le Haut Moyen Age', *Annales ESC*, May–June 1972, pp. 525–9. The term 'allod' may be etymologically linked to 'odal' by metathesis: at any rate the limits of allodial ownership are indicated, in an extreme form, by Viking *odal* possession.

9. Jones, *A History of the Vikings*, p. 148.

at Stamford Bridge. Symbolically, the fruits of this expedition were reaped three weeks later at Hastings by the Normans, a Danish overseas community that had made its own the new military and social structures of European feudalism.[10] The original Viking invasions had precipitated the crystallization of feudalism amidst the disintegration of the Carolingian Empire in the 9th century. It had now been perfected and hardened into a full-scale institutional system, and proved decisively superior to the improvised, ramshackle thrusts of the traditional Viking campaigns. Heavy cavalry conquered England, where long ships had been repelled. The relationship of forces between the far North and the rest of Western Europe was henceforward inverted: from now on Western feudalism was to exercise a slow and constant pressure on Scandinavia, and gradually alter it to its own pattern. To start with, the halting of Viking expansion overseas in itself inevitably led to radical endogenous changes within Scandinavia. For it meant that the supply of slave labour now effectively ceased, and with it the old social structures increasingly broke up.[11] For once there was no longer a constant reserve of forced labour from abroad, social differentiation could only proceed by progressive subjection of the *bondi* farmers to the local nobility, and the emergence of dependent tenants cultivating the lands of a racinated aristocracy, now territorial rather than maritime in its social power. The corollary of this process was the gradual stabilization of royal rule, and the conversion of regional *jarlar* into provincial governors, subordinating the work of the local *thing*. The gradual introduction of Christianity into Scandinavia, a conversion which was not completed until the late 12th century, everywhere assisted and accelerated the transition from traditional semi-tribal communities to monarchical state systems: the Norse pagan religions that had been the indigenous ideology of the old clan order, naturally fell with it. These internal changes were already visible during the 12th century. The full external impact of European feudalism on the Northern confines of the continent were felt in the 13th century. The first, victorious use of heavy cavalry was at the battle of Fotevik in

10. Whose feat of launching a successful feudal invasion by sea was, of course, in debt to their Scandinavian background.

11. Slavery eventually disappeared in Iceland during the 12th, in Denmark during the 13th, and in Sweden during the 14th century: Foote and Wilson, *The Viking Achievement*, pp. 77–8.

1134, when German mercenary knights demonstrated their prowess in Scania. But it was not until after the Danish army of Waldemar II – the most powerful Scandinavian ruler of the Middle Ages – had been crushed by a host of Norther German princes at Bornhöved in 1227, because of the latter's equestrian superiority, that the military organization of feudalism was finally transplanted into the North, with all its social consequences.[12] Schleswig became the first proper fief to be granted by the Danish monarchy in 1253. Heraldic arms, title-systems and dubbing ceremonies soon followed. In 1279–80 the Swedish aristocracy achieved juridical tax-exemption (*frälse*) in exchange for formal obligation of knight-service (*rusttjänst*) to the monarch. It thereby became a separate legal class along continental lines, invested in fiefs (*länar*) by royal rulers. The consolidation of the local aristocracies into a-feudal nobility was followed by a steady degradation of the condition of the peasantry in all the Scandinavian countries, during the centuries of late mediaeval depression. By 1350, the yeomanry owned only two-fifths of the land in Norway.[13] In the 14th century, the Swedish nobility forbade the former *bondi* class to wear arms, and strove to tie them to the land, passing laws demanding compulsory labour services from the vagrant rural population.[14] The *thingar* were demoted to limited judicial functions, and central political power became concentrated in a magnate council or *råd*, which typically dominated the mediaeval polity of this period. The trend towards a continental pattern was unmistakable by the time of the Union of Kalmar, which in 1397 formally joined the three Scandinavian realms in a single state.

Nevertheless, Scandinavian feudalism never succeeded in making up for its very late start. It proved incapable of wholly erasing the powerful rural institutions and traditions of an independent peasantry, whose folk rights and farmer assemblies were still a living memory in the countryside. There was a further critical determinant of this Nordic

12. Erik Lönroth, 'The Baltic Countries', in *The Cambridge Economic History of Europe*, III, Cambridge 1963, p. 372.

13. Foote and Wilson, *The Viking Achievement*, p. 88.

14. Musset, *Les Peuples Scandinaves au Moyen Age*, pp. 278–80. *Frälse* meant 'free', and was originally the opposite of 'slave', when it was customarily applied to the farmer class of *bondi*. The semantic shift of the word to denote noble privileges, over and against peasant obligations, condensed the whole social evolution of later mediaeval Scandinavia. See Foote and Wilson, *The Viking Achievement*, pp. 126–7.

exceptionalism: most of the area was virtually immune from foreign invasions throughout the later Middle Ages and early modern epoch; so the coefficient of feudal warfare, whose constant attrition had invariably depressive effects on peasant liberties, was considerably lower than elsewhere. Denmark presents a special case, since it was an extension of the continental land-mass and hence far more subject to German influences and intrusions through the border zone of Schleswig-Holstein, and eventually became aligned quite closely to the social pattern of its Imperial hinterland. Even so, the Danish peasantry was not fully enserfed until very late, in the 17th century, and was emancipated again a hundred years later. Norway, which ultimately fell under rule from Copenhagen, became dominated by a Danish-speaking aristocracy, but retained a more traditional rural structure.

It was Sweden, however, which represented the purest example of the general type of Scandinavian social formations in the later mediaeval epoch. For throughout this period, it was the most backward area in the region.[15] It had been the last country to preserve slavery, which had actually persisted until the early 14th century – it was formally abolished only in 1325; the last country to be christianized; and the last country to achieve a unified monarchy, which proved weaker than that of its neighbours. When knight service was introduced in the late 13th century, it did not acquire the oppressive weight of its Danish counterpart, both because of the strategic shelter of the Swedish latitude and because the local topography – a carpet of forests, lakes and rivers – was always inhospitable to mounted cavalry. Thus rural relations of production were never fully feudalized. By the end of the Middle Ages, despite the encroachment of aristocracy, clergy and monarchy, the Swedish peasantry was still in possession of half the cultivated surface of the country. Although this was later to be declared the *dominium directum* of the monarch by royal lawyers and was hedged with regal restrictions on leasing and dividing of plots,[16] in practice it formed a

15. The Swedish land laws of the 13th and 14th centuries reveal a society still strikingly similar in many respects to that depicted by Tacitus in his account of Germany in the 1st century; the two main differences being the disappearance of tribes and the existence of a central state authority: K. Wuhrer, 'Die schwedischen Landschaftsrechte und Tacitus' Germania', *Zeitschrift der Savigny-Stiftung für Rechtsgeschichte (Germ. Abteilung)*, LXXXIX, 1959, pp. 1–52.

16. These restrictions are stressed by Oscar Bjurling, 'Die ältere schwedische

broad allodial sector which owed taxes to kings, but no further dues and services. The other half of the peasantry tilled lands owned by the monarchy, the church and the nobility, owing feudal rents and services to its respective landlords. Swedish nobles declared themselves 'kings over their own peasants' in the late 15th century (Recess of Kalmar 1483), and asserted in the 17th century that the peasantry as a class were *mediate subditi*;[17] but again in practice, the actual relationship of class forces on the ground never allowed these claims to be made good. For serfdom proper never became established in Sweden, and seigneurial justice was virtually unknown: courts were either royal or popular. Manorial codes (*gårdsrätt*) and prisons became important only for a brief decade in the 17th century. Thus it was no accident that when an Estates system emerged in the early modern epoch, Sweden was the only major country in Europe where the peasantry was represented in it. The incomplete feudalization of rural relations of production, in its turn, had inevitably limiting effects on the noble polity itself. The fief system imported from Germany never reproduced the strict continental pattern. Rather, traditional administrative offices of the monarchy, to which leading nobles had been appointed, were now assimilated to fiefs, with a regional devolution of sovereignty; but these *län* remained revocable by the royal ruler, and did not become the hereditary quasi-property of the nobles invested in them.[18] This lack of an articulated feudal hierarchy did not, however, mean a particularly powerful monarchy at its summit: on the contrary, as elsewhere in Europe at the time, it signified an extremely weak royal apex to the polity. There was no ascendant feudal monarchy in later mediaeval Sweden, but rather a reversion in the 14th and 15th centuries to conciliar rule by a *råd* of magnates, for whom the Union of Kalmar, nominally presided over by a Danish dynasty in Copenhagen, provided a conveniently distant screen.

Landwirtschaftspolitik im Überblick', *Zeitschrift für Agrargeschichte und Agrarsoziologie*, Jg 12, Hft I, 1964, pp. 39–41. But they do not alter the fundamental significance of the small-holding peasantry, in any comparative perspective.

17. For the famous dictum of Per Brahe to this effect, see E. Hecksher, *An Economic History of Sweden*, Cambridge U.S.A. 1954, p. 118.

18. Michael Roberts, *The Early Vasas*, Cambridge 1968, p. 38; Lucien Musset, *Les Peuples Scandinaves au Moyen Age*, pp. 265–7.

4

The Feudal Dynamic

Feudalism in Western Europe, then, emerged in the 10th century, expanded during the 11th century, and reached its zenith in the late 12th and 13th centuries. Having traced something of its varied paths of implantation in the major West European countries, we can now consider the remarkable overall economic and social progress that it represented.[1] By the 13th century, European feudalism had produced a unified and developed civilization that registered a tremendous advance on the rudimentary, patchwork communities of the Dark Ages. The indices of this advance were multiple. The first and most fundamental of them was the great jump forward in the agrarian surplus yielded by feudalism. For the new rural relations of production had permitted a striking

1. A full awareness of the dynamism of the feudal mode of production has been one of the most important gains of mediaeval historiography in the last decades. Just after the Second World War, Maurice Dobb could repeatedly write, in his classic *Studies in the Development of Capitalism*, of the 'low level of technique', the 'meagre yield from land', the 'inefficiency of feudalism as a system of production', and the 'stationary state of labour productivity of the time' (London 1967, reedition, pp. 36, 42–3). Despite warnings in Engels, such views were at that time probably widespread among Marxists; although it should be noted that Rodney Hilton specifically demurred, criticizing Dobb for 'a tendency to assume that feudalism was always and inevitably backward as an economic and social system . . . In actual fact, until about the end of the thirteenth century, feudalism was, on the whole, an expanding system. In the ninth century and even earlier there were a number of technical innovations in productive methods which were a great advance on the methods of classical antiquity. Vast areas of forest and marsh were brought into cultivation, population increased, new towns were built, a vigorous and progressive artistic and intellectual life was to be found in all the cultural centres of Western Europe.' (*The Modern Quarterly*, Vol. 2, No. 3, 1947, pp. 267–8.) Today, most writers, Marxist and non-Marxist, would agree with Southern's general emphasis when he speaks of the 'secret revolution of these centuries': see his remarks in *The Making of the Middle Ages*, pp. 12–13, for the significance of this period of European development for world history.

increase in agricultural productivity. The technical innovations which were the material instruments of this advance were, essentially, the use of the iron-plough for tilling, the stiff-harness for equine traction, the water-mill for mechanical power, marling for soil improvement and the three-field system for crop rotation. The immense significance of these invention for mediaeval agriculture, in which the prior ideological transformations wrought by the Church were of great importance, is indisputable. But they should not be isolated as fetishized and determinant variables in the economic history of the epoch.[2] In fact, it is clear that the simple existence of these improvements was no guarantee of their widespread utilization. Indeed, there is a gap of some two or three centuries between their initial sporadic appearance in the Dark Ages and their constitution into a distinct and prevalent system in the Middle Ages.[3] For it was precisely only the formation and consolidation of new *social relations of production* which could set them to work on a general scale. It is only after the crystallization of a developed feudalism in the countryside that they could become widely appropriated. It is in the internal dynamic of the mode of production itself, not the advent of a new technology which was one of its material expressions, that the basic motor of agrarian progress must be sought.

We have seen at the outset that the feudal mode of production was defined, among other characteristics, by a scalar *gradation* of property, which was therefore never cross-divisible into homogeneous and exchangeable units. This organizing principle generated the eminent domain and the revocable fief at the knightly level: at the village level, it determined the division of land into the demesne and peasant

2. Lynn White's volume, *Mediaeval Technology and Social Change*, London 1963, the lengthiest study of feudal inventions, does precisely this: the mill and the plough become demiurges of whole historical epochs. White's fetishism of these artefacts and handling of evidence has been caustically criticized by R. H. Hilton and P. H. Sawyer, 'Technical Determinism: the Stirrup and the Plough', *Past and Present*, No. 24, April 1963, pp. 90–100.

3. Duby comments that improved ploughs and harnesses were still a rarity among the European peasantry of the 9th and 10th centuries, and that equine traction did not become widespread before the 12th century: *Rural Economy and Country Life in the Mediaeval West*, p. 21. Duby's greater caution contrasts with White's free-wheeling conjectures: the difference in their dating is not a matter simply of chronological accuracy, but of the causal position of technique within feudal agriculture. This point is developed above.

virgates, over which the lord's rights were in their turn differentiated by degree. It was just this division which shaped the dual forms of class confrontation between lords and peasants in the feudal mode of production. For on the one hand, the lord naturally sought to maximize labour services on his manor, and dues in kind from the peasant strips outside it.[4] The level of organization achieved by the feudal noble on his demesne was of often critical importance for the application of new techniques: the most obvious example of this, amply documented by Bloch, was the introduction of the water-mill, which needed a catchment of a certain size to be profitable, and so gave rise to one of the first and most long-lived of all seigneurial *banalités* or exploitative monopolies – the obligation of the local peasantry to take their grain to be ground in the lord's mill.[5] Here the feudal lord was indeed, in Marx's words, 'the manager and master of the process of production and of the entire process of social life'[6] – in other a functional necessity of agrarian advance. At the same time, of course, this advance was achieved to the repressive profit of the mill proprietor and at the cost of the villein. Other *banalités* were more purely confiscatory in character, but most derived from coercive use of the superior means of production controlled by the nobility. The *banalités* were deeply hated throughout the Middle Ages, and were always one of the first objects of popular attack during peasant uprisings. The direct role of the lord in managing and supervising the process of production, of course, declined as the surplus itself grew: from early on, reeves and bailiffs administered large estates for a higher nobility that had become economically parasitic. Below the magnate level, however, the smaller

4. Van Bath suggests that a balance had to be struck between demesne and virgate exploitation of perhaps 1:2, in order not to exhaust villein labour and thereby endanger demesne cultivation itself, unless there was additional hired labour available. *The Agrarian History of Western Europe*, pp. 45–6. Eastern European experience does not appear to confirm this hypothesis, since as we shall see, labour services there could be very much higher than in the West.

5. Bloch traced the emergence and significance of the latter in a famous essay, 'The Advent and Triumph of the Water-Mill', now reprinted in *Land and Work in Mediaeval Europe*, London 1967, pp. 136–68. The *banalités* were typically introduced in the 10th and 11th centuries, after the manorial system had become established, in a subsequent turn of the seigneurial screw.

6. *Capital*, Vol. III, pp. 860–1. Marx's reference is retrospective to the whole epoch before the advent of capitalism.

nobles and ministerial intermediaries typically exerted close pressure on land and labour for a greater output at the disposal of the proprietors: and the social and economic importance of this stratum tended to rise steadily during the mediaeval period. From 1000 onwards, the aristocratic class as a whole was consolidated by new patterns of inheritance designed to protect noble property against division, and all sections of it developed a growing appetite for the consumption of amenities and luxuries which acted as a powerful goad to expansion of supply from the countryside, as well as to the introduction of novel exactions such as the *taille* that first came to be levied on the peasantry towards the end of the 11th century. One typical sign of the seigneurial role in the development of the feudal economy in this epoch was the spread of viticulture during the 12th century: wine was an elite beverage, and vineyards were characteristically aristocratic ventures, involving a higher degree of skilled labour and of profitability than grain crops.[7] More generally, within the manorial system as a whole, net productivity on the demesne probably remained substantially higher than on the peasant plots that surrounded it;[8] evidence not only of the appropriation of the best soil by the ruling class, but also of the relative economic rationality of its exploitation of it.

On the other hand, it was in the class of immediate producers themselves that lay the mass impetus of mediaeval agrarian development. For the feudal mode of production that had emerged in Western Europe generally afforded the peasantry the minimal space to increase the yield at its own disposal, within the harsh constraints of manorialism. The typical peasant had to provide labour rents on the seigneurial demesne – often up to three days a week – and numerous additional dues; he was nevertheless free to try to increase output on his own strips in the rest of the week. Marx observed that: 'The productivity of the remaining days of the week, which are at the disposal of the direct producer himself, is a variable magnitude which must develop with the course of his experience . . . The possibility is here presented for definite economic development.'[9] The feudal dues levied on the

7. Duby, *Guerriers et Paysans*, pp. 266–7.

8. M. Postan, 'England', *The Cambridge Economic History of Europe*, Vol. I, *The Agrarian Life of the Middle Ages*, p. 602; *The Mediaeval Economy and Society*, p. 124.

9. *Capital*, Vol. III, p. 774.

production of the peasant plots themselves tended to acquire a certain regularity and stability, whose customary character could only be altered by the lords as a result of radical shifts in the local balance of forces between the two classes.[10] A margin was thereby created for the results of improved productivity to accrue to the direct producer. Thus the high Middle Ages were marked by a steady spread of cereal cultivation, and a shift within it towards the finer crop of wheat, that was essentially the work of a peasantry that consumed bread as its staple food. There was gradual transition to the use of horses for ploughing, faster and more efficient than the oxen that had preceded them, if also more expensive. More and more villages came to possess forges for local production of iron tools, as a scattered rural artisanate developed.[11] The improvements in technical equipment thus created tended to lower the demand for labour services on noble demesnes, allowing a corresponding rise in inputs on peasant plots themselves. At the same time, however, as population grew with the expansion of the mediaeval economy, the average size of peasant holdings steadily diminished because of fragmentation, dropping from perhaps some 100 acres in the 9th century to 20 or 30 acres in the 13th century.[12] The normal upshot of this process was increasing social differentiation in the villages, with the main dividing-line running between families that owned plough-teams and those that did not; an incipient kulak stratum usually confiscated most of the benefits of rural progress within the village, and often tended to reduce the poorest peasants to the position of dependent labourers working for them. However, both prosperous

10. R. H. Hilton, 'Peasant Movements in England before 1381', in *Essays in Economic History*, Vol. II, ed. E. M. Carus-Wilson, London 1962, pp. 73–5. Marx emphasised the necessity of this regularity for the coherence of the mode of production as a whole: 'Here as always it is in the interest of the ruling section of society to sanction the existing order as law and to legally establish its limits through usage and tradition. Apart from all else, this, by the way, comes about of itself as soon as the constant reproduction of the basis of the existing order and its fundamental relations assumes a regulated and orderly form in the course of time. Such regulation and order are in themselves indispensable elements of any mode of production, if it is to assume social stability and independence from mere chance and arbitariness.' *Capital*, Vol. III, pp. 773–4.

11. See Duby, *Guerriers et Paysans*, pp. 213, 217–21.

12. Rodney Hilton, *Bond Men Made Free*, London 1973, p. 28.

and pauper peasants were structurally opposed to the lords who battened on them, and constant, silent rent struggles between the two were waged throughout the feudal epoch (occasionally erupting into open warfare, of course; although this was on the whole infrequent in the centuries now under consideration). The forms of peasant resistance were extremely varied: appeals to public justice (where it existed, as in England) against exorbitant seigneurial claims, collective non-compliance with labour services (proto-strikes), pressures for outright rent reductions, or chicanery over weights of produce and measures of land.[13] The lords, whether lay or ecclesiastical, for their part resorted to legal fabrication of new dues, straightforward coercive violence to secure rent increases, or seizure of communal or disputed lands. Rent struggles could thus be generated from either pole of the feudal relationship, and tended to stimulate productivity at both ends.[14] Both

13. For these different forms of struggle, some clandestine and some overt, see R. H. Hilton, *A Mediaeval Society: The West Midlands*, pp. 154–60; 'Peasant Movements in England before 1381', pp. 76–90; 'The Transition from Feudalism to Capitalism', *Science and Society*, Fall 1953, pp. 343–8; and Witold Kula, *Théorie Economique du Système Féodale*, The Hague–Paris, 1970, pp. 50–3, 146.

14. Duby, by contrast, attributes the central economic impetus of the epoch to the peasantry alone. In his view, the nobility led the growth of the European economy in the period from 600 to 1000 by its accumulation of booty and land in war; the peasantry led the growth of the economy in the period from 1000 to 1200 by its advance of rural cultivation, amidst a new peace; the urban bourgeoisie led the growth of the period from 1200 onwards by trade and manufactures in the towns: *Guerriers et Paysans*, passim. The somewhat suspect symmetry of this schema is not, however, sustained by his own evidence. It is very doubtful whether the overall incidence of warfare seriously declined after 1000 (as he at one point concedes, p. 207); while the active seigneurial role in the economy of the 11th and 12th centuries is amply documented by Duby himself. On the other hand, it is difficult to see why the military activities of the nobility should be ascribed such economic preeminence in the period before 1000, at the expense of peasant labours. In practice, Duby's vocabulary oscillates significantly in its location of the 'mainsprings of economic dynamism' in each phase (compare the apparently contradictory formulations on pp. 160 and 169, and on pp. 200 and 237, which successively assign causal priority to war and to cultivation in phase 1, and to lesser nobles and to peasants in phase 2). These oscillations reflect real difficulties of analysis, within Duby's masterly survey. In fact, it is doubtless impossible to impute accurate economic ratios to the subjective roles of the contending classes of the time: it was the objective structure of the mode of production that set in motion their respective, variant performances in the form of antagonistic social struggle.

lords and peasants were objectively engaged in a conflictual process whose overall consequences were to drive the whole agrarian economy forward.

One area of social conflict was especially important in its consequences for the development of the mode of production as such. Disputes over land were naturally endemic in a situation where village communal ground was by no means prime agricultural soil and large regions of terrain were virgin forest, swamp or heath. Reclamation and conversion of uncultivated soil were therefore the most fruitful single avenue of expansion of the rural economy in the Middle Ages, and the most dramatic expression of the improved productive capacity of feudal agriculture. In fact, a vast movement of occupation and colonization of new lands occurred from 1000 to 1250. Both lords and peasants participated vigorously in this sweeping process. Peasant clearances were generally piece-meal extensions of the existing boundaries of arable land, at the expense of surrounding woods or pastures. Noble reclamations were usually later and larger undertakings, mobilizing greater resources for the recovery of more difficult terrain.[15] The most arduous retrieval of remote waste-lands was the work of the great monastic orders, above all the Cistercians, whose frontier abbeys provided tangible proof of the benefits of Catholic anti-naturalism. The life-span of a monastery was not that of a baron: it did not have to recoup the labour investment necessary for difficult reclamations within a single generation; the most remote and intractable regions that were recovered for tillage or pasturage, needing longer-term economic projections, were thus often undertaken by religious orders. These in turn, however, were otherwise often especially oppressive to the peasantry, since their clerical communities were more firmly resident than knights or barons, who might often be away on military expeditions. The conflicting pressures and claims which arose from competition for new areas was thus a further form of class struggle on the land. In some cases, to gain a labour draft for the assarting of forests or heaths, nobles freed peasants from servile status: for major enterprises, their agents or *locatores* typically had to promise special feudal exemptions to recruits. In other cases, peasant clearances were subsequently

15. See Duby's account, *Rural Economy and Country Life in the Mediaeval West*, pp. 72–80.

seized and expropriated by nobles, and the small-holders on them therewith reduced to villeinage.

More generally, in the later 12th and 13th centuries sharply contradictory movements could be observed in the rural society of Western Europe. On the one hand, demesne lands contracted and labour services on them diminished in most regions, with the notable exception of England. Seasonal labourers, paid in wages but prescribed customary duties, became more frequent on seigneurial estates; while leasing of manorial reserves to peasant tenants increased greatly at the expense of direct home cultivation. In certain areas, especially perhaps Northern France, communities of peasants and villages purchased enfranchisement from lords anxious to realize their revenues in cash.[16] On the other hand, the same epoch also witnessed a renewed wave of enserfment, which deprived previously free social groups of their liberty and lent a new hardness and precision to the juridical definitions of lack of freedom, with the formulation of the doctrine of 'glebe serfdom' for the first time from the late 11th century onwards. Free peasant holdings, which unlike villein tenures were subject to partible inheritance, were simultaneously worn down by dominical pressures in many regions, becoming converted into dependent tenancies. Allodial holdings generally receded and dwindled in this epoch, which saw a further spread of the fief system.[17] These conflicting agrarian trends were all manifestations of the silent social struggle for land which gave its economic vitality to the age. It was this hidden yet ceaseless and restless tension between the rulers and the ruled, the military masters of society and the direct producers beneath them, which lay behind the great mediaeval expansion of the 12th and 13th centuries.

The net result of these dynamic pressures, innate to the Western feudal economy, was to increase total output very considerably. The increment of acreage under cultivation naturally cannot be quantified on a continental scale, because of the impossibility of assessing any average ratios, given the diversity of climates and soils; although there is no doubt that nearly everywhere it was very considerable. But the

16. Such purchases were usually the work of rich peasants dominating villages in regions drawn into market relationships, whether in France or Italy: Hilton, *Bond Men Made Free*, pp. 80–5.

17. Boutruche, *Seigneurie et Féodalité*, II, pp. 77–82, 102–4, 276–84.

improvement in yields has been estimated somewhat more precisely, if still cautiously, by historians. Duby's calculation is that between the 9th and the 13th centuries, average harvest/seed yields increased at a minimum from 2.5 : 1 to 4 : 1, and that the portion of the harvest at the disposal of the producer thus effectively doubled: 'A great change in productivity, the only one in history until the great advances in the eighteenth and nineteenth centuries, occurred in the countryside of Western Europe between the Carolingian period and the dawn of the thirteenth century. . . . Mediaeval agriculture had at the end of the thirteenth century reached a technical level equivalent to that of the years which immediately preceded the agricultural revolution.'[18] The dramatic quickening of the forces of production in turn set off a corresponding demographic boom. The total population of Western Europe probably more than doubled between 950 and 1348, from some 20,000,000 to 54,000,000.[19] It has been calculated that average life-expectation, which had been some 25 years in the Roman Empire, rose to 35 years by the 13th century in feudal England.[20] It was in the midst of this multiplying society that trade revived after its long decline during the Dark Ages, and ever more numerous towns sprang up and prospered as intersection points for regional markets and centres for manufactures.

The rise of these urban enclaves cannot be separated from the agrarian leaven surrounding them. It is quite incorrect to divorce the two in any analysis of the High Middle Ages.[21] For one thing, the majority of the new towns were in origin either promoted or protected by feudal lords, for whom a natural objective was to corner local

18. *Rural Economy and Country Life in the Mediaeval West*, pp. 103–2. Duby's epochal claim seems overstated here: see Van Bath's estimates of yields in post-mediaeval agriculture, below pp. 261–2. But his emphasis on the magnitude of mediaeval growth itself commands a general consensus.

19. J. C. Russell, *Late Ancient and Mediaeval Populations*, Philadelphia 1958, pp. 102–13. The populations of France, Britain, Germany and Scandinavia actually appear to have trebled over these centuries; it was slower growth rates in Italy and Spain that pulled the total average down.

20. R. S. Lopez, *The Birth of Europe*, London 1967, p. 398.

21. A frequently expressed view is that, in Postan's words, the towns of this epoch were 'non-feudal islands in the feudal seas' (*The Mediaeval Economy and Society*, p. 212). Such a description is incompatible with any comparative analysis of mediaeval cities, within a wider historical typology of urban development.

markets or scoop off profits from long-distance trade by concentrating it under their aegis. For another, the steep rise in cereal prices from 1100 to 1300 – a slope of some 300 per cent – provided the propitious inflationary ground-work for the sale of all urban commodities. However, once economically founded and launched, the mediaeval towns soon gained a relative autonomy, which took a visible political form. Initially dominated by seigneurial agents (England) or resident petty nobles (Italy), they subsequently threw up typically urban patriciates proper, for the most part recruited from the ranks of former feudal intermediaries or successful merchants or manufacturers.[22] These new patrician strata controlled an urban economy in which production itself came to be tightly regulated in guilds, which generally emerged in the last decades of the 12th century. In these corporations, there was no separation between the artisan producer and the means of production, and small masters formed a plebeian mass immediately below the merchant-manufacturer oligarchy itself. Only in the Flemish and Italian towns did a sizeable wage-earning class of urban labourers appear beneath this artisanate, with a separate identity and interests. The pattern of municipal government varied according to the relative weight of 'manufacturing' or 'mercantile' activity in the cities concerned. Where the former was of central importance, the artisan guilds eventually tended to win some participation in civic power (Florence, Basle, Strasburg, Ghent); while where the latter were decisively predominant, the city authorities usually remained exclusively merchant (Venice, Vienna, Nuremburg, Lubeck).[23] Large-scale manufactures were concentrated essentially in the two densely populated regions of Flanders and North Italy. Woollen textiles were naturally the main growth sector, productivity in which probably more than trebled with the introduction of the horizontal pedal-loom. However, the greatest profits reaped by mediaeval urban capital were undoubtedly from long-distance trade and usury. Given the continued (although diminished)

22. J. Lestocquoy, *Aux Origines de la Bourgeoisie: Les Villes de Flandre et de l'Italie sous le Gouvernement des Patriciens (XIe–XVe Siècles)*, Paris 1952, pp. 45–51, discusses the origins of the Florentine, Genoese and Sienese oligarchies. A. B. Hibbert, 'The Origin of the Mediaeval Town Patriciate', *Past and Present*, No. 3, February 1953, pp. 15–27, is the best general analysis of the problem.

23. See the comments in Guy Fourquin, *Histoire Economique de l'Occident Médiéval*, Paris 1969, pp. 240–1.

predominance of a natural economy and the still rudimentary transport and communications network in Europe, the opportunities for buying cheap and reselling dear in imperfect markets were disproportionately lucrative. Mercantile capital could realize very high profits simply by mediating between separated spheres of use-values.[24] The Champagne fair-system linking the Low Countries to Italy from the 12th century to the early 14th century became a famous pivot of these inter-regional transactions.

Moreover, the structural *fusion* of economy and polity that defined the feudal mode of production was necessarily not confined to seigneurial extraction of the agrarian surplus only. Extra-economic coercion of a military-political character was likewise freely utilized by the patrician oligarchies who came to rule the mediaeval towns: armed expeditions to enforce monopolies, punitive raids against rivals, campaigns to impose tolls and levies on the neighbouring countryside. The highpoint of this application of political violence for the forcible domination of production and exchange was, of course, reached with the annexationism of the Italian cities, with their greedy subjection and extortion of provisions and labour from their conquered rural *contado*. The anti-seigneurial character of the urban sorties in Lombardy or Tuscany did not make them in any strict sense anti-feudal: they were rather urban modalities of the general mechanism for surplus extraction typical of the age, directed against competing rural practitioners. Nevertheless, the corporate urban communities undoubtedly represented a vanguard force in the total mediaeval economy, for they alone were devoted solely to commodity production and rested exclusively on monetary exchange. Indeed, the very scale of the profits made from the other great commercial vocation of the merchants is witness to their pilot role in this respect, amidst the general rarefaction of money at the time. The pinnacle of patrician fortunes was in banking, where astronomic rates of interest could be earned from extortionate loans to princes and nobles short of liquid cash. 'Usury lives in the pores of production, as it were, just as the gods of Epicurus lived in the space between worlds', Marx remarked. 'Money is so much harder to obtain, the less the commodity-form constitutes the general form of products. Hence the usurer knows no other barrier than the capacity

24. See Marx, *Capital*, III, pp. 320–5.

of those who need money to pay or resist.'[25] The 'parasitic' character of these operations did not necessarily render them economically unproductive, however: fruitful tributaries of investment into manufactures or transport frequently ran from the lush rivers of usury. The return of gold coinage to Europe in the mid 13th century, with the simultaneous minting in 1252 of the januarius and florin in Genoa and Florence, was the resplendent symbol of the commercial vitality of the cities.

It was they, too, which restored to feudal Europe the command of the surrounding seas – a decisive gift for its growth. The urban economy of the Middle Ages was throughout indissociable from maritime transport and exchange: it was no accident that its two great regional centres, in Northern and Southern Europe, were both close to the sea-board. The first precondition of the ascent of the Italian towns was their establishment of naval supremacy in the Western Mediterranean, which was cleared of Islamic fleets in the early 11th century. This was followed by two further international breakthroughs – the domination of the Eastern Mediterranean with the victory of the First Crusade, and the opening of regular Atlantic trade-routes from the Mediterranean to the Channel.[26] It was the sea-power of Genoa and Venice which now ensured Western Europe a constant trade surplus with Asia – a surplus that financed its return to gold. The scale of wealth accumulated in these Mediterranean cities can be judged from a simple comparison: in 1293, the maritime taxes of the single port of Genoa yielded $3\frac{1}{2}$ times the entire royal revenues of the French monarchy.[27]

The structural condition of possibility of this urban power and prosperity was, as we have seen, the parcellization of sovereignty peculiar to the feudal mode of production in Europe. This alone permitted the *political* autonomy of the towns and their emancipation from direct seigneurial or monarchical control, which separated Western Europe fundamentally from the Oriental States of the same

25. *Capital*, III, p. 585.

26. Bautier, *The Economic Development of Mediaeval Europe*, pp. 96–100, 126–30, rightly emphasizes the importance of these advances.

27. Lopez, *The Birth of Europe*, pp. 260–1. The year was an exceptional one in Genoa: receipts were four times the level of those of 1275, and twice those of 1334. But the possibility of such a peak is still striking enough.

epoch, with their much larger metropolitan concentrations. The most mature form taken by this autonomy was the *commune*, an institution that is a reminder of the irreducible difference between town and country even within their feudal unity. For the commune was a confederation founded by an oath of reciprocal loyalty between equals: the *conjuratio*.[28] This sworn pledge was an anomaly in the mediaeval world: for although the feudal institutions of vassalage and liegeancy had an emphatically mutual character, they were bonds of obligation between superiors and inferiors in an express hierarchy of rank. Inequality defined them even more than reciprocity. The urban *conjuratio*, founding pact of the commune and one of the nearest actual historical approximations to a formal 'social contract', embodied a new principle altogether – a community of equals. It was naturally hated and feared by nobles, prelates and monarchs: the *commune* was a 'new and detestable name' for Guibert de Nogent in the early 12th century.[29] In practice the commune was, of course, restricted to a narrow elite within the towns; while its example inspired inter-city Leagues in North Italy and the Rhineland, and eventually by extension knightly Leagues in Germany. Nevertheless, the germinal novelty of the institution derived from the self-government of autonomous towns. It dated precisely from the conjuncture in which the Lombard cities threw off the overlordship of their episcopal rulers and so snapped the chain of feudal dependence into which they had previously been integrated. Communes on the Italian model never became universalized in Europe: they were the privilege only of the most advanced economic regions. Thus the two other great clusters in which they were to be found were Flanders and (a century later) the Rhineland. In both these zones, however, they existed under charters of autonomy from feudal suzerains; whereas the Italian towns had demolished Imperial suzerainty

28. Weber, *Economy and Society*, III, pp. 1251–62. Weber's specific comments on mediaeval cities are nearly always accurate and acute, but his general theory prevented him from ever grasping the structural reasons for their dynamism. He attributed the urban capitalism of Western Europe essentially to the later competition between closed nation-states: *General Economic History*, London 1927, p. 337.

29. A phrase that caught the eye of both Marx (*Selected Correspondence*, p. 89) and Bloch (*Feudal Society*, p. 354). For Jacques de Vitry, another prelate, they were 'violent and pestilential': Lopez, *The Birth of Europe*, p. 234.

over Lombardy once and for all in the 12th century. They were also important for a century or so in the vassal regions outside the royal demesne in Northern France, where their influence ensured tolerant treatment of the *bonnes villes* of the Centre and South by the monarchy.[30] In England, on the other hand, where the prominence of foreign merchant communities was a sign of the relative weakness of the local burgher class, towns were too small to acquire the economic importance necessary for political emancipation, with the exception of London which as a capital was kept fairly directly under royal control.[31] No communes proper ever became established in the island, with important consequences for later constitutional developments. However, throughout Western Europe the urban centres gained basic charters and a corporate municipal existence. In every country the mediaeval towns represented an absolutely central economic and cultural component of the feudal order.

It was on these dual foundations of impressive agrarian progress and urban vitality that the stately aesthetic and intellectual monuments of the High Middle Ages were raised, the great cathedrals and the first universities. Van Bath comments: 'In the twelfth century a period of exuberant development broke out in western and southern Europe. In the cultural as well as the material field a high point was reached in the years between 1150 and 1300 that was not equalled again till much later. This advance took place not only in theology, philosophy, architecture, sculpture, glasswork and literature, but also in material welfare.'[32] The origins of Gothic architecture, the supreme artefact of this cultural 'exuberance', were a fitting expression of the unitary energies of the epoch: its homeland was Northern France, the cradle of feudalism since Charlemagne, and its inaugurator was Suger – Abbot, Regent and Patron, whose triple vocation was to reorganize and rationalize the demesne of St Denis, to consolidate and extend the power of the Capetian monarchy for Louis VI and VII, and to launch on Europe an aerial style of building of which his own religious

30. C. Petit-Dutaillis, *Les Communes Françaises*, Paris 1947, pp. 62, 81.

31. London received a formal charter of liberties from Edward III in 1327; but by the later Middle Ages, the city was in general securely subordinated to the central power of the monarchy.

32. *The Agrarian History of Western Europe*, p. 132.

verse was the poetic programme.[33] These inward accomplishments of Western mediaeval civilization had their outer reflection in its geographical expansion. The thrust of the feudal mode of production at its height produced the international crusading expeditions of 1000 to 1250. The three great prongs of this expansion were into the Baltic, the Iberian peninsula, and the Levant. Brandenburg, Prussia and Finland were conquered and colonized by German and Swedish knights. The Moors were driven from the Tagus to the Sierra Granada; Portugal was cleared *in toto* and a new kingdom founded there. Palestine and Cyprus were seized from their Muslim rulers. The conquest of Constantinople itself, definitively breaking the remains of the old Eastern Empire, seemed to consummate and symbolize the triumphant vigour of Western feudalism.

33. See Erwin Panofsky's exhilarating essay on Suger in *Meaning in the Visual Arts*, New York 1955, pp. 108-45.

5

The General Crisis

In fact, within the next hundred years, a massive general crisis struck the whole continent. It will be seen that it is this crisis which has often retrospectively appeared to be the watershed dividing the destinies of Europe. Its causes have yet to be systematically studied and analysed, although by now its phenomenal elements are well established.[1] The deepest determinant of this general crisis probably lay, however, in a 'seizure' of the mechanisms of reproduction of the system at a barrier point of its ultimate capacities. In particular, it seems clear that the basic motor of rural reclamation, which had driven the whole feudal economy forwards for three centuries, eventually over-reached the objective limits of both terrain and social structure. Population continued to grow while yields fell on the marginal lands still available for conversion at the existing levels of technique, and soil deteriorated through haste or misuse. The last reserves of newly reclaimed land were usually of poor quality, wet or thin soil that was more difficult to farm, and on which inferior crops such as oats were sown. The oldest lands under plough were, on the other hand, liable to age and decline

1. The best general account of the crisis is still Leopold Génicot, 'Crisis: from the Middle Ages to Modern Times', in *The Agrarian Life of the Middle Ages*, pp. 660–741. See also R. H. Hilton, 'Y Eut-Il une Crise Générale de la Féodalité?', *Annales ESC*, January–March 1951, pp. 23–30. Duby has recently criticized the 'romantic' idea of a general crisis on the grounds that in certain sectors significant cultural and urban progress was registered in the last centuries of the Middle Ages. 'Les Societes Médiévales: Une Approche d'Ensemble', *Annales ESC*, January–February 1971, pp. 11–12. This is to confuse the concept of crisis with that of retrogression, however. No general crisis of any mode of production is ever simply a vertical decline. The limited emergence of new relations and forces of production was not only compatible with the nadir of the depression in the mid 14th century, but was often an integral aspect of it, particularly in the towns. There is no need to question the existence of a general crisis, merely because it has been embroidered in romantic literature.

from the very antiquity of their cultivation. The advance of cereal acreage, moreover, had frequently been achieved at the cost of a diminution of grazing-ground: animal husbandry consequently suffered, and with it the supply of manure for arable farming itself.[2] Thus the very progress of mediaeval agriculture now incurred its own penalties. Clearance of forests and wastelands had not been accompanied by comparable care in conservation: there was little application of fertilizers at the best of times, so that the top soil was often quickly exhausted; floods and dust-storms became more frequent.[3] Moreover, the diversification of the European feudal economy with the growth of international trade had led in some regions to a decrease of corn output at the expense of other branches of agriculture (vines, flax, wool or stock-breeding), and hence to increased import dependence, and its attendant dangers.[4]

2. Much the best discussion of these processes within later feudal agriculture is now to be found in Postan, *The Mediaeval Economy and Society*, pp. 57–72. Postan's book is devoted to England, but the implications of his analysis are general in scope.

3. Postan, 'Some Economic Evidence of Declining Population in the Later Middle Ages', *Economic History Review*, No. 3, 1950, pp. 238–40, 244–6; Van Bath, *The Agrarian History of Western Europe*, pp. 132–44. These facts are clear evidence of a crisis of the forces of production within the prevalent relations of production. They indicate precisely what Marx meant by a structural contradiction between the two. An alternative explanation of the crisis, once tentatively advanced by Dobb and Kosminsky, is both empirically questionable and theoretically reductionist. They argued that the general crisis of feudalism in the 14th century was caused essentially by a linear escalation of noble exploitation from the 11th century onwards, which eventually provoked cumulative peasant revolts and hence a breakdown of the old order. See E. A. Kosminsky, 'The Evolution of Feudal Rent in England from the 11th to the 15th Centuries', *Past and Present*, No. 7, April 1955, pp. 12–36; M. Dobb, *Studies in the Development of Capitalism*, pp. 44–50; Dobb is more nuanced. This interpretation does not seem to square with the general trend of rent relationships in Western Europe in this epoch; moreover it tends to inflect Marx's theory of complex objective contradictions into a simple subjective contest of class wills. The *resolution* of structural crises in a mode of production always depends on the direct intervention of the class struggle; but the *germination* of such crises may well take all social classes by surprise in a given historical totality, by deriving from other structural levels of it than their own immediate confrontation. It is their clash within the unfolding emergency which, as we shall see in the case of the feudal crisis, then determines its outcome.

4. This trend can be exaggerated, however. Bautier, for example, virtually reduces the whole economic crisis of the 14th century to an adverse side-effect of

Against the background of this increasingly precarious ecological balance, demographic expansion could tip into over-population at the first stroke of harvest misfortune. The opening years of the 14th century were soon studded with such disasters: 1315–16 were years of European famine. Lands began to be abandoned and the birth rate fell, even before the cataclysms which overtook the continent later in the period. In some regions, such as Central Italy, rent-racking of the peasantry was already weakening its rate of reproduction by 13th century.[5] At the same time, the urban economy now hit certain critical obstacles to its development. There is no reason to believe that the petty commodity production on which its manufactures rested was yet seriously hampered by the guild restrictions and patrician monopolism which ruled the towns. But the basic medium of circulation for commodity exchange was undoubtedly gripped by crisis: from the early decades of the 14th century onwards, there was a pervasive scarcity of money which inevitably affected banking and commerce. The underlying reasons for this monetary crisis are obscure and complex. But one central factor in it was an objective limit of the forces of production themselves. As in agriculture, so in mining a technical barrier was reached at which exploitation became unviable or deleterious. The extraction of silver, to which the whole urban and monetary sector of the feudal economy was organically connected, ceased to be practicable or profitable in the main mining zones of Central Europe, because there was no way of sinking deeper shafts or refining impurer ores. 'Silver-mining came almost to an end in the fourteenth century. In Goslar there were complaints of a rise in the ground water-level; there was also trouble with water in the Bohemian mines. The recession had already begun in Austria as early as the thirteenth century. Mining

---

beneficial progress in agricultural specialization, the result of a developing international division of labour: *The Economic Development of Mediaeval Europe*, pp. 190–209.

5. D. Herlihy, 'Population, Plague and Social Change in Rural Pistoia, 1201–1450', *Economic History Review*, XVIII, No. 2, 1965, pp. 225–44, documents this phenomenon in Tuscany. The rural economy of Central Italy was, on the other hand, rather atypical of Western Europe as a whole: it would be unwise to generalize rent-relationships from the Pistoian case. It should be noted that the result of Tuscan super-exploitation was peasant infertility, rather than rebellion.

activity in Deutschbrod ceased in 1321, in Freisach about 1350, and in Brandes (French Alps) about 1320.'[6] The shortage of metals led to repeated debasements of coinage in one country after another, and hence to spiralling inflation.

This in turn provoked a widening scissors in the relationship between urban and agricultural prices.[7] The decline in population led to a contraction of demand for subsistence commodities, so that grain prices slumped after 1320. Urban manufactures and high cost goods produced for seigneurial consumption, by contrast, enjoyed a comparatively inelastic and elite clientele, and became progressively more expensive. This contradictory process affected the noble class drastically, for its mode of life had become ever more dependent on the luxury goods produced in the towns (the 14th century was to see the apogee of feudal display with Burgundian court fashions, which spread throughout Europe), while demesne cultivation and servile dues from its estates yielded progressively decreasing incomes. The result was a decline in seigneurial revenues, which in its turn unleashed an unprecedented wave of warfare as knights everywhere tried to recoup their fortunes with plunder.[8] In Germany and Italy, this quest for booty in a time of dearth produced the phenomenon of unorganized and anarchic banditry by individual lords: the ruthless *Raubrittertum* of Swabia and the Rhineland and the marauding *condottieri* who spread from the Romagna throughout Northern and Central Italy. In Spain, the same pressures generated endemic civil war in Castile, as the nobility split between rival factions over issues of dynastic succession and royal power. In France, above all, the Hundred Years' War – a murderous combination of civil war between the Capetian and Burgundian houses and an international struggle between England and France, also involving Flanders and the Iberian powers – plunged the richest country in Europe into unparalleled disorder and misery. In England, the epilogue of final continental defeat in France was the

6. Van Bath, *The Agrarian History of Western Europe*, p. 106.

7. See H. Miskimin, 'Monetary Movements and Market Structures – Forces for Contraction in Fourteenth and Fifteenth Century England', *Journal of Economic History*, XXIV, December 1964, No. 2, pp. 483–90; Génicot, 'Crisis: from the Middle Ages to Modern Times', p. 692.

8. For the crisis of noble incomes, see the discussion in Fourquin, *Histoire Economique de l'Occident Médiéval*, pp. 335–40.

baronial gangsterism of the Wars of the Roses. War, chivalrous vocation of the noble, became his professional trade: knight service increasingly gave way to mercenary captains and paid violence. The civil population were everywhere the victims.

To complete a panorama of desolation, this structural crisis was over-determined by a conjunctural catastrophe: the invasion of the Black Death from Asia in 1348. This was an event from outside European history, which shattered against it in something like the same way that European colonization did to American or African societies in later centuries (the impact of the epidemics in the Caribbean perhaps provides a comparison). Passing from the Crimea via the Black Sea to the Balkans, the plague travelled like a typhoon through Italy, Spain and Portugal, curved northwards through France, England and the Low Countries, and then finally swung back east again through Germany, Scandinavia and Russia. With demographic resistance already weakened, the Black Death cut a swathe through the population of perhaps a quarter of the inhabitants of the continent. Thereafter, outbreaks of pestilence became endemic in many regions. Combined with these repeated ancillary plagues, the toll by 1400 was perhaps two-fifths.[9] The result was a devastating scarcity of labour, just when the feudal economy was gripped by grave endogenous contradictions. These accumulated disasters unleashed a desperate class struggle on the land. The noble class, threatened by debt and inflation, was now confronted by a sullen and diminishing labour force. Its immediate reaction was to try to recuperate its surplus by riveting the peasantry to the manor or battering down wages in both towns and countryside. The Statutes of Labourers decreed in England in 1349–1351, directly after the Black Death, are among the most glacially explicit programmes of exploitation in the whole history of European

9. Russell, *Late Ancient and Mediaeval Population*, p. 131. In reaction against traditional interpretations, it is fashionable among modern historians to deprecate emphasis on the impact of the epidemics of the 14th century on European economy and society. By any comparative standards, this attitude shows a strangely defective sense of proportion. The combined casualties of the two World Wars in this century inflicted far less damage to life than did the Black Death. It is difficult even to conceive of what the consequences of a net loss of 40 per cent of the total population of Europe within the space of two generations would have been in a later epoch.

class struggle.[10] The French Ordonnance of 1351 essentially repeated provisions similar to the English Statutes.[11] The Cortes of Castile, assembled in Valladolid, decreed regulation of wages in the same year. The German princes soon followed suit: similar controls were imposed in Bavaria in 1352.[12] The Portuguese monarchy passed its laws of the *seismarías* two decades later, in 1375. However, this seigneurial bid to reinforce servile conditions and make the producing class pay the costs of the crisis now met with wild, violent resistance – often led by better educated and more prosperous peasants, and mobilizing the deepest popular passions. The muffled, localized conflicts that had characterized the long feudal upswing suddenly fused into great regional or national explosions during the feudal depression, in mediaeval societies that were by now much more economically and politically integrated.[13] The penetration of the countryside by commodity exchange had weakened customary relationships, and the advent of royal taxation now often overlaid traditional noble exactions in the villages: both tended to centralize popular reactions to seigneurial extortion or repression, into major collective movements. Already in the 1320's, West

10. 'Whereas it was lately ordained by our lord the king and by assent of the prelates, earls, barons and others of his council, against the malice of servants, who were idle, and not willing to serve after the pestilence without excessive wages, that such manner of servants, as well men as women, should be bound to serve, receiving the customary salary and wages in the places where they ought to serve in the 20th year of the reign of the king that now is, or five or six years before, and that the same servants refusing to serve in such a manner should be punished by imprisonment of their bodies . . . the servants, having no regard to the ordinance, but to their ease and singular covetousness, do withdraw themselves from serving great men and others, unless they have livery and wages double or treble of what they were wont to take in the 20th year and earlier, to the great damage of the great men and impoverishment of all the commonalty.' A. R. Myers (ed.), *English Historical Documents, Vol. IV, 1327–1485*, London 1969, p. 993. The Statute applied to all those who did not own enough land for their own subsistence, obliging them to work for lords at fixed wages: hence it struck at small-holders as such.

11. E. Perroy, 'Les Crises du XIVe Siècle', *Annales ESC*, April–June 1949, pp. 167–82. Perroy points out that there was a triple determination of the mid-century depression in France: a cereal crisis because of bad harvests in 1315–20, a financial and monetary crisis to leading successive devaluations in 1335–45, and then the demographic crisis from the epidemics of 1348–50.

12. Friedrich Lütge, 'The Fourteenth and Fifteenth Centuries in Social and Economic History', in G. Strauss (ed.), *Pre-Reformation Germany*, London 1972, pp. 349–50.   13. See Hilton, *Bond Men Made Free*, pp. 96 ff.

Flanders had been the theatre of a ferocious peasant war against the fiscal exactions of its French suzerain, and the dues and tithes of its local nobility and church. In 1358, Northern France was aflame with the Grande Jacquerie, perhaps the greatest peasant rising recorded in Western Europe since the Bacaudae, set off by military requisitioning and pillage during the Hundred Years' War. Then in 1381, there erupted the Peasants' Revolt in England, precipitated by a new poll tax, with the most advanced and sweeping goals of all these upheavals: nothing less than the straightforward abolition of serfdom and the abrogation of the existing legal system. In the next century, it was the turn of the Calabrian peasantry to rebel against its Aragonese masters, in the great rising of 1469–75. In Spain, the *remença* serfs in Catalonia broke loose against the spread of the 'evil customs' imposed on them by their baronial lords, and a bitter civil war ensued in 1462 and again in 1484.[14] These were only the major episodes of a continent-wide phenomenon, which stretched from Denmark to Majorca. Meanwhile, in the most developed urban regions of all, Flanders and North Italy, there were autonomous communal revolutions: in 1309, the small masters and weavers of Ghent seized power from the patriciate and defeated the noble army which set out to crush them at Courtrai. In 1378, Florence experienced a yet more radical upheaval, when the famished Ciompi wool-combers – not artisans, but wage-workers – established a brief dictatorship.

All of these revolts of the exploited were defeated, with the partial exception of the *remença* movement, and politically repressed.[15] But their impact on the final outcome of the great crisis of feudalism in Western Europe was nevertheless a profound one. For one of the most

14. There had already been serious trouble in both these areas in the 14th century: in the Neapolitan lands under the Angevin rule of Robert I (1309–43), and in Catalonia in the 1380's.

15. One peasantry alone successfully defied the feudal class in Europe. The case of Switzerland is frequently ignored in discussions of the great rural insurrections of late mediaeval Europe. But, although the Swiss cantonal movement certainly represents in many respects a *sui generis* historical experience, distinct from that of the peasant revolts in England, France, Spain, Italy or the Low Countries, it cannot be altogether separated from them. It was one of the central episodes of the same epoch of agrarian depression and social struggle on the land. Its historical significance is discussed in the sequel to this study, *Lineages of the Absolutist State*, pp. 301–302.

important conclusions yielded by an examination of the great crash of European feudalism is that – contrary to widely received beliefs among Marxists – the characteristic 'figure' of a crisis in a mode of production is not one in which vigorous (economic) forces of production burst triumphantly through retrograde (social) relations of production, and promptly establish a higher productivity and society on their ruins. On the contrary, the forces of production typically tend to *stall* and *recede* within the existent relations of production; these then must themselves first be radically changed and reordered *before* new forces of production can be created and combined for a globally new mode of production. In other words, the relations of production generally change *prior* to the forces of production in an epoch of transition, and not vice versa. Thus the immediate aftermath of the crisis of Western feudalism was not any rapid release of new technology in either industry or agriculture; this was to occur only after a considerable interval. The direct and decisive consequence was rather a pervasive social alteration of the Western countryside. For the violent rural upheavals of the epoch, even in their defeat, led imperceptibly to changes in the balance of class forces on the land. In England, rural wages had markedly declined with the proclamation of the Statute of Labourers: after the Peasants' Revolt, they started to rise in an ascending curve which continued throughout the whole of the next century.[16] In Germany, the same process was evident. In France, the economic chaos wrought by the Hundred Years' War dislocated all factors of production, and wages therefore initially remained comparatively stable, adjusted to decreased levels of output; but even there, they started to rise appreciably by the end of the century.[17] In Castile, wage-levels quadrupled in the decade 1348–58 after the Black Death.[18] Far from the general crisis of the feudal mode of production worsening the condition of the direct producers in the countryside, it thus ended by ameliorating it and emancipating them. It proved, in fact, the turning-point in the dissolution of serfdom in the West.

16. E. Kosminsky, 'The Evolution of Feudal Rent in England from the 11th to the 15th Centuries', p. 28; R. Hilton, *The Decline of Serfdom in Mediaeval England*, London 1969, pp. 39–40.

17. E. Perroy, 'Wage-Labour in France in the Later Middle Ages', *Economic History Review*, Second Series, VIII, No. 3, December 1955, pp. 238–9.

18. Jackson, *The Making of Mediaeval Spain*, p. 146.

The reasons for this immensely significant outcome are undoubtedly to be found, first and foremost, in the dual articulation of the feudal mode of production which has been emphasized from the outset of this survey. It was above all the *urban* sector, structurally sheltered by the parcellization of sovereignty in the mediaeval polity, that had now developed to a point where it could decisively alter the outcome of the class struggle in the rural sector.[19] The geographical location of the great peasant revolts of the later Middle Ages in the West tells its own story. In virtually every case, they occurred in zones with powerful urban centres, which objectively acted as a ferment on these popular upheavals: Bruges and Ghent in Flanders, Paris in Northern France, London in South-Eastern England, Barcelona in Catalonia. For the presence of major cities always meant a radiation of market relationships into the surrounding countryside: and in a transitional epoch, it was the strains of a semi-commercialized agriculture that proved most acute for the fabric of rural society. In South-East England, tenants were actually outnumbered by landless servants and labourers in the districts most affected by the Peasants' Revolt.[20] Rural artisans were prominent in war in Flanders. The Paris and Barcelona regions were the most economically advanced areas of France and Spain respectively, with the highest density of commodity exchange in each country. Moreover, the role of the cities in the peasant revolts of the time was not limited to their sapping effects on the traditional seigneurial order in their vicinity. Many of the towns actively supported or assisted the rural rebellions in one way or another, whether out of inchoate popular sympathy from below, or self-interested patrician calculation from above. The poor commoners of London rallied to the Peasants' Revolt in social solidarity; while the wealthy burghers of Etienne Marcel's regime in Paris lent tactical aid to the Jacquerie in pursuit of their own political ends. The merchants and guilds

19. The structural interconnections between the rural predominance and urban autonomy of the feudal mode of production in Western Europe can be seen vividly from the paradoxical example of Palestine. There, virtually the entire Crusader community – magnates, knights, merchants, clergy and artisans – was concentrated in towns (rural production was left to indigenous peasants). Consequently, it was one area where there was no municipal autonomy whatever, and no local estate of burghers ever emerged.

20. Hilton, *Bond Men Made Free*, pp. 170–2.

of Barcelona remained aloof from the *remença* risings; but the
weavers of Bruges and Ypres were natural allies of the peasants
of maritime Flanders. Thus both objectively and often subjectively,
the cities affected the character and course of the great revolts of the
age.

However, it was not merely or mainly in these climactic explosions
that the cities intervened in the fate of the country: they never ceased
to do so in conditions of surface social peace as well. For in the West,
the relatively dense network of towns exerted a constant gravitational
influence on the balance of social forces in the countryside. For, on the
one hand, it was the prevalence of these market centres that rendered a
flight from serfdom a permanent possibility for discontented peasants.
The German maxim *Stadtluft macht frei* (town air makes a man free)
was the rule for city governments throughout Europe, since runaway
serfs were a positive labour input for urban manufactures. On the other
hand, the presence of these towns put constant pressure on the em-
battled nobles to realize their incomes in monetary form. The lords
both needed cash and, beyond a certain point, could not risk driving
their peasants wholesale into vagrancy or urban employment. They
therefore were compelled to accept a general relaxation of servile ties
on the land. The result was a slow but steady commutation of dues into
money rents in the West, and an increasing leasing-out of the demesne
to peasant tenants. This process developed earliest, and farthest, in
England, where the proportion of free peasantry had always been
relatively high; there servile customary tenures had become silently
converted into non-servile leases by 1400, and villeinage had passed
over into copy-holding.[21] The next century probably witnessed a
substantial rise in the total real incomes of the English peasantry,
combined with sharply accentuated social differentiation within it, as a
stratum of kulak yeomen gained dominance in many villages and wage-
labour spread in the countryside. Manpower shortage was still so acute
in agriculture, however, that while cultivated acreage contracted,
agrarian rents declined, cereal prices fell and wages rose: fortunate, if
ephemeral, conjuncture for the direct producer.[22] The nobility reacted

21. R. H. Hilton, *The Decline of Serfdom in Mediaeval England*, pp. 44 ff.
22. M. Postan, 'The Fifteenth Century', *Economic History Review*, Vol. IX,
1938–9, pp. 160–7, describes this concatenation. Postan has recently suggested

by increasingly switching to pasturage to supply the woollen industry that had developed in the new cloth towns, already starting a movement of enclosures; and by the complex system of paid retinues and hired violence, the 'indenture' and the 'letter patent', which has been designated the 'bastard feudalism' of the 15th century,[23] and whose main theatre of operations was the Yorkist-Lancastrians Wars. The new conjuncture was probably more propitious to the knight class, who profited from the retainer system, than to the traditional magnate lines.

The process of commutation took the form of a direct transition from labour services to money rents in England. On the continent, there was generally a somewhat slower evolution from labour services to rents in kind, and then to money rents. This was true both of France, where the final effect of the Hundred Years' War was to leave the peasant in possession of his plots, and of South-Western Germany.[24] The French pattern was distinguished by two peculiarities. Lords resorted to outright sale of emancipation more frequently than anywhere else, to reap the maximum immediate profit from the transition. At the same time, belated royal justice and Roman law combined to make peasant tenures after emancipation more securely heritable than in England, so that petty proprietorship eventually became deeply entrenched; whereas in England, the gentry were able to prevent this, keeping copyhold leases insecure and temporary, and thereby permitting easier eviction of the peasantry from the land at a later

---

that increased peasant prosperity may also have led for a time to a decrease in the level of commercialization in the countryside, as village households retained more of the agrarian product for their own consumption: *The Mediaeval Economy and Society*, pp. 201–4.

23. K. B. MacFarlane, 'Bastard Feudalism', *Bulletin of the Institute of Historical Research*, Vol. XX, No. 61, May–November 1945, pp. 161–81.

24. Kohachiro Takahashi, 'The Transition from Feudalism to Capitalism', *Science and Society*, XVI, No. 41, Fall 1952, pp. 326–7. The evolution from labour services to money rents was a more direct one in England, because the island had not experienced the earlier continental shift towards rents in kind during the 13th century; labour exactions consequently had survived longer in their original form there than elsewhere. For the oscillations in England during the 12th and 13th centuries (relaxation, followed by intensification, of dues), see M. Postan, 'The Chronology of Labour Services', *Transactions of the Royal Historical Society*, XX, 1937, pp. 169–193.

date.[25] In Spain, the struggle of the Remença peasants of Catalonia against the 'six evil customs' eventually ended with the 'Sentence of Guadelupe' in 1486, when Ferdinand of Aragon formally emancipated them from these burdens. They acquired stable possession of their plots, while their lords retained jurisdictional and legal rights over them; to discourage the example of rebellion, those who had participated in the *remença* risings were simultaneously fined by the monarch.[26] In Castile, as in England, the landowning class reacted to the labour shortages of the 14th century by widespread conversion of land to sheep-farming, which henceforward became the dominant branch of agriculture on the Meseta. Wool production was generally one of the most important seigneurial solutions to the agrarian crisis; European output may have increased some three to five times in the late mediaeval period.[27] In Castilian conditions, glebe serfdom no longer had much economic rationale, and in 1481 the Cortes of Toledo finally granted serfs the right to abandon their lords, and thereby abolished their bonds of adscription. In Aragon, on the other hand, where pastoralism had never been of much importance, towns were weak and a more rigid feudal hierarchy existed, repressive manorialism was not seriously shaken in the later Middle Ages, and glebe serfdom remained entrenched.[28] In Italy, the Communes had nearly always consciously combatted seigneurial jurisdictions by separating the functions of lord and landlord in their *contado*. Bologna, for example, had emancipated its serfs with a ringing declaration as early as 1257. In fact, serfdom had fairly generally disappeared in Northern Italy by the early 14th century, two or three generations before the same process occurred in France or England.[29] This precocity only confirms the rule that it was the solvent of the towns which fundamentally assured the disintegration of serfdom in the West. In Southern Italy, on the other

25. M. Bloch, *Les Caractères Originaux de l'Histoire Rurale Française*, pp. 131–133. Bloch points out that just because of this peasant entrenchment the French lords strove strenuously to reconstitute large demesnes from the 15th century onwards, by legal and economic means, with considerable success: pp. 134–54.

26. Vicens Vives, *Historia de los Remensas en el Siglo XV*, pp. 261–9.

27. Bautier, *The Economic Development of Mediaeval Europe*, p. 210.

28. For the character and persistence of serfdom in Aragon, see Eduardo de Hinojosa, 'La Servidumbre de la Gleba en Aragón', *La España Moderna*, 190, October 1904, pp. 33–44.

29. Philip Jones, 'Italy', in *The Agrarian Life of the Middle Ages*, pp. 406–7.

hand, with its overwhelmingly baronial character, the disastrous depopulation of the 14th century led to internecine noble anarchy and a new wave of seigneurial jurisdictions. There was widespread reversion of arable to pasturage, and a growth in the size of latifundia. The Calabrian rising of the 1470's, unlike virtually all other rural rebellions in Western Europe, lacked any urban resonance: the peasantry gained no liberties and the countryside was sunk in a long economic depression. The early and unqualified ascendancy of the cities in Northern Italy, on the other hand, accelerated the advent of the first large-scale forms of commercial farming with wage-labour, pioneered in Lombardy, and the development of short-term leases and share-cropping, which began to spread slowly northwards across the Alps into Western and Southern France, Burgundy and the Eastern Netherlands, in the course of the century. The demesne tilled by servile labour was an anachronism in France, England, Western Germany, Northern Italy and most of Spain by 1450.

II. Eastern Europe

East of the Elbe

On the other side of the Elbe, the economic result of the great crisis was diametrically opposite. It is now necessary to turn to the history of the vast regions to the East of the heartland of European feudalism, above the line of the Danube, and to the differential nature of the social formations which had developed there.[1] For our purposes, the most fundamental characteristic of the whole planar zone stretching from the Elbe to the Don can be defined as the permanent *absence* of that specific Western synthesis between a disintegrating tribal-communal mode of production based on primitive agriculture and dominated by rudimentary warrior aristocracies, and a dissolving slave mode of production, with an extensive urban civilization based on commodity exchange, and an imperial State system. Beyond the line of the Frankish *limes*, there was no structural fusion of disparate historical forms comparable to that which occurred in the West.

This central fact was the basic historical determinant of the uneven development of Europe, and of the persistent retardation of the East. The immense and backward regions beyond the Carpathians had always lain outside the bounds of Antiquity. Greek civilization had skirted the shores of the Black Sea with scattered colonies in Scythia. But these tenuous maritime outposts never established any penetration of the Pontic hinterland, and were eventually pushed aside by Sarmatian occupation of the South Russian Steppes, leaving only archaeological traces behind them.[2] Roman civilization accomplished the

1. Below the Danube, the Balkan peninsula formed a distinct region, set apart from the rest of the East by its integration into the Byzantine Empire. Its separate fate will be discussed in a later consideration of South-Eastern Europe.

2. Rostovtsev, in his first important work, emphasized that Oriental influences were always more important than Greek in Southern Russia, which was never

decisive feat of conquering and colonizing most of the land-mass of
Western Europe – but this momentous geographical extension of the
structures of classical Antiquity was never repeated to any comparable
depth in Eastern Europe. Trajan's annexation of Dacia represented the
only significant advance into the interior of the continent here; a
modest gain, soon relinquished. The Eastern hinterland was never
integrated into the Roman imperial system.[3] It did not even possess the
military and economic contacts with the Empire that Germany always
retained, although beyond it. Roman diplomatic, commercial and
cultural influences remained deep in Germany after the evacuation of
the legions, and Roman knowledge of it intimate and accurate. There
was no such relation between the Empire and the barbarian territories
in the East. Tacitus, admirably informed of German social structure
and ethnography, had virtually no notion of the peoples who lay
beyond them. The space further east was mythical and blank: *cetera iam
fabulosa.*[4]

It is thus no accident that very little is still known today about the

---

durably hellenized: *Iranians and Greeks in South Russia,* Oxford 1922, pp. viii–ix.
For a modern survey of the Black Sea colonies, see J. Boardman, *The Greeks Overseas,* London 1964, pp. 245–78.

3. It is noticeable that Dacia formed an isolated salient, jutting vulnerably out
from the line of the imperial frontiers into the Transylvanian highlands: no attempt
was made to occupy the intervening gaps formed by the plains towards Pannonia
in the west and Wallachia in the east. It is possible that Roman reluctance to
penetrate further into the interior of Eastern Europe was related to the comparative lack of naval access to the region, compared with the extended coast-line of
Western Europe, and hence can be seen as a function of the intrinsic structure of
classical civilization. It is perhaps significant that Augustus and Tiberius seem to
have envisaged a strategic expansion of Roman power in Central Europe from the
Baltic to Bohemia, for this line potentially permitted a pincer movement from the
North and South, using amphibious expeditions along the North Sea and up the
German rivers, of the type conducted by Drusus and Germanicus. The key
Bohemian campaign of A.D. 6 may have been based on a projected juncture of
Tiberius's army advancing up from Illyricum with a second army moving up the
Elbe: Wells, *The German Policy of Augustus,* p. 160. The depths of Eastern
Europe beyond the Elbe did not offer the same sort of access. In the event, even
the absorption of Bohemia proved too much for Roman forces. Another reason
for the failure of the Empire to expand into the regions further to the East may
have been the steppe character of much of the terrain, typically inhabited by
Sarmatian nomads – a natural setting discussed below.

4. *quod ego ut incompertum in medio relinquam* – 'the rest are legends, which I
abandon as unverified': the last words of the *Germania,* at which Tacitus breaks off.

tribal migrations and displacements in Eastern Europe in the early Christian era, although these were on an enormous scale. It is clear that the great plains north of the Danube – once the habitation of Ostrogoths, Visigoths or Vandals – were partially emptied by the *Völkerwanderungen* of the Germanic tribes during the 5th century into Gaul, Italy, Spain and North Africa. There was, in effect, a general shift of the Germanic populations westwards and southwards, clearing the ground for the advance of another ethnic group of tribal and agricultural peoples behind them. The Slavs probably originated in the Dnieper-Pripet-Bug region, and started to expand into the vacuum in the East left by the Germans from the 5th and 6th centuries onwards.[5]

A great demographic surge must have occurred in their remote homelands to explain the tidal character of this movement. By the end of the 6th century, Slav tribes had occupied virtually the whole of the immense expanse from the Baltic to the Aegean, and back to the Volga. The exact tempo and distribution of these migrations remain obscure: their general social outcome in the succeeding centuries, however, is clear enough.[6] The Slav agricultural communities slowly evolved towards a more differentiated internal structure, along the path already earlier taken by the Germans. Tribal organization gave way to nucleated settlements of villages which grouped associated families together, with increasingly individualized property. Warrior aristocracies with larger landholdings produced, first military chieftains with exceptional and tribal powers only, then more stable princely leaders with authority over larger confederations. The retinues or bodyguards of these leaders everywhere formed the embryo of a landed ruling class dominating a non-servile peasantry. In this respect, the Russian *druzhina* was essentially similar to the Germanic *Gefolgschaft*, or the Scandinavian *hirdh*, despite the local variations within and between

5. F. Dvornik, *The Slavs. Their Early History and Civilization*, Boston 1956, pp. 3–45, who tends to locate the original Slav homelands somewhat farther west, between the Vistula and the Oder; and L. Musset, *Les Invasions: Le Second Assaut contre L'Europe Chrétienne (VII–IXe Siècles)*, pp. 75–9, who comments: 'This immense progression resembles the inundation of empty lands more than a conquest' (p. 81).

6. For a typical sketch, see S. H. Cross, *Slavic Civilization through the Ages*, pp. 17–18.

them.[7] Prisoner of war slavery was often another characteristic of these rudimentary social formations, providing captive household and field labour for the clan nobility, in the absence of a serf class. Communal political institutions, with folk assemblies or justice, often survived to coexist with a hereditary social hierarchy. Agriculture remained extremely primitive, slash-burn techniques long prevailing amidst the unending forests. There was initially little urban development. In other words, the evolution of the Slav peoples in the East was a more or less faithful reproduction of the evolution of the Germanic peoples who had preceded them, prior to the latters' irruption into the Roman Empire and assimilation of its much more advanced civilization, in a catastrophic dissolution of both respective anterior modes of production. This halting 'unaided' development underlines the imprescriptible importance of Antiquity in the formation of Western feudalism.

7. Frantisek Graus, 'Deutsche und Slawische Verfassungsgeschichte', *Historische Zeitschrift*, CXLVII, 1963, pp. 307–12.

2

The Nomadic Brake

At the same time, the slow growth of the agrarian Slav communities in the East towards stable State systems was repeatedly interrupted and shattered by successive waves of nomadic invasions from Central Asia, which swept across Europe, often to the very borders of the West from the Dark Ages onwards. These invasions, which exercised a fundamental influence on the history of Eastern Europe, were the ransom of the geography of the region. For not only was it territorially adjacent to the Asian frontiers of pastoral nomadism, and therefore repeatedly bore the brunt of nomadic military assaults on Europe, from which the West was by its interposition buffered. But much of it also shared a topographical similarity with the Asian steppe-lands from which nomadic peoples periodically poured outwards. From the coast of the Black Sea to the forests above the Dnieper, and the Don to the Danube, a wide belt of territory including most of the modern Ukraine and Crimea, and tapering into Rumania and Hungary, formed a flat European grass-land that lent itself naturally to pastoralism, while – less arid than the Asian steppe proper – also permitting settled agriculture.[1] This zone formed the broad Pontic corridor through which nomadic confederations again and again rode to pillage and conquer the settled agrarian societies beyond, and of which they themselves became in kaleidoscopic succession the masters. The development of stable agriculture amidst the forests of Eastern Europe was thus always hindered by the protusion of the wedge of semi-steppe land into it from Asia, and the destructive nomadic attacks drawn on by the latter.

1. For description and discussion of the Pontic grass-lands, see D. Obolensky, *The Byzantine Commonwealth*, London 1971, pp. 34–7; W. H. McNeill, *Europe's Steppe Frontier 1500–1800*, Chicago 1964, pp. 2–9.

The first and most famous of these shocks was the lurid drive of the Huns, which set in motion the fall of the Roman Empire itself, in the 5th century, by churning up the whole Germanic world. While Teutonic tribes fled *en masse* in their path across the imperial borders, the Hunnic ruler Attila established a predatory realm beyond the Danube, pillaging Central Europe. Then in the 6th century, the Avars sacked their way through the East, establishing their dominion over the local Slavic populations. In the 7th century, the Bulgar cavalry was the scourge of the Pannonian and Transdanubian plains. In the 9th and 10th centuries, it was the Magyar nomads who laid waste whole regions from their strongholds in Eastern Europe. In the 11th and 12th centuries, the Petchenegs and Cumans successively preyed on the Ukraine, the Balkans and the Carpathians. Finally, in the 13th century, the Mongol armies overran Russia, smashed the Polish and Hungarian resistance to them, and after wintering at the gates of the West, turned to ravage the Balkans on their way back to Asia. This last and greatest assault left the most permanent social and political mark. The Golden Horde, a Turkic offshoot of Genghis Khan's host settled near the Caspian, kept a tributary yoke on Russia for 150 years thereafter.

The pattern and frequency of these invasions thus made them one of the basic coordinates of the formation of Eastern Europe. If much of Eastern European history can be defined in the first instance by the absence of classical Antiquity, it is differentiated from that of Western Europe in the second instance by the pressure of Nomadic pastoralism. The early history of Western feudalism is that of a synthesis between the dissolving primitive-communal and slave modes of production, social formations centred on the fields and the cities. The early history of Eastern feudalism is in some respects that of the lack of any possible such synthesis between settled-agrarian and predator pastoral societies, modes of production of the fields and the steppes. The impact of the nomadic invasions should not, of course, be exaggerated: but that they significantly retarded the internal evolution of the agrarian societies of Eastern Europe is clear. To bring out the character of this impact, some comment is necessary on the peculiarities of nomadic economic and social organization. For nomadic pastoralism represents a distinct mode of production, with its own dynamic, limits and contradictions, that should not be confused with those of either tribal or feudal agriculture.

Historically, it dominated the Asian borderlands beyond Europe in the Dark and Middle Ages, demarcating the outer frontiers of the continent. This nomadism did not simply constitute a primordial form of economy, earlier and cruder than that of sedentary peasant agriculture. Typologically, it was probably a later evolution, in those semi-arid and arid regions where it classically developed.[2] In fact, the particular paradox of nomadic pastoralism was that it represented in certain respects a more highly specialized and skilled exploitation of the natural world than pre-feudal agriculture, yet one whose inherent limits were also narrower. It was a path of development that branched off from primitive agrarian cultivation, achieved impressive initial gains, but eventually proved a cul-de-sac, while peasant agriculture slowly revealed its far greater potential for cumulative social and technical advance. But in the intervening period, nomadic societies often possessed a critical political superiority over sedentary societies in the organization and wielding of power, when the two were in conflict: this paramountcy in turn, however, had strict and self-contradictory limitations. The Turkic and Mongol pastoralists of this epoch were by the very logistics of their mode of production and military strength necessarily always far outnumbered by the Slavic agricultural populations when they dominated them, and their rule was usually an ephemeral one, except where exercised close to their homelands.

Nomadic social formations were defined by the mobile character of their basic means of production: herds, not land, always constituted the fundamental wealth of transhumant pastoralism, and articulated the nature of its property system.[3] Nomadic societies thus typically combined individual ownership of livestock, with collective appropriation

2. Owen Lattimore, *Inner Asian Frontiers of China*, New York 1951, pp. 61–5, 361–5; *Nomads and Commissars*, New York 1962, pp. 34–5.

3. This basic position was upheld by S. E. Tolybekov, in his important essay, 'O Patriarkhal'no-Feodal'nykh Otnosheniyakh U Kochevykh Narodov', *Voprosy Istorii*, January 1955, No. 1, p. 77 – in contradistinction to other Soviet specialists who participated in a discussion of nomadism in the pages of the same journal, initiated by the report of L. P. Potapov, 'O Sushchnosti Patriarkhal'no-Feodal'nykh Otnosheniyakh U Kochevykh Narodov Srednei Azii i Kazakhstana', *Voprosy Istorii*, June 1954, No. 6, pp. 73–89. All other participants – L. P. Potapov, G. P. Basharin, I. Ya. Zlatkin, M. M. Efendiev, A. I. Pershits, S. Z. Zimanov – argued that land, not herds, constituted the fundamental means

of land. Animals belonged to households, while their pastures were the usufruct of agnatic clans or tribes. Moreover, not only was landed property collective: it was not a fixed possession, unlike the soil of an agrarian society which is the object of permanent occupation and tillage. For nomadic pastoralism precisely signified a constant shifting of flocks and herds from one pasturage to another in a complicated seasonal cycle. In Marx's words: 'Among nomadic pastoral tribes the earth, like all other conditions of nature, appears in its elementary boundlessness, e.g. in the Asian steppes and the Asian high plateaux. It is grazed and consumed by the herds, which provide the nomadic peoples with their subsistence. They regard it as their property, though never fixing that property. . . What is *appropriated* and *reproduced* is here only the herd and not the soil, which is always used in temporary commonalty wherever the tribe breaks its wanderings.'[4] 'Ownership' of land thus meant the enjoyment of an intermittent and regulated traversal of it; in Lattimore's phrase, 'the right to move, not the right to camp is the decisive "property" '.[5] Transhumance was a system of cyclical use, not of absolute domain. Social differentiation could thus proceed quite rapidly within nomadic societies, without necessarily rupturing their clannic unity. For the wealth of a pastoral aristocracy was based on the size of its herds, and could remain compatible for a long time with a communal cycle of migration and pasturage. Even the poorest nomads typically owned some animals themselves, so that a

---

of production of nomadic social formations, and this position was endorsed by an editorial statement at the conclusion of the debate (*Voprosy Istorii*, January 1956, No. 1, p. 77). The disagreement occurred within a general consensus that nomadic societies were in essence 'feudal', although with an admixture of 'patriarchal' survivals – hence the notion of 'patriarchal feudalism' to designate nomadic social structures. Tolybekov was deemed by his colleagues to have weakened the force of this classification unduly, by emphasizing the divergences between nomadic and seigneurial types of property. In fact, nomadism manifestly represents a separate mode of production altogether, that is not assimilable to agrarian feudalism, as Lattimore has long rightly maintained: *Inner Asian Frontiers of China*, pp. 66 ff. It is fairly clear that Marx himself believed nomadic pastoralism to constitute a distinct mode of production, as can be seen from his comments on pastoral societies in his 1857 Introduction: *Grundrisse der Kritik der Politischen Okonomie (Einleitung)*, pp. 19, 27. He mistakenly, however, referred to the Mongols as engaged primarily in cattle-breeding.

4. K. Marx, *Pre-Capitalist Formations*, pp. 88–9.
5. Lattimore, *Inner Asian Frontiers of China*, p. 66.

propertyless class of dependent producers was normally precluded, although rank-and-file nomadic households characteristically owed various dues and services to clan chiefs and notables. Constant internecine warfare on the steppes also led to the phenomena of attached 'subject' clans, co-migrating in a subordinate role with a victor clan;[6] while military captives could also become domestic slaves, although these were never numerous. Clan assemblies gathered for important decisions; tribal leadership was customarily semi-elective.[7] The aristocratic stratum characteristically controlled the allocation of pastures and the regulation of transhumances.[8]

Nomadic societies, thus organized, revealed remarkable skill in the utilization of their inhospitable environment. The typical clan mustered a carefully variegated combination of herds, including horses, cattle, camels and sheep – the last of which provided the main social form of wealth. Each of these needed distinctive skills in treatment, and separate sorts of grazing-land. Likewise, the complex annual cycles of migration demanded exact knowledge of the gamut of different terrains, in their respective seasons. The practised exploitation of these mixed means of production involved a notable degree of collective discipline, integrated task-performance and technical expertise. To take the most obvious example: the nomad's mastery of horsemanship probably embodied a higher level of work-skill than any single labour technique in mediaeval peasant agriculture. At the same time, however, there were extremely rigid limits to the nomadic mode of production. To start with, it could support only a small labour-force: nomadic peoples were always vastly outnumbered by their herds, since the ratio

6. B. Ya. Vladimirtsov, *Obshchestvennyi Stroi Mongolov. Mongol'skii Kochevoi Feodalizm*, Leningrad 1934, pp. 64–5. Vladimirtsov's work on the Mongols was a pioneering study in the field, whose influence remains great on Soviet scholarship to this day. The 1956 editorial in *Voprosy Istorii* cited above pays tribute to it, although rejecting Vladimirtsov's notion of a special nomadic feudalism, distinct from that of settled societies (op. cit., p. 75).

7. Vladimirtsov, *Obshchestvennyi Stroi Mongolov*, pp. 79–80.

8. I. Ya. Zlatkin, 'K Voprosu o Sushchnosti Patriarkhal'no-Feodal'nykh Otnoshenii u Kochevykh Narodov', *Voprosy Istorii*, April 1955, No. 4, pp. 78–9. Zlatkin emphasizes that the dependent nomad – whose incidence and degree of subjection he overstates – was bound to the person of his itinerant lord, not to the soil: 'these relations, so to speak, nomadized together with the nomad' (p. 80).

of animals to men necessary to maintain transhumance in the semi-arid steppes was very high. No major increases in productivity comparable to those of arable farming were possible, because the basic means of production was not soil – qualitatively and directly malleable – but herds which depended on land, that was not itself touched by nomadism, and which therefore essentially permitted only quantitative augmentation. The fact that in the nomadic mode of production the basic objects and means of labour were largely identical – livestock – posed insurmountable limits to the yield of labour. Pastoral cycles of production were much longer than agricultural, and lacked interludes for the development of rural crafts: moreover all clan members participated in them, including chiefs, thereby preventing the emergence of a division of manual and mental labour, and hence of literacy.[9] Above all, nomadism by definition virtually excluded the formation of towns or urban development, where sedentary agriculture always ultimately promoted them. Beyond a certain point, the nomadic mode of production was therefore vowed to stagnation.

Nomadic societies were thus usually hungry and poor, in their barren homelands. They were rarely self-sufficient, usually exchanging products with neighbouring agricultural communities, in a meagre trading-system.[10] But they had one avenue of expansion to which they typically had spectacular recourse: tribute and conquest. For the horsemanship which was the basic economic skill of nomadic pastoralists also equipped them preeminently for warfare: they inevitably provided the best cavalry in the world. It was they who first developed mounted archery, and from Attila to Genghis Khan, it was their supremacy in this arm which was the secret of their formidable military power. The peerless ability of nomadic cavalry to cover vast distances at high speed, and their capacity for tight command and organization on long-distance expeditions, were further decisive weapons in war.

The structural characteristics of nomad social formations thus tended to generate a typical cycle of predatory expansion and contraction, in which steppe clans could suddenly spiral up into huge empires,

9. See the excellent analysis by Tolybekov, 'O Patriarkhal'no-Feodal'nykh Otnosheniyakh', pp. 78–9.

10. M. M. Efendiev, A. I. Pershits, 'O Sushchnosti Patriarkhal'no-Feodal'nykh Otnoshenii u Kochevikov-Skotovodov', *Voprosy Istorii*, November 1955, No. 11, pp. 65, 71–2; Lattimore, *Inner Asian Frontiers of China*, pp. 332–5.

and then as quickly subside back again into dusty obscurity.[11] The process would typically begin with raids on adjacent trading-routes or centres, the immediate objects for control and pillage – virtually all nomadic peoples showing a keen sense of monetary wealth and commodity circulation.[12] The next phase was characteristically the fusion of rival clans and tribes on the steppe into confederations, for external aggression.[13] Then actual wars of conquest would be launched, often unfolding one after another across immense spaces and involving the migrations of whole peoples. The end-result could be a nomadic empire on a vast scale: in the extreme case of the Mongols an imperial territory larger than any other single state system before or since. The nature of these empires, however, doomed them to a short life. For they were invariably built on elementary tribute – the straightforward extortion of treasure and manpower from the conquered societies beneath them, which were usually socially more advanced than the nomadic overlord society itself, and were left otherwise unmodified by it. Monetary booty was the prime object of what the Rumanian historian Iorga called these 'predator states':[14] their tax-system was simply designed to sustain the occupying nomad troops and provide a lavish income for the new steppe aristocracy, in command of the tributary state. Secondarily, the subject societies were often forced to provide conscripts for a greatly expanded nomadic military system,

11. The most vivid study of this process is E. A. Thompson, *A History of Attila and the Huns*, Oxford 1948, which traces the development the first major nomadic invasion of Europe.

12. Marx once commented: 'Nomad races are the first to develop the money form, because all their worldly goods consist of movable objects and are therefore directly alienable; and because their mode of life, by continually bringing them into contact with foreign communities, solicits the exchange of products'. *Capital*, Vol. I, p. 88. Naturally, he was wrong to believe that nomadic social formations were the first to invent money.

13. Vladimirtsov, *Obshchestvennyi Stroi Mongolov*, p. 85. This phase also produced in the case of the Mongols a genuinely close parallel to the retinue phenomenon in pre-feudal social formations – contra-clan groups of free warriors or *nokod*, in the service of tribal leaders. Vladimirtsov, op. cit., pp. 87–96.

14. See N. Iorga, 'L'Interpénétration de l'Orient et de l'Occident au Moyen Age', *Bulletin de la Section Historique*, XV (1929), Academia Romana, p. 16. Iorga was one of the first European historians to grasp the importance and specificity of these States for the history of the Eastern regions of the continent; later Rumanian historians have been much indebted to him.

and artisans for a newly constructed nomad political capital.[15] Collection of taxes; control of trade-routes; rounding up of recruits; deportation of craftsmen: the administrative operations of nomadic states were essentially limited to these. They were thus purely parasitic constructs, with no roots in the system of production on which they battened. The tributary state merely scooped an exorbitant surplus from the existing system of distribution, without otherwise substantially altering the subject economy and society, other than by blocking and stunting its development. Nomadic society itself, however, underwent rapid and drastic changes with the establishment of such an empire.

Military conquest and fiscal exploitation inevitably stratified the original clan communities sharply; the passage from a tribal confederation to a tributary state automatically generated a princely dynasty and ruling nobility, cleft from commoner nomads organized in regular armies commanded by them. In cases where the original territorial base of nomadism was preserved, the creation of permanent field armies itself divided nomadic society vertically; a large section of it was henceforward split off from its pastoral homeland, for privileged duty as garrison troops in the conquered territories abroad, where riches were greater. It thereby tended to become progressively sedentarized and assimilated to the more developed or more numerous populations under its control. The final result could be a complete denomadization of the occupying army and administration, and a religious and ethnic fusion with the local ruling class.[16] Social and political disintegration by the whole empire usually followed, as the poorer and more primitive nomadic clans at home pulled away from the privileged and demoralized branches abroad. In cases where a whole nomadic people migrated to form an empire over new lands, the same dilemmas reappeared: either the nomadic nobility gradually abandoned pastoralism altogether and merged with the indigenous

15. See the descriptions in G. Vernadsky, *The Mongols and Russia*, Yale 1953, pp. 118, 213, 339–41. The Mongol armies also enlisted artisans for their engineer corps.

16. Lattimore, *Inner Asian Frontiers of China*, pp. 519–23, which focuses mainly on the Mongol example. Complete cultural assimilation, of course, occurred neither among the Mongol nor Manchu conquerors of China: a separate ethnic identity was preserved in each case, till the overthrow of the respective dynasties created by them.

landowning class, or the whole community remained semi-pastoralist and superimposed on the subject peoples, in which case the demographic superiority of the latter would eventually lead to a successful revolt and destruction of the conquerors.[17] For the numerical layer of nomadic control over conquered populations was always very thin, because of the inherent logistics of nomadism itself: in the ultimate case of Genghis Khan's dominions, the ratio of Mongols to tributary peoples was 1:100.[18] Nomadic empires, whether expeditionary or migratory, were fated to the same cycle of expansion and disintegration, because transhumant pastoralism as a mode of production was structurally incompatible with stable tributary administration as a political system. Nomadic rulers either ceased to be nomads or to rule. Transhumant pastoralism could and did exist in a precarious symbiosis with sedentary agriculture in the arid steppe-zones themselves, each preserving its own separate character and terrain and depending on the other for a limited exchange of products. But it could never form a *synthesis* with it, when pastoralist clans established a predator state over settled agrarian populations in their own territory.[19] No new

17. Thompson, *A History of Attila and the Huns*, pp. 177–83, describes the Hunnic case. Thompson was mistaken, however, in supposing that the Huns relinquished pastoralism after creating their Pannonian Empire along the Danube. Its existence was too brief for this. The Hungarian scholar Harmatta has pointed out that any rapid abandonment of horse-breeding would have undermined the immediate basis of Hun military power in Central Europe. J. Harmatta, 'La Société des Huns à l'Epoque d'Attila', *Recherches Internationales*, No. 2, May–June 1957, pp. 194, 230.

18. Vernadsky, *The Mongols and Russia*, pp. 130–1.

19. Brown has recently compared the respective fates of the Roman and Chinese Empires, confronted with their barbarian invaders, condemning the rigid inability of the former to assimilate its Germanic conquerors and outlive them as a civilization, by contrast with the elastic capacity of the latter to tolerate and absorb its Mongol overlords: *Religion and Society in the Age of Saint Augustine*, pp. 56–7, *The World of Late Antiquity*, p. 125. Such a comparison, however, is a paralogism, which reveals the limits of the 'historical psychology' that is the distinctive mark, and merit, of Brown's fecund work. For the difference between the two outcomes was not a function of the subjective cultural attitudes of classic Roman and Chinese civilizations, but of the material nature of the conflicting social formations in Europe and Asia respectively. Extensive desert nomadism could never fuse with the intensive irrigated agriculture of the Chinese imperial State, and the whole economic and demographic polarity between the two was consequently altogether different from that which gave rise to the Romano-Germanic synthesis in Western Europe. The reasons for the impossibility of any

social or economic forms ever emerged. The nomadic mode of production remained a historical dead-end.

If such was the typical course of a complete cycle of nomadic conquest, there were nevertheless certain important variations within the common pattern of the specific pastoralist peoples who descended on Eastern Europe from the Dark Ages onwards, which can be briefly indicated. The central geographical magnet for the armies of mounted archers which successively rode into the continent was the Pannonian plain of modern Hungary. For the Alföld region stretching across the Danube and the Tisza, the Hungarian *puszta*, was the topographical zone in Europe which in some ways most closely resembled the steppe-lands of Central Asia: a flat, treeless savannah ideal for horse-breeding to this day.[20] Moreover, the Pannonian *puszta* offered natural strategic advantages, because of its locale in the centre of Europe; it provided a territorial base from which radial attacks could be made in any direction on the rest of the continent. Thus the Huns established their Empire there; the Avars pitched their circular camps in the same region; the Bulgars selected it as their first resting-place; the Magyars eventually made it their permanent homeland; the Petchenegs and Cumans sought final refuge among them; and the Mongols when they invaded Europe came to a halt and wintered there. Of these peoples, only the Magyar nomads became sedentarized, after their defeat at Lechfeld in 955, eventually settling as a permanent agricultural community in the Danubian basin. The Hunnic Empire was destroyed without a trace by a revolt of the subject population, mainly Germanic tribes, at the Nedao in the mid 5th century, and the Huns effectively disappeared from history. The Avar Empire was overthrown by its Slav tributary population in the 7th century, leaving no ethnic remnant behind in Europe. The Bulgars, another Turco-Tartar people, were evicted from Pannonia, but installed a khanate in the South-East Balkans whose nobility eventually became assimilated to their subject population and

---

comparable synthesis are set out by Lattimore, *Inner Asian Frontiers of China*, pp. 512 ff.

20. The sociological peculiarities of this region, some of which lasted right down to this century, emerge very clearly from A. N. J. Den Hollander, 'The Great Hungarian Plain. A European Frontier Area', *Comparative Studies in Society and History*, III, 1960–1, pp. 74–88, 155–69.

Slavicized in the 9th century. The Petchenegs and Cumans, after dominating the modern regions of Southern Ukraine and Rumania for two centuries, were finally dispersed in the 11th and 13th centuries by Byzantine and Mongol armies respectively, their European remnants fleeing to Hungary, where the Magyar ruling class integrated them to strengthen its cultural and ethnic separation from Slav neighbours. Finally, the Mongol armies withdrew to the Gobi in the 13th century, to participate in the dynastic struggle after the death of Genghis Khan; but a Turkic sub-section of the Mongol hosts, the Golden Horde, clamped a predator overlord system on Russia for 150 years before being shattered in its turn by an incursion of Tamerlane into its Caspian domain. The unique longevity of the Golden Horde's power was due essentially to its geographical fortune. Russia was the nearest European country to the Asian steppes, and the only one which could be subjected to tributary rule by nomad conquerors from the border-lands of pastoral territory itself. The Golden Horde's capital near the Caspian was poised for military intervention and control within agrarian Russia, while itself remaining within steppe-country – thereby avoiding the dilemmas of either direct super-imposition or distant garrisoning in the conquered country.

The impact of these successive nomadic assaults on Eastern Europe was naturally uneven. But the general effect, of course, was to retard and thwart the indigenous development of both forces of production and state systems in the East. Thus the Avar Empire overlaid and manipulated the great Slav migrations of the 6th century, so that no commensurate political forms emerged from their territorial advances – in contrast with the state formation of the epoch of the German migrations in the West. The first autochthonous Slav State, the shadowy Greater Moravia of the 9th century, was levelled by the Magyars. The major political order of the early mediaeval East, Kievan Russia, was first critically weakened by Petcheneg and Cuman attacks on its flanks, and then obliterated completely by the Mongols. Poland and Hungary were by comparison only bruised by the Mongol invasion; yet the defeats of Legnitsa and Sajo ended Piast unification for a generation in the one, and disrupted the Arpad dynasty in the other, leaving both countries in disorder and disarray. The revived Bulgarian State – a long since Slavicized polity – was brought to an abrupt close by the Mongol withdrawal through it. In some ways, the region worst affected of all was the area of modern Rumania, which was so continually subject to nomadic depredation and domination that no native state system at all emerged before the expulsion of the Cumans in the 13th century; its whole intervening history after the Roman retreat from Dacia in the 3rd century remains shrouded in darkness as a consequence. The nomadic pall was a recurrent background to the formation of the mediaeval East.

3

The Pattern of Development

The interior evolution of the East European social formations can now be considered, against this general historical context. Marx once wrote, in a letter to Engels discussing Polish development, that: 'here serfdom can be shown to have arisen in a purely economic way, without the intermediate link of conquest and ethnic dualism'.[1] This formula indicates accurately enough the nature of the problem posed by the emergence of feudalism East of the Elbe. As we have seen, it was fundamentally characterized by the absence of Antiquity, with its urban civilization and slave mode of production. However, to speak of a 'purely economic' path of feudalism in Eastern Europe is an over-simplification, which neglects the fact that the Eastern lands became precisely part of the continent that came to be *Europe* and therefore could not escape certain general determinations – structural and superstructural – of the feudal mode of production that had arisen in the West. The initial pattern of the Slav agrarian communities which occupied most of the Eastern half of the continent above the Danube has already been indicated. Some centuries after the migrations, these remained amorphous and primitive, their development unquickened by any prior contact with urban or imperial forms, or any subsequent fusion with them, given the lack of any legacy from classical Antiquity. Tribe and clan remained the basic units of social organization for a long time; ancestral paganism was untouched; agrarian techniques were rudimentary, with a predominance of slash-burn cultivation amidst the sylvan wilderness of the Eastern plains, up to the 8th century; no native states like those of the Marcomanni and Quadi which had once briefly existed along the Roman *limes*, were yet recorded. Gradually, however,

1. Marx-Engels, *Selected Correspondence*, London 1965, p. 95.

social differentiation and political stratification proceeded. The slow transition to regular arable farming increased the surplus available for the full crystallization of a warrior nobility, divorced from economic production. Clan aristocracies consolidated their dominance, acquiring larger landholdings and using war captives as slave-labour to till them. A small peasantry with its own individual property sometimes retained popular institutions of assembly and justice, but was otherwise subject to their power. Princes and chiefs now emerged, grouping their followers in the familiar armed retinues that henceforward formed the nucleus of a stabilized ruling class. This maturation of a social and political hierarchy was soon accompanied by an impressive multiplication of modest towns, in the 9th and 10th centuries – a phenomenon common to Russia, Poland and Bohemia. These were initially fortified tribal centres, at least in Poland, dominated by local castles.[2] But they also naturally became the focus of regional trade and crafts, and in Russia – where less is known about their political organization – revealed a comparatively advanced urban division of labour. The Scandinavians, when they arrived in Russia, called it *Gardariki* – the land of the towns, because they found so many trading centres there. The appearance of these Polish *gródy* and Russian *goroda* was perhaps the most significant development in the Slav lands of this period, given the complete prior absence of urbanization in the East. It was the farthest point of the endogenous social evolution of Eastern Europe in the Dark Ages.

For the ulterior political development of the whole region was now to come under critical exogenous influence. Both the rise of Western European feudalism and the impact of Scandinavian expansionism were to be largely felt beyond the Elbe. Henceforward, in fact, the continental proximity of more advanced economic and social systems adjacent to it must always be remembered in assessing the course of events in Eastern Europe itself. The profound influence these exercised, in different ways, on the political structures and state systems of the mediaeval East, can be seen from the consistency of the philological

2. Henryk Lowmianowski, 'La Genèse des Etats Slaves et Ses Bases Sociales et Economiques', *La Pologne au Xe Congrès International des Sciences Historiques à Rome*, Warsaw 1955, pp. 29–53 – a summary of present views on early Slav development.

evidence for it.[3] Thus virtually all key Slavonic words for higher political rank and dominion in this period – the vocabulary of the state superstructure itself – are derived from Germanic, Latin or Turanian terms. The Russian *tsar* – 'Emperor' – is borrowed from Roman *caesar*. The Polish *krol*, South Slav *kral* – 'king' – is taken from the eponymous name of Charlemagne himself, *Carolus Magnus*. The Russian *knyaz* – 'prince' – derives from the Old German *kuning-az*, while *druzhina* (Polish *drużyna*) – 'retinue' – perhaps comes from the Gothic *dringan*. The Russian and South Slav *boyar* – 'noble' – is a Turanian word, adopted from the nomad aristocracy of the steppes, first designating the Bulgar ruling class. The Czech *rytiry* – 'knight' – is the German *reiter*. The Polish and Czech words for 'fief' – *lan* and *lan* – are likewise simply transcriptions of the German *lehen*.[4] This massive predominance of foreign (nearly always Western, Germanic or Roman) terms tells its own story. Conversely, it is significant that perhaps the most important purely Slav word in the superstructural sphere – Russian *voevoda* or Polish *wojewoda* – means simply 'he who leads warriors': the tribal military chieftain of the early phase of social development described by Tacitus. This term survived to become transmuted into a formal title in the Middle Ages (misleadingly rendered

3. Today, this evidence is often ignored, by polite convention, because of German chauvinist claims that it proved early Slav societies were 'incapable' of indigenous State-formation, which led East European historians to deny or minimize it. The echoes of these controversies are by no means silenced yet, as can be seen by consulting F. Graus, 'Deutsche und Slawische Verfassungs-geschichte', *Historische Zeitschrift*, CXLVIII, 1963, pp. 265–317. The pre-occupations inspiring them are, of course, entirely foreign to historical material-ism. To state the obvious truth that the Slav social formations were in general more primitive than their Germanic counterparts in the early Middle Ages, and borrowed politically from them, is not to endow either group with any inherent 'ethnic' characteristics, but merely to assert that the former started along a com-parable path of evolution later than the latter, for determinate historical reasons, which in themselves in no way dictated their respective ulterior trajectories, which were naturally marked by uneven and interverted development. It should be unnecessary to repeat these truisms.

4. F. Dvornik, *The Slavs in European History and Civilization*, New Brunswick 1962, pp. 121, 140; L. Musset, *Les Invasions. Le Second Assaut contre L'Europe Chrétienne*, p. 78; George Vernadsky, *Kievan Russia*, Yale 1948, p. 178; K. Wuhrer, 'Die Schwedischen Landschaftsrechte und Tacitus' Germania', *Zeit-schrift des Savigny-Stiftung für Rechtsgeschichte (Germanistische Abteilung)*, LXXXIX, 1959, pp. 20–1.

into English as 'palatine'). Otherwise, the vocabulary of rank was nearly all borrowed from abroad.

There was a second external catalyst in the formation of the state structures in the East. This was the Christian Church. Just as the transition from tribal communities to territorial polities was invariably accompanied by religious conversion in the epoch of the German settlements of the West, so in the East too the foundation of princely states punctually coincided with the adoption of Christianity. As we have seen, the abandonment of tribal paganism was normally an ideological precondition of the supersession of clannic principles of social organization, and the establishment of centralized political authority and hierarchy. The successful work of Church emissaries from the outside – Catholic or Orthodox – was thus an essential component of the process of State formation in Eastern Europe. The princedom of Bohemia was founded by the Premyslid dynasty, when its first ruler Vaclav, who ruled from 915 to 929, became an ardent Christian. The first unitary Polish State was created when the Piast potentate Mieszko I simultaneously adopted the Catholic faith and the ducal title in 966. The Varangian realm in Kievan Russia achieved its completed form when the Rurik prince Vladimir accepted Orthodox baptism in 988, in order to obtain an imperial marriage with the sister of the Byzantine Emperor Basil II. The Hungarian nomads were similarly sedentarized and organized into a royal state, with the conversion of the first Arpad ruler Stephen, who – like Mieszko – received both his creed (996–7) and his monarchy (1000), the one in exchange for the other, from Rome. In all these cases, princely adoption of Christianity was followed by an official Christianization of their subjects: it was an inaugural act of state. In many cases, a popular pagan reaction broke out later, in Poland, Hungary and Russia, mingling religious and social protest against the new order.

Religious innovation was an easier step in the consolidation of royal states, however, than the passage from a retainer to a landed nobility. It has been seen that the emergence of a retinue-system everywhere marks a signal rupture with bonds of kinship as the basic principle of social organization; a retinue represents the threshold for a transition from a tribal to a feudal aristocracy. Once such a princely retinue is formed – a cross-clan group of nobles constituting the personal military entourage of the ruler, who are economically maintained by his household and share in his war booty in exchange for loyal service in combat and administration – it typically becomes the prime initial instrument of royal government. Yet for a feudal nobility proper to develop out of a military retinue, a further crucial step is necessary: its territorialization as a landowning class. In other words, a compact group of royal guards and warriors must be dispersed to become seigneurial lords with provincial estates, held as fiefs in vassalage to their monarch. This structural passage was invariably a very hazardous one, since the final phase of the whole movement always threatened to cancel the gains of the first phase, by producing an anarchic local nobility recalcitrant to any centralized royal authority. The danger then fatally arose of a disintegration of the original monarchical State itself, whose unity was paradoxically assured with less difficulty in the less advanced household-retinue stage. The implantation of a stable and integrated fief system was thus an extremely difficult process. It had only emerged after centuries of confused and inchoate gropings in the West, during the Dark Ages, and was finally consolidated amidst a general breakdown of unitary royal authority in the 10th century – half a millennium after the Germanic invasions. Thus it is no surprise that in the East, too, there was no linear progress from the first dynastic States of the Premyslids, Piasts and Ruriks, to fully-fledged feudal systems. On the contrary, in each case – Bohemia, Poland and Russia – there was an eventual relapse back into confusion and disorder: a political regression in which both princely power and territorial unity were fragmented or eclipsed.[5] Viewed in a comparative perspective, these vicissitudes of the early Eastern state systems were rooted in the problems of forging a cohesive seigneurial nobility within a unitary royal polity. This in turn presupposed the creation of an enserfed

5. Eastern European experience is a salutary warning against the inflated claims made by local historians for the Anglo-Saxon State in England, often presented as having virtually completed a successful transition to feudalism on the eve of the Norman invasion, because of the unitary character of its royal government. In fact, no stable dynastic succession or coherent fief system had emerged in Anglo-Saxon England, whose relative advance might well subsequently have collapsed into disorder and regression such as overtook the early Slav states, in the common absence of a classical heritage. It was the Norman Conquest, product of the Romano-Germanic synthesis of the Western mainland, which in practice precluded such a relapse.

peasantry, fixed to the land and furnishing the surplus for a developed feudal hierarchy. By definition, a fief system could not emerge until a servile labour-force existed to provide the immediate producers for it. In the West, the final emergence and generalization of serfdom had occurred, once again, only in the course of the 10th century, after the whole experience of the Dark Ages and the Carolingian Empire which concluded them. The typical rural economy of the prolonged epoch from the 5th to the 9th century had been – as we have seen – very mixed and fluid in character, with coexistent slave, small-holder, free tenant and-dependent peasant elements in it. In the East, there was no anterior slave mode of production, so that the starting-point for any evolution towards serfdom was necessarily different, and ruder. But there too, rural society in the first era after state-systems were established was everywhere heterogeneous and transitional: the mass of the peasantry had not yet experienced enserfment. Eastern feudalism was only born after its own necessary period of labour.

If this was the general pattern of early development in the East, there were naturally important variations in the economic, political and cultural trajectory of different regions within it that must be noted. Russia represents the most interesting and complex case, because there something like a flickering 'Eastern' shadow of the Western synthesis did appear to occur. The first Russian State was created in the late 9th and early 10th centuries by Swedish traders and pirates sailing down the river routes from Scandinavia.[6] There they found a society that had already produced many local towns in the forests, but no regional unity or polity. The Varangian merchants and soldiers who came upon it soon established their political supremacy over these urban centres, linking the Volkhov and Volga waterways to create a single zone of economic transit from the Baltic to the Black Sea, and founding a State whose axis of political authority ran from Novgorod to Kiev along it. The Varangian State centred on Kiev was, as we have seen elsewhere, commercial in character: it was set up in order to control the trade routes between Scandinavia and the Black Sea, and its main export

6. Russian national sentiment has repeatedly led, both in the 19th and 20th centuries, to denials of the Scandinavian origins of the Kievan State (or indeed, derivation of the word 'Rus' itself). The anachronism of such 'patriotic' historiography needs no demonstration here: it has its counterpart in English myths of 'continuity', alluded to earlier.

traffic was slaves – destined for the Muslim world or Byzantium. A slave emporium was formed in Southern Russia, whose catchment area was the whole Slav East and which served both the Mediterranean and Persian lands conquered by the Arabs, and the Greek Empire. The Khazar State further to the East which had previously dominated the lucrative export trade to Persia was eliminated, the Varangian rulers thus gaining direct access to the Caspian routes as well.[7] These major commercial operations of the Kievan State helped to give Europe its new and permanent word for slaves: *sclavus* first appears in the 10th century. Varangian traders also shipped out wax, furs and honey – henceforward Russian export staples throughout the Middle Ages: but these were subordinate items. The urban development of Kiev, which set it apart from any other centre in Eastern Europe, was essentially founded on a trade that by now represented a growing anachronism within the Western economy.

However, if the Norse rulers of Kiev provided the initial political impetus and commercial experience for the first Russian State, it was the close diplomatic and cultural contact across the Black Sea with Byzantium which contributed most to the relative superstructural sophistication of Kievan Russia. Here a limited parallelism with the impact of the Roman Empire on the Germanic West is most evident. In particular, both written language and religion – the two basic components of any ideological system, in that epoch – were imported from Byzantium. The early Varangian princes in Kiev had conceived their capital as a base for piratical expeditions against Byzantium and Persia, but especially the former – a glittering prize for plunder. Their attacks were twice repulsed, however, in 860 and 941; and shortly thereafter the first Varangian ruler to bear a Slav name, Vladimir, adopted Christianity. The Glagolitic and Cyrillic alphabets had been invented by Greek priests specifically for the languages of the Slavonic peoples, and the cause of their conversion to the Orthodox faith. Kievan Russia now adopted both script and creed, and with them the Byzantine institution of a State Church. Greek clergy were dispatched to the

7. There is a balanced discussion of the nature of the Varangian role in Russia in Musset, *Les Invasions. Le Second Assaut*, pp. 99–106, 261–6. It may be noted that the Slavonic word for a town, *gorod*, is ultimately the same as the Old Norse term *gardr*, but it is not certain whether the former derived from the latter: Foote and Wilson, *The Viking Achievement*, p. 221.

Ukraine to man an ecclesiastical hierarchy, which gradually became as slavicized as the ruling house and its retainers were to be. This Church was later to be the medium for an ideological transplantation of the autocratic imperial tradition of the Eastern Empire, even after the subsequent disappearance of the latter. The administrative and cultural influence of Byzantium thus seemed to permit a precarious Russian synthesis in the East which might be compared to the Frankish synthesis in the West, both in its precocious achievements and in its inevitable downfall, followed by chaos and regression.[8] However, the limits of such comparisons are evident. There was no common territorial ground between Kiev and Byzantium, which could be the soil of an actual fusion. The Greek Empire, which was itself now remote from its Roman predecessor, could only transmit partial and distant impulses across the Euxine. Thus it is natural that no organic feudal hierarchy such as the Carolingian Empire gestated ever appeared in Russia during this epoch. It is rather the heteroclite and amorphous nature of the Kievan society and economy that is striking. A ruling class of princes and boyars, derived from the Varangian *druzhina*, collected tribute and controlled trade in the towns, where there typically subsisted oligarchic councils or *vechya*, the remnants of former folk assemblies. The boyars owned large estates with a mixed workforce of slaves, peon *zakupy* or peasants in debt bondage, and hired labourers. Side by side with these estates, a considerable free peasantry organized in village communes existed.[9]

The Kievan State reached the zenith of its power with the rule of Iaroslav, in the early 11th century (1015–36), the last of its princes

8. Marx coupled the Carolingian with the Varangian Empires in *The Secret Diplomatic History of the Eighteenth Century*, London 1969, p. 109. But this is work of phobic fabulation, certainly the worst piece of historical writing ever composed by Marx; its errors are legion. When it was first republished at the turn of the century, Ryazanov wrote a sober critique of it, as a Marxist scholar: 'Karl Marx über den Vorsprung der Vorherrschaft Russlands in Europa', *Die Neue Zeit* (*Ergänzungshefte No. 5*), 5 March 1909, pp. 1–64. The contemporary editor of the text has failed to indicate the most minimal distance from it.

9. A comprehensive account of Kievan social structure can be found in Vernadsky, *Kievan Russia*, pp. 131–72; but marred by Vernadsky's belief that 'capitalism' and 'democracy' were in some sense latent in the commercial system and council survivals of the Kievan State, fanciful category errors inherited from Rostovtsev.

with Scandinavian connections and Varangian ambitions: it was in his reign that its final external adventures were launched, a military attack on Byzantium and an expedition into Central Asia. From the mid 11th century, the Rurik dynasty and its nobility were completely Russianized. Soon, the great trade-routes to the South were cut – first by the Cuman occupation of the Southern Ukraine and then by the Crusades. The Italian cities now seized control of both Islamic and Byzantine trade. Once an economic outpost of Byzantium, Kiev declined together with the Greek metropolis to the South. The result of this isolation was a marked shift in the evolution of the Kievan social formation. The contraction of trade was inevitably accompanied by a sinking of the towns and an enhancing of the importance of local rural landowners. Deprived of their commercial incomes from the slave-trade, the boyar class turned inwards to compensate themselves with enlarged domains and an increased agrarian surplus.[10] The consequence was marked economic pressure on the peasantry, which now began to decline towards serfdom. Simultaneously, the political unity of the Kievan State started to break up into mediatized principalities which mauled one another as the House of Rurik disintegrated into dynastic quarrels. Seigneurial localism developed together with increasing degradation of the peasantry.

The path of development in the Czech and Polish lands was naturally affected in the main by German rather than by Scandinavian or Byzantine influences; but within this more westerly environment, a comparable evolution is discernible. The initial social formations of those regions were not unlike that of early Kievan Russia, without the extensive river commerce that was the basis of its exceptional urban growth. Thus local aristocracies presided over a mixture of immediate producers – including small-holders, slaves and peons – very widely in the East, a reflection of the transition from simple social structures, whose clan warriors had used slave prisoners to till their lands in the absence of a dependent peasantry, towards differentiated State systems with increasing subordination of the whole rural labour force via

10. K. R. Schmidt, 'The Social Structure of Russia in the Early Middle Ages', *XIe Congrès International des Sciences Historiques*, Uppsala 1960, Rapports III, p. 32. Schmidt discusses rival historiographic emphases on the agrarian or commercial wealth of the Kievan ruling classes, from Kliuchevsky onwards.

mechanisms of peasant indebtedness or practices of commendation. In Poland, Silesia, Bohemia or Moravia, agricultural techniques often remained extremely primitive, with slash-burn cultivation and field pasturage still practised by a heterogeneous population of free-holders, tenants and slaves. The first political structure to emerge was a somewhat spectral Bohemian State in the early 7th century, established by the Frankish merchant Samo who led the local Slav revolt which overthrew the Avar Empire in Central Europe. Samo's State, which was probably a trade-controlling realm like that of the early Varangians in Russia, failed to convert the population of the region and did not last long.[11] Two hundred years later, a more solid structure emerged further to the east, the Greater Moravian State of the 9th century.

This princedom rested on numerous castles and aristocratic fortifications, and was an important power on the confines of the Carolingian Empire, whose diplomatic alliance was sought by Byzantium against Frankish expansionism. It was there that the Orthodox brothers Cyril and Methodius were dispatched to the ruler, Rastislav, on the mission of instruction and conversion for which they created the Slavonic alphabet. Eventually, their efforts were trumped by Catholic priests from Rome. The Czech lands, however, became the first beach-head of Christian conversion in the East, before the Moravian State was overwhelmed by a Magyar invasion in the early 10th century. It was in Bohemia, less gravely damaged by nomadic devastation, that a political recovery henceforward gradually occurred. By the early 11th century, a Czech State had once again appeared – this time with a more advanced social structure that included an early version of a fief system. The Ottonian Renovation had led to a great increase in German pressure on the eastern marches of the Empire. Bohemian political development was henceforward always subject to the contradictory impact of German intervention and influence in the Czech lands. On the one hand, this accelerated the formation of feudal institutions (by imitation) and stimulated the attachment of the Slav nobility to its own local State,

11. G. Vernadsky, 'The Beginnings of the Czech State', *Byzantion*, 1944–5, XVII, pp. 315–28, argues – against all the evidence – that Samo was a Slav merchant 'dedicated to the idea of inter-slavic cooperation', an improbable mission that is another instance of the ravages of nationalism in the field of Dark Age historiography.

symbolized by the fervent cult of its patron saint, Wenceslas.[12] On the other hand, it checked the consolidation of a stable monarchy – since German Emperors from Otto I onwards claimed Bohemia as a fief of the Empire, and exacerbated dynastic rivalries within the Czech aristocracy. For the unitary Bohemian State was soon compromised by a long and debilitating struggle between the Premyslid and Slavnikovic families for political dominance, which plunged the country into repeated civil wars.[13] By the later 12th century, Bohemian fiefs were heritable and the peasantry increasingly subjected to seigneurial dues, as a provincial aristocracy took root in the countryside. By the same process, central political power was weakened and compromised, as Bohemia receded into princely disputes and divisions.

In Poland, tribal and clan organization lasted longer: by the 9th century a vague regional confederation of the Polanes existed with its centre at Gniezno. It was not until the advent of the Piast leader Mieszko I in the late 10th century that the first unitary Polish state was formed. Mieszko adopted Christianity in 966, and imposed it on his domains, as the organizing religion of the new political system.[14] The successful mission in Poland was the work of the Roman Church, which brought with it Latin, henceforward the official literary language of the country (an index of the comparative abruptness of the change in social and cultural levels attendant on the emergence of the Piast State, contrasting with the earlier and slower evolution of Bohemia; the Polish nobility, in fact, was to use Latin as its current written language long after it fell into desuetude in the post-mediaeval West). Mieszko was confirmed in his ducal title by the Papacy in exchange for his religious allegiance. His duchy rested on a well-integrated and extensive retinue system – a *druzyna* of some 3,000 nobles, who were stationed either in the ruler's entourage or in the regional garrisons of fortified *grody* with which the country was covered. The use of these royal retainers as castle commandants represented an effective intermediate

12. F. Graus, 'Origines de l'Etat et de la Noblesse en Moravie et en Bohème', *Revue des Etudes Slaves*, Vol. 39, 1961, pp. 43–58.

13. F. Dvornik, *The Slaves. Their Early History and Civilization*, pp. 115, 300.

14. Aleksander Gieysztor, 'Recherches sur les Fondements de la Pologne Médiévale: État Actuel des Problèmes', *Acta Poloniae Historica*, IV, 1961, pp. 19–25.

device in the passage from a household to a landed aristocracy. The early Piast State benefited from the incipient urban development of the previous pagan century, and derived respectable revenues from local trading centres. Mieszko's son Boleslaw I rapidly developed Piast power, expanding the Polish realm geographically by annexing Silesia and marching into the Ukraine, and claiming the royal title. But here too, early State solidity and political unity proved a deceptive promise. The Polish monarchy, like the Bohemian, was the target of constant German diplomatic and military manoeuvres. The German Emperors claimed imperial jurisdiction over both regions, and eventually succeeded in blocking the consolidation of royal authority in Poland, where the monarchical title was retroceded by Mieszko II, and vassalizing it in Bohemia, which became a formal fief of the Empire.[15] Moreover, the rapidity with which the Piast State had been constructed proved to be its internal undoing. In 1031, there was a violent social and religious upheaval, combining a pagan reaction against the Church, a peasant revolt against the increase of seigneurial pressures, and an aristocratic rising against the power of the ruling dynasty. The Polish lords evicted Mieszko II from the country, and divided it into provincial voyevodships. His son Casimir was restored with Bohemian and Kievan help, but the central State was henceforward gravely weakened. In the 12th century, Piast devolution of power into regional appanages eventually undid it altogether. Poland now split into innumerable petty duchies, while small peasant property declined and predial exactions multiplied in the countryside. Clerical and noble lands still englobed only some 45 per cent of the rural population, but the trend was clear.[16] In Poland, as elsewhere, the condition of the native peasantry was slowly deteriorating in the direction of servitude towards the 12th century. This process was common to Russia, Livonia, Poland, Bohemia, Hungary and Lithuania. In general, it took the form of a steady extension of large estates by the local aristocracies, a decline in the number of free-holders, an increase in peasant tenancy, and then a gradual convergence of dependent tenants and captive or

15. For German policy in this period, see especially F. Dvornik, *The Making of Central and Eastern Europe*, London 1949, pp. 194–6, 217–35, and *The Slavs: Their Early History and Civilization*, pp. 275–92.

16. H. Lowmianski, 'Economic Problems of the Early Feudal Polish State', *Acta Poloniae Historica*, III, 1960, p. 30.

penal slaves into a single unfree rural mass, factually under seigneurial jurisdictions but not yet formally servile.[17]

This process, however, was to be suddenly halted and reversed. During the 12th and 13th centuries, as we have seen, Western feudalism expanded rapidly outwards, from Spain to Finland, from Ireland to Greece. Two of these advances were especially important and lasting, those achieved in the Iberian peninsula and in the Transalbingian East. But whereas the Reconquista in Spain and Portugal evicted an advanced, if decaying civilization and involved little if any immediate economic improvement of the terrain newly won (the ultimate overseas dynamism of both still lay well in the future), the mainly German colonization of the East wrought a dramatic growth of output and productivity in the lands affected by it. The forms of this colonization varied greatly. Brandenburg and Pomerania were occupied by marcher lords or princes from Northern Germany. Prussia and Livonia were conquered by crusading military organizations, the Teutonic Order and the Knights of the Sword. Bohemia, Silesia and to some extent Transylvania were gradually peopled with immigrants from the West who formed townships and villages side by side with the Slav inhabitants, without drastic changes in the political status quo. Poland and Lithuania likewise received Germanic communities, mainly urban merchants and artisans. The pagan Baltic tribes – Pruzzi and others – were subdued *manu militari* by the Teutonic Order, and a so-called 'Wendish Crusade' was launched against the Obodrite Slavs between the Elbe and the Oder. But apart these two sectors, the bulk of the colonization was a relatively peaceful affair that was often encouraged by the local Slav aristocracies, anxious to settle their own sparsely populated spaces with a new and comparatively skilled labour force.[18]

The specific conditions of this colonization determined its peculiar impact on the social formations of the East. Land was abundant, if heavily forested and not always of very good quality (the soil of the Baltic littoral was sandy): population, on the other hand, was scarce. It has been calculated that the total inhabitants of Eastern Europe,

17. Jerome Blum, 'The Rise of Serfdom in Eastern Europe', *American Historical Review*, LXVII, No. 4, July 1957, pp. 812–15.

18. The Teutonic Order itself was invited to Prussia by the Polish Duke of Mazovia, in 1228.

including Russia, perhaps numbered some 13,000,000 at the beginning of the 13th century, compared with some 35,000,000 in the smaller zone of Western Europe.[19] Labour and skills had to be transported to the West, in organized convoys of settlers recruited from the densely populated regions of the Rhineland, Swabia, Franconia and Flanders. The need for them was so pressing, and the problems of marshalling their transit so great, that the nobles and clergy who inspired the drive to the East had to grant the peasants and burghers who settled the new lands considerable social rights. The deftest peasantry in Europe for the diking and drainage work that was so essential for reclamation of uncultivated regions was to be found in the Netherlands, and particular efforts were made to attract them to the East. The Northern Netherlands, however, was a corner of Europe which had never known a proper manorial system, and whose peasantry were already much freer from servile dues than the French, English or German counterparts in the 12th century. 'Flemish law' had therefore to be accepted along with them, and soon exercised a general influence on the statute of the colonial peasantry, who were numerically mostly German and had not known such liberty in their homelands.[20] Thus in the newly colonized East, there was little manorial jurisdiction over the peasantry, who were given inheritable tenures with rents in kind attached, but few labour services; moreover, cultivators were permitted to sell the usufruct of their plots and leave their settlements altogether. Villages formed rural communities governed by hereditary mayors (often the initial organizer of the emigration), not by seigneurial fiat. These settlements rapidly changed the whole agrarian pattern from the Elbe to the Vistula and beyond. Forests were cleared, iron ploughs and the three-field system were introduced for the first time: husbandry receded and grain cultivation became widespread for the first time. A considerable timber export trade developed. Under the impact of this process, with its manifestly higher yields and surplus, both the indigenous nobility and the crusader orders increasingly came to accept the norms of peasant agriculture introduced from the West.

19. Russell, *Late Ancient and Mediaeval Population*, p. 148.
20. M. Postan, 'Economic Relations between Eastern and Western Europe', in Geoffrey Barraclough (ed.), *Eastern and Western Europe during the Middle Ages*, London 1970, p. 169.

Thus the condition of the native peasantry in Poland, Bohemia, Silesia, Pomerania and elsewhere, which had been dipping downwards towards serfdom before the onset of the German colonization, now registered a recovery by assimilation to that of the newcomers; while the Prussian peasantry initially enserfed by the Teutonic Order were emancipated in the course of the succeeding century. Autonomous villages with their own mayors and courts sprang up, rural mobility was enlarged, and productivity rose correspondingly.

The increase in cereal production and timber felling in its turn stimulated an even more important result of the Eastern colonization: the growth of towns and trading entrepots along the Baltic coast in the 13th century – Rostock, Danzig, Wismar, Riga, Dorpat and Reval. These urban centres were independent and turbulent communes, with a prosperous export trade and a lively political life. Just as 'Flemish law' had exerted an ameliorating pull on social relations in indigenous agriculture, so 'German law' modelled on the Charter of Magdeburg exercised an analogous influence on the statute of the traditional towns of the East. In Poland, in particular, towns which were often hosts to sizeable colonies of German merchants and craftsmen now received the Rights of Magdeburg: Poznan, Cracow and the recent foundation of Warsaw were all beneficiaries of this process.[21] In Bohemia, a denser network of urban colonization by German burghers occurred, based on the mining and metallurgical industries of the area, and with more significant participation by Czech artisans and traders. Thus, in the 13th century, the colonial East was the frontier society of European feudalism, an impressive projection of its own expansive dynamism, which at the same time had some of the advantages over the parent system that the frontier societies of European capitalism were later to have in America or Oceania: greater equality and mobility. Carsten sums up the characteristics of its prime thus: 'The manorial system proper with its restrictions of freedom and its private jurisdictions had not been transferred to the East, nor had serfdom. The peasants' position was far better than it was in the West, and this included the native population. Class distinctions in the East were less sharp, noblemen moved into the towns and became burghers, while burghers acquired estates and village mayors held fiefs. The whole structure of

21. Roger Portal, *Les Slaves*, Paris 1965, p. 75.

society, as might be expected of a colonial area, was much freer and looser than it was in Western Europe. It only seemed a question of time until the East would no longer be backward but would belong to the most developed parts of Europe. Indeed, this already applied to the Hanseatic towns along the coast of the Baltic, especially to the Wendish towns and to Danzig.'[22]

Russia, which lay beyond the confines of German penetration proper, nevertheless underwent an evolution with certain curious parallels in these centuries, although with a different tempo and in a different context. This was the result of the break-up of the Kievan State in the 12th and 13th centuries, under the pressure of external misfortunes and internal weaknesses. As we have seen, the Crusades cut off the Black Sea trade-routes to Constantinople and the Islamic world, on which Kievan commerce had traditionally thrived. From the East, Cuman raids were a constant menace, while at home the princely 'seniorate' system led to a tangle of civil wars and disorders.[23] Kiev itself was sacked in the mid-12th century by the Prince of Suzdal. Then, seventy years later, there occurred the hurricane shock of the last great nomad invasion from Central Asia: virtually the whole of Russia, apart from the North-West, was ravaged and subjugated by the Mongols, shortly after the death of Genghis Khan. Perhaps a tenth of the population perished in this disaster. The consequence was a permanent shift in the axis of Russian civilization from the Kievan basin to the hitherto largely uninhabited and virgin forests of the Oka-Volga triangle to the North-East, approximately at the same time as the widening demographic seepage across the Elbe.

In the gradual recomposition of a Russian social formation in the

---

22. F. L. Carsten, *The Origins of Prussia*, Oxford 1954, p. 88.

23. Dvornik offers two contradictory explanations for the peculiarly intricate Kievan appanage system, which led to these disorders. He initially attributes it to a Germano-Scandinavian institution, the 'tanistry', whereby a ruler was succeeded not by his son but by his youngest brother, and the latter by his eldest nephew, otherwise found only in Vandal Africa and Norse settlements in Scotland. Elsewhere, however, he assimilates it to the 'seniorate' hierarchy of Piast dukes in Poland and the Czech succession systems of the 12th century, and asserts that it was a Slav principle that a country was the patrimony of the ruling house, all of whose members should share in its government. Compare *The Slavs: Their Early History and Civilization*, p. 213, and *The Slavs in European History and Civilization*, pp. 120–1.

North-East, many of the same social effects as those which marked the Baltic zone occurred. The reclamation and colonization of vast unpopulated spaces halted the descent of the Russian peasantry towards permanent servile dependence, which had been well under way in the last centuries of the Kievan State. Princes were obliged to offer exemptions from dues, communal rights and personal mobility to peasants, to induce them to settle the recently cleared lands. Nobles and monasteries followed suit, if with closer manorial controls over the new villages. Political authority became further sub-divided and feudalized among territorial lords, while the peasants beneath them gained greater freedom.[24] The farther the distance from the main sites of political power in the Central region, the greater was the degree of liberty which the peasantry won in this way: it was characteristically fullest in the remote Northern forests, where seigneurial jurisdictions only fitfully reached. At the same time, the shift of the demographic and economic axis of the country to the Oka-Volga triangle greatly stimulated the trading towns of Novgorod and Pskov to the North-West, in the intermediate zone between Russia and German-colonized Livonia. Henceforward Central Russia provided the cereal supplies for the Novgorod trading empire, with its tributary exactions over the Sub-Arctic tribes to the North and its pivotal role in Baltic commerce. Although ruled by a municipal assembly, Novgorod was not in fact a merchant commune comparable to the German towns on the coast: the *veche* was dominated by landowning boyars very unlike the Hansa burghers. However, German influence was powerful in the city, which had a large foreign merchant community and – uniquely for Russian towns, before or afterwards – a Western-inspired guild system for its artisans. Novgorod thus provided the strategic linkage which connected Russia and the other lands of Eastern Europe into an inter-communicating economic system.

24. There is a good analysis of this dual development in Marc Szeftel's essay, 'Aspects of Russian Feudalism', in Rushton Coulborn (ed.), *Feudalism in History* Princeton 1956, pp. 169–73.

4

The Crisis in the East

The crisis of European feudalism started later and was probably in absolute dimensions more mitigated in the East; while in Russia it was staggered over a distinct time-sequence. But its relative impact may if anything have been even greater: for it struck a much more recent and fragile social structure than in the West. The blow was more diffuse: but the resistance to it was weaker. It is necessary to keep both these contradictory aspects of the general Eastern crisis in mind, for it is their combination alone which renders intelligible its course and outcome. Conventional accounts tend to collapse the whole feudal depression of the 14th and 15th centuries into an unduly homogeneous continental slump. Yet it is clear, in the first instance, that the basic mechanism of the feudal crisis in the West – an 'over-reaching' and 'stalling' of the forces of production at the barrier limit of existing social relations of production, leading to a demographic collapse and economic recession – would not in itself be replicated in the East. For there the implantation of new agrarian techniques and social organization was still relatively fresh, and had by no means attained the boundaries of possible expansion. The type of dense overpopulation that existed in the West by 1300 was unknown in the East. Large tracts of cultivable territory had yet to be opened up along the Vistula or the Oder when marginal lands were already contracting round the Rhine, the Loire or the Thames. There was thus little probability of a simultaneous endogenous repetition of the Western crisis in the East. In fact, for a considerable period in the 14th century, Poland and Bohemia seemed to have reached a political and cultural zenith. Czech urban civilization achieved its apogee under the Luxemburg dynasty, before its spiral downwards into the Barons' League and the Hussite

Wars.[1] In its brief coruscation under Charles IV, Bohemia was the Burgundy of Eastern Europe. Poland escaped the great plague, and was the victor in the Thirteen Years' War; Casimir III was the contemporary and counterpart of Charles IV; the Jagellonian house united Poland with Lithuania to form the largest territorial state in the continent. In Hungary too, the Angevin rulers Charles Robert and Louis I organized a powerful feudal monarchy, whose influence and prestige were considerable throughout the region, and which under Louis was united in a personal union with Poland. But this political vitality could not long withstand the change of economic climate that came over Eastern Europe, lagged after that in the West but visibly linked to it. For the evidence makes it clear that by the early 15th century, there was a synchronic depression in both parts of Europe.

What were the real reasons for the crisis in the East? First and foremost, of course, in the vast arc of territories affected by German colonization, there was the sudden faltering of the whole economic and demographic impulse transmitted by it. Once the homelands of feudalism in the West were gripped by recession on a wide front, their projections into the borderlands of the East were correspondingly enfeebled. The momentum of settlement now slackened and died out. By the early 14th century, there were already ominous signs of deserted villages and abandoned fields in Brandenburg and Pomerania. In part, these were due to migration further east by peasants grown accustomed to mobility. But such shifts in themselves indicated one of the dangers of the whole colonization process. Just because land was abundant, it could be briefly exploited and then left behind, in a recurring trail of the type that was to create dustbowls in other continents and epochs. The sanded soil of the Baltic littoral was particularly prone to exhaustion unless carefully treated: thus here, too, inundation and erosion gradually set in. Moreover, the decline in cereal prices in the West because of the precipitous fall in demand inevitably affected the East, where a modest volume of grain exports had already begun. The rye

1. Bohemian prosperity in this period was based on the discovery of the Kutna Hora silver mines, which became the major European supplier after 1300, amidst the general shut-downs elsewhere: R. R. Betts, 'The Social Revolution in Bohemia and Moravia in the Later Middle Ages', *Past and Present*, No. 2, November 1952, p. 31.

index in Königsberg during the next century closely reflected the decline of wheat prices registered in the Western cities.[2] At the same time, as we have seen, the bottlenecks in mining technique affected the stocks of mintable metals throughout the continent, even if Bohemian mines were less affected than Saxon. Devaluation of the coinage and a drop in seigneurial incomes, keenly felt in Brandenburg, Poland and elsewhere, were a common result. Nor was the East spared the concomitant scourges of the great crisis in the West, the terrible 'effects' of the depression which became the 'causes' of its reiteration. Pestilence, dearth and war swept across the Eastern plains scarcely less than elsewhere. There were 11 major outbreaks of the plague in Prussia between the 1340s and the 1490s.[3] There were 20 visitations in Russia from 1350 to 1450:[4] the Muscovite ruler Simeon himself died of it, together with his brother and two sons, in 1353. Poland, alone of any major area of Europe, by and large escaped the Black Death. Bohemia was not so fortunate. The crop-failures of 1437–9 in Prussia were the worst in a century. Meanwhile, military struggles ravaged all the main regions of the East. The Ottomans overran Serbia and Bulgaria in the late 14th century, subjecting them to a local history separate from that of the rest of Europe. Over 150 campaigns were waged across Russia, against Mongols, Lithuanians, Germans, Swedes and Bulgarians. Continual border raids and feuds depopulated the frontiers between Brandenburg and Pomerania. Polish forces crushed the Teutonic Order at Grünewald in 1410 with an army drawn from all over Eastern Europe, and invaded Prussia in 1414, 1420 and 1431–3. After two decades of smouldering peace, a final and far more deadly conflict was engaged in 1453: the Thirteen Years' War, which shattered the Teutonic Order and ruined East Prussia utterly for a generation. Massive depopulation and desertion of holdings was the outcome of this ferocious and protracted struggle. In Bohemia, the long Hussite Wars of the early 15th century had much the same effect, levelling and grinding down the rural economy as rival armies marched and counter-marched across it. Nor was this supreme drama of the late Middle Ages confined merely to the Czech lands. The Emperor Sigismund's hired hosts

2. Van Bath, *The Agrarian History of Western Europe*, p. 139.
3. Carsten, *The Origins of Prussia*, p. 103.
4. Blum, *Lord and Peasant in Russia*, p. 60.

were raised from all over Europe to suppress the insurgent Hussite Leagues, while the Taborite armies of Prokop the Shaven extended the war against the Empire and the Church deep into Austria, Slovakia, Saxony, Silesia, Brandenburg, Poland and Prussia, their itinerant columns and waggoned gun platforms wreaking a path of destruction all the way to Leipzig, Nuremburg, Berlin and Danzig.

Moreover, while in the West social revolts had succeeded military conflicts, or been separate by-blows of them (the Grande Jacquerie), in the East the two were inextricably mingled: the major wars and insurrections formed a single process. The two great conflagrations in the Baltic and Bohemia were also violent civil wars. The peasants in Ermland had already revolted during a brief pause in the Prusso-Polish conflict. The Thirteen Years' War itself, however, was a savage and generalized social upheavel in which the merchant towns of Danzig and Torun allied with the rural gentry and ruthless, foot-loose mercenaries in a rebellion to bring down the military bureaucracy of the Teutonic Order. In the late 14th century, Bohemia too was already the scene of turbulent baronial conflicts during the reign of Wenceslas IV, with roving bands of paid thugs prowling the countryside: it was in these ugly feuds that John Zizka, the future commander of the Hussite cause, found his military training, before serving in a group which fought at Grünewald for the Polish monarch. Then, from 1419 to 1434, the Hussite Wars themselves exploded, an event without precedent in mediaeval history, pitting burghers, squires, artisans and peasants against noble landowners, urban patricians, the dynasty and foreign troops, in an extraordinary social and proto-national struggle waged under the pennants of religion.[5] The Articles of the community of rural poor who founded the city of Tabor in the Bohemian hills

5. Frederick Heymann, *John Zizka and the Hussite Revolution*, Princeton 1965, is the major work available in a non-Czech language on the Hussite Wars. A warm and well-written study, it is unduly brief in social analysis and stops with Zizka's death in 1424. Heymann justly emphasizes the unprecedented character of the Hussite upheaval, but commits an anachronism in claiming it as the first of the great chain of modern revolutions, the predecessor of the Dutch, English, American and English, pp. 477–9. It clearly belongs to another historical series. Josef Macek, *The Hussite Movement in Bohemia*, Prague 1958, is a much more thorough exploration of the class composition of the contending forces, but is essentially only a sketch summarizing the author's full-scale scholarly works in Czech.

express perhaps the profoundest cry for an impossible liberation in the whole history of European feudalism.[6] Radical millenarianism was soon suppressed within the Hussite bloc, but the loyalty of the peasants and craftsmen who provided the soldiers of the Hussite cause, under their leaders Zizka and Prokop, did not waver. It was 15 years before this unique armed insurrection, which deposed an Emperor, defied the Papacy and defeated five crusades against it, was finally stifled, and the country regained a moribund peace. The once strong monarchies of Poland, Bohemia and Hungary had all disintegrated into baronial usurpation and disorder, with increasing seigneurial pressures on the peasantry, by the early 15th century. There was a brief, concerted recovery in all three countries at mid-century, with the rise of George of Podebrody in the Czech lands, the accession of Matthias Corvinus in Hungary, and the reign of Casimir IV in Poland – all competent rulers who for a period restored royal authority, checking the slide towards nobiliary fragmentation. But by the end of the century, all three kingdoms had relapsed once again into a common debility. Their decline was now irremediable. In Poland, the monarchy was to be auctioned by the *szlachta*, in Bohemia and Hungary it was annexed by the Hapsburgs. No local dynastic state ever re-emerged in this zone.[7]

Russia, on the other hand, entered into its own distinct crisis before the rest of the East, with the disintegration of the Kievan state and the Mongol conquest, and started to recover in advance of it as well. The worst phase of the 'moneyless' epoch, when economic activity shrank so much that autochthonous coinage disappeared completely, was over by the second half of the 14th century. A slow and spasmodic re-assemblage of the Central Russian lands, first under the leadership of Suzdal and then of Moscow, occurred even while the Mongol tributary yoke prevailed; although its initial success should not be exaggerated,

6. 'In this time no king shall reign nor any lord rule on earth, there shall be no serfdom, all interests and taxes shall cease, nor shall any man force another to do anything, because all shall be equal, brothers and sisters.' The Taborite Chiliast Articles of 1420, in Macek, *The Hussite Movement in Bohemia*, p. 133.

7. For this pattern, see R. R. Betts, 'Society in Central and Western Europe: Its Development towards the End of the Middle Ages', *Essays in Czech History*, London 1969, pp. 255–60: one of the most important comparative essays on Eastern and Western European agrarian evolution in this epoch.

since for another century the Mongols proved capable of inflicting condign punishment for undue Russian autonomy. Moscow was resoundingly sacked in 1382 in revenge for the Mongol defeat at Kulikovo two years earlier. Moreover, the Mongols made a practice of deporting artisans for their own benefit to their Asiatic encampment of Sarai-Batu by the Caspian Sea; it has been calculated that as a result of their raids, the number of Russian towns fell by half, and urban handicraft production was for a period virtually eliminated.[8] The ceaseless civil wars between the princely states during the gradual process of reunification (more than 90 are recorded between 1228 and 1462) also contributed their part to agrarian recession and abandonment of settlements: although perhaps more ambiguous than elsewhere in Eastern Europe, the phenomenon of *pustoshi* – empty lands – was still widespread in the 14th and 15th centuries.[9] Beyond the reach of German emigration, within the radius of Mongol tutelage, Russian development should not be mechanically aligned with that of the Baltic littoral or the Polish plains: it had its own rhythm and its own anomalies. Sarai was naturally more important for it than Magdeburg. But the broad analogy of its trajectory, amidst these differences, nevertheless seems indisputable.

The agrarian depression in the East had one further, and fatal, consequence. More recent and less robust, the trading towns of the Baltic, Poland and Russia were far less able to resist a sudden dearth and contraction of their hinterland than the larger and older urban centres of the West. The latter, indeed, represent the one notable sector of the Western economy which despite all its crises did ultimately forge ahead, past popular tumults and patrician bankruptcies,

8. Blum, *Lord and Peasant in Russia*, pp. 58–61.

9. Hilton and Smith, in their illuminating introduction to R. E. F. Smith (ed.), *The Enserfment of the Russian Peasantry*, Cambridge 1968, p. 14, cast doubts on Blum's interpretation of documentary references to the *pustoshi*, arguing that these could equally well indicate lands awaiting new clearance and settlement, not deserted holdings. They question to what extent there was a demographic or economic recession in Russia during the 13th and 14th centuries (pp. 15, 26). Russell, on the other hand, calculates a net decline in population of 25 per cent from 1340 to 1450, from 8 to 6 million, equivalent to the losses in Italy in the same period; and necessarily a graver setback, since Russian population growth had already been 'notably slow' in the preceding epoch. *Population in Europe 500–1500*, pp. 19, 21.

through the 14th and 15th centuries. Total urban population in Western Europe in fact probably grew up to 1450, for all the casualties of epidemics and famines. The Eastern cities, however, were far more exposed. The Hansa towns may have equalled the Italian ports by 1300 in their volume of their turnover. The value of their trade, however, composed largely of cloth imports and sylvan and natural-agricultural exports (timber, hemp, wax or furs), was much smaller;[10] nor did they control any rural *contado*, needless to say. Furthermore, they were now faced with intense maritime competition from Holland; Dutch ships started to navigate the Sound in the 14th century and by the end of the 15th century they were logging 70 per cent of the traffic that passed through it. It was precisely to meet this challenge that the German towns from Lübeck to Riga formally constituted themselves the Hanseatic League for the first time in 1367. Federation did not avail them, however. Squeezed between Dutch competition at sea and the agrarian depression on the land, the Hansa towns were eventually crippled. With their decline, went the mainspring of local commercial vitality beyond the Elbe.

It was fundamentally this weakness of the towns that allowed the nobles to adopt a solution to the crisis that was structurally barred to them in the West: a manorial reaction that slowly destroyed all peasant rights and systematically reduced tenants to serfs, working on large seigneurial demesnes. The economic rationale of this situation, diametric opposite of that which was finally adopted in the West, lay in the relationship between land and labour in the East. The demographic collapse, although in absolute terms probably less severe than in the West, put a relatively even greater strain on what was anyway an endemic shortage of labour. Given the vast underpopulated spaces of Eastern Europe, peasant flight was an acute danger to lords everywhere, while land remained potentially very abundant. At the same time, there were few opportunities of switching to less labour-intensive forms of agriculture, such as the wool-industry which had come to the aid of hard-pressed lords in England or Castile: arable farming and cereal cultivation remained the obvious avenues of production in the Eastern environment even before a large export trade got under way.

10. Henri Pirenne, *Economic and Social History of Mediaeval Europe*, London 1936, pp. 148–52.

The land/labour ratio thus in itself solicited the noble class towards forcible restrictions of peasant mobility and the constitution of large manorial estates.[11] But the economic profitability of such a path was not the same as its social possibility. The existence of urban municipal independence and power of attraction, even in a diminished form, was a manifest obstacle to the coercive imposition of a generalized serfdom on the peasantry: it has been seen that it was precisely the objective 'interposition' of cities in the overall class structure that blocked any final intensification of servile bonds as a response to the crisis in the West. The precondition of the ruthless regressive conversion of the countryside that ensued in the East was thus the annihilation of the autonomy and vitality of the towns. The noble class was well aware that it could not succeed in crushing the peasants until it had eliminated or subjugated the towns. It now proceeded to do so, implacably. The Livonian towns actively resisted the introduction of serfdom; the Brandenburger and Pomeranian towns, always more subject to baronial and princely pressures, did not. Both, however, were indifferently defeated in their struggle with seigneurial adversaries in the course of the 15th century. Prussia and Bohemia, where towns had traditionally been stronger, were – significantly enough – the only zones in the East which witnessed real peasant uprisings and violent social resistance to the noble class in this epoch. Yet by the end of the Thirteen Years' War, all Prussian towns except Königsberg were ruined or annexed by Poland: Königsberg did oppose the onset of serfdom thereafter, but was helpless to stem it. The ultimate defeat of the Hussites, in whose armies poor peasants and artisans had marched side by side, likewise sealed the fate of the autonomous towns in Bohemia: some fifty magnate families monopolized political power in the late 15th century, and from 1487 onwards launched a relentless attack on the enfeebled urban centres.[12]

In Russia, where the trading cities of Novgorod and Pskov had never possessed a municipal structure comparable to those of other

11. This fundamental proposition was classically advanced by Dobb, *Studies in the Development of Capitalism*, pp. 53–60, and has lately been developed by Hilton and Smith, *The Enserfment of the Russian Peasantry*, pp. 1–27.

12. F. Dvornik, *The Slavs in European History and Civilization*, New Brunswick 1962, p. 333.

European towns, since they were dominated throughout by land-owning boyars and provided no guarantees of personal freedom within their boundaries, the gathering concentration of noble power in the Suzdal and Muscovite states nevertheless dealt with them in similar spirit. The independence of Novgorod was broken by Ivan III in 1478; the cream of its boyars and merchants were deported, their estates confiscated and redistributed, and a royal governor or *namestnik* henceforward ruled the city directly for the tsar.[13] Vassily III shortly afterwards subdued Pskov. The new towns created in Central Russia were military and administrative centres under the control of the princes from the start. The most systematically anti-urban policies of all were pursued by the Polish gentry. In Poland, the noble class cut out local entrepots to deal directly with foreign merchants, fixed price-ceilings on urban-produced goods, appropriated manufacturing and processing rights for itself (brewing), banned townsmen from ownership of land and – of course – prevented any reception of fugitive peasants in the towns: all measures which struck at the very existence of a city economy. A slow and general desiccation of town life throughout Eastern Europe was the inevitable result of this process, repeated in country after country. The process was limited in Bohemia by the timely alliance of the German urban patriciate with the Czech feudal lords against the Hussites, and in Russia, where towns had never enjoyed the corporate liberties of the Hanseatic ports, and hence posed no comparable threat to seigneurial power: Prague and Moscow survived with the largest populations in the region. In the German-colonized lands of Brandenburg, Pomerania and the Baltic, on the other hand, deurbanization was so complete that as late as 1564, the largest single town in Brandenburg, Berlin, numbered a pitiful 1,300 houses.

It was this historic defeat of the towns that cleared the way for the imposition of serfdom in the East. The mechanisms of seigneurial reaction were long drawn out, and were codified in most areas some time after the substantive changes had been operated in practice. But the general pattern was everywhere the same. During the course of the 15th and 16th centuries, peasants in Poland, Prussia, Russia, Branden-

13. For this episode, see G. Vernadsky, *Russia at the Dawn of the Modern Age*, Yale 1955, pp. 54–63.

burg, Bohemia and Lithuania were gradually restricted in their mobility; punishments were inflicted for flights; debts were used to tie them to the soil; dues were screwed up.[14] For the first time in history, the East now witnessed the emergence of a true manorial economy. In Prussia, the Teutonic Order decreed the expulsion at harvest-time of all those without fixed abode from the towns in 1402; the return of runaway peasants to their lords in 1417; the regulation of wage-maximums for labourers in 1420. Then during the Thirteen Years' War, the Order alienated lands and jursidictions wholesale to the mercenaries whom it had hired to fight the Poles and the Union, with the result that a territory previously dominated by small-holders paying rent in kind to a military bureaucracy which had then appropriated and marketed it, now saw transfers of land on a massive scale to a new nobility and the consolidation of large demesnes and seigneurial jurisdictions. By 1494, the Prussian landowners had won the right to hang fugitives without trial. Eventually, the debilitated Order dissolved itself in the early 16th century, amidst the suppression of peasant rebellions and secularization of church estates, its remnant knights merging with the local aristocracy to form a single *junker* class, henceforward presiding over a peasantry deprived of its customary rights and irreversibly tied to the soil. In Russia, the attack on the rural poor was similarly linked to a reshuffling within the feudal class itself. The rise of the service-estate or *pomest'e* at the expense of the allodial patrimony or *votchina* under the auspices and in the interests of the Muscovite State produced a new stratum of ruthless gentry landowners

14. For a panorama of this whole process, see Blum's article 'The Rise of Serfdom in Eastern Europe', *American Historical Review*, July 1957 – a pioneering essay, whatever reservations its explanatory schema may inspire. In effect, Blum proposes four basic reasons for the ultimate enserfment of the East European peasantry: the increased political power of the nobility, the growth of seigneurial jurisdictions, the impact of the export market, and the decline of the towns. The first two of these merely redescribe the phenomenon of enserfment, they do not explain it. The third, as we shall see, is empirically implausible. The fourth is the only really valid cause listed, although it has itself, of course, to be explained. In general, Blum's article lacks either a sufficient temporal depth or comparative width to situate the phenomenon of Eastern serfdom fully. This can only be done once the differential historical formation of the two zones of Europe is properly established. However, its deficiencies in this respect do not detract from the signal merits of Blum's essay otherwise, which remains a milestone in discussion of the problem.

from the late 15th century onwards; here there was a temporary decrease in the average size of the feudal estates, combined with an intensification of exactions from the peasantry. Dues and services were steadily hoisted, while the *pomeshchiki* clamoured against peasant patterns of mobility. In 1497, Ivan III's administrative code formally abrogated the traditional right of the debt-free peasants to leave estates of their own volition, and restricted their departures to a week on either side of St George's Day. Under his successor Ivan IV in the next century, departures were increasingly forbidden altogether, at first under the pretext of provisional 'national emergencies' because of the catastrophes of the Livonian Wars; then, as time went on, they became normal and absolute.

In Bohemia, the redistribution of land after the Hussite upheavals, which led to the dispossession of a Church which had hitherto owned one third of the cultivated surface of the country, produced enormous noble latifundia and a simultaneous quest for stable and dependent labour to work them. The wars had led to great depopulation and shortage of manpower. Consequently, there was an immediate trend towards coercive restrictions of peasant movement. In 1437, three years after the defeat of Prokop at Lipan, the Land Court gave a ruling for the pursuit of fugitives; in 1453 the *Snem* reenacted the same principle; formal and legal adscription was then decreed by a Statute of 1497 and the Land Ordinance of 1500.[15] In the next century, labour services were intensified and the typical development of pond-fisheries and brewing on the Czech estates added further emoluments to seigneurial revenues,[16] but the survival of a respectable urban enclave in the economy seems to have limited the local degree of rural exploitation (labour services were lower here than elsewhere). In Brandenburg, the banning of seasonal migration by Poland in 1496 seriously aggravated the labour problem of the German landowners there, and helped to precipitate the expropriation of small peasant holdings and the forcible integration of the rural work-force into the domains which were to be

15. R. R. Betts, 'Social and Constitutional Development in Bohemia in the Hussite Period', *Past and Present*, No. 7, April 1955, pp. 49–51.

16. A. Klima and J. Macurek, 'La Question de la Transition du Féodalisme au Capitalisme en Europe Centrale (16e–18e Siècles)', *10th International Congress of Historical Sciences*, Uppsala 1960, p. 100.

the great characteristic of the next century.[17] In Poland, the manorial reaction went furthest of all. There, the gentry had extorted special jurisdictional and other rights for the monarchy in exchange for supplying the money-grants necessary to win the wars with the Teutonic Order. The reaction of the landowning class to the labour shortages of the epoch was the Statutes of Piotrkow, which for the first time formally tied peasants to the soil and forbade towns henceforward to receive them. It was in the 15th century that there was a rapid growth of feudal *folwarky* or demesnes, which developed with particular density along the riparian routes to the Baltic. There was thus a general juridical drive towards serfdom throughout Eastern Europe in this epoch. The adscriptive legislation of the 15th and 16th centuries did not, in fact, achieve the enserfment of the Eastern peasantries all at once. There was in every country a considerable gap between the legal codes banning rural mobility and the social realities of the countryside; this was equally true of Russia, Bohemia or Poland.[18] The instruments for enforcing glebe serfdom were often still defective, village flights continuing even after the most repressive measures were decreed against them – sometimes illicitly connived at by large magnates themselves, anxious to entice labour from smaller landowners. The political machinery for a rigorous and complete enserfment did not yet exist in Eastern Europe. But the decisive turn had been taken: the new laws anticipated the future economy of the East. Henceforward, the position of the peasantry was to sink inexorably downwards.

The steady degradation of the peasantry in the 16th century coincided with the spread of export agriculture, as Western markets came to be supplied increasingly with cereals from the manorial estates of the East. From 1450 or so onwards, with the economic recovery of the

17. Hans Rosenberg, 'The Rise of the Junkers in Brandenburg-Prussia 1410–1653', *American Historical Review*, Vol. XLIX, October 1943 and January 1944, p. 231.

18. Compare the very similar comments in R. H. Hellie, *Enserfment and Military Change in Muscovy*, Chicago 1971, p. 92; W. E. Wright, *Serf, Seigneur and Sovereign – Agrarian Reform in Eighteenth Century Bohemia*, Minneapolis 1966, pp. 8–10; Marian Malowist, 'Le Commerce de la Baltique et le Problème des Luttes Sociales en Pologne aux XVe et XVe Siècles', *La Pologne au Xe Congrès International des Sciences Historiques*, pp. 133–9.

West, grain exports for the first time overtook timber along the Vistula. The grain trade is often adduced as the most fundamental reason of all for the 'second serfdom' of Eastern Europe.[19] The actual evidence, however, does not seem to warrant such a conclusion. Russia, which exported no wheat until the 19th century, experienced a seigneurial reaction no less than Poland or Eastern Germany, which had a flourishing trade from the 16th century onwards. Moreover, within the exporting zone itself, the drive towards serfdom chronologically antedates the take-off of the grain trade, which occurred only after the pick-up of cereal prices and expanded Western consumption with the general boom of the 16th century. The *Gutsherrschaft* specialized in rye exports was, of course, itself not unknown in Pomerania or Poland already in the 13th century: but it was never a statistically dominant pattern, and did not become so in the next two centuries either. The real heyday of Eastern export agriculture, of the manorial estates sometimes abusively termed 'plantation business concerns', was the 16th century. Poland, the main producer country of the region, exported some 20,000 tons of rye a year at the start of the 16th century. A hundred years later, this had risen over eight times, to 170,000 tons in 1618.[20] The annual number of ships passing through the Sound increased from an average of 1,300 to 5,000 in the same period.[21] Corn prices in Danzig, the main port for the cereal traffic, were consistently 30–50 per cent above those in the inland centres of Prague, Vienna and Ljubljana, indicating the commercial pull of the export market; although the general level of Eastern grain prices was still only about half that in the West itself, by the later 16th century.[22] However, the role of the Baltic trade in the cereal economy of Eastern Europe should not be exaggerated. In fact, even in Poland – the main country in-

19. See, for example, M. Postan, in *Eastern and Western Europe in the Middle Ages*, pp. 170–4; Van Bath, *The Agrarian History of Western Europe*, pp. 156–7; K. Tymieniecki, 'Le Servage en Pologne et dans les Pays Limitrophes au Moyen Age', *La Pologne au Xe Congrès International des Sciences Historiques*, pp. 26–7.

20. H. Kamen, *The Iron Century. Social Change in Europe 1550–1660*, London 1971, p. 221.

21. J. H. Parry, 'Transport and Trade Routes', *Cambridge Economic History of Europe*, Vol. IV, *The Economy of Expanding Europe in the Sixteenth and Seventeenth Centuries*, Cambridge 1967, p. 170.

22. Aldo de Maddalena, *Rural Europe 1500–1750*, London 1970, pp. 42–3; Kamen, *The Iron Century*, pp. 212–13.

volved – grain exports accounted for only some 10–15 per cent of total output, at their peak; for much of the 16th century, the proportions were well below this.[23]

The impact of the export trade on social relations of production should not be underestimated, but it characteristically seems to have taken the form of an *increase in the rate* rather than an *innovation in the type* of feudal exploitation. It is thus significant that labour services – transparent index of the degree of surplus extraction from the peasantry – jumped very considerably from the 15th to the 16th centuries in both Brandenburg and Poland.[24] By the end of the 16th century, they were running at some three days a week in Mecklenburg, while in Poland no less than six days in every week were on occasion exacted from pauperized villeins, often deprived of any plots of their own altogether. For together with an intensification of the rate of exploitation, the advent of large-scale export farming inevitably also led to seizure of village lands and a general expansion of the arable surface. Demesne lands increased 50 per cent in the Middle Mark from 1575 to 1624.[25] In Poland, the ratio of demesne to peasant cultivation on the gentry estates climbed to levels virtually unknown in the mediaeval West: between 1500 and 1580, the average was something between 2:3 and 4:5, involving increasing reliance on hired labour.[26] The stratum of once prosperous peasants or *rolniki* were now everywhere eliminated.

At the same time, of course, the Baltic corn trade accelerated the anti-urban propensities of the local landowners. For the export flow freed them from dependence on local towns: they now acquired a market which assured them steady revenues in cash, and ready supplies

23. W. Kula, *Théorie Economique du Système Féodal*, pp. 65–7. See also Andrzej Wyczanski, 'Tentative Estimates of Polish Rye Trade in the Sixteenth Century', *Acta Poloniae Historica*, IV, 1961, pp. 126–7. The estimate used by Kula was originally calculated for Pre-Partition Poland in the 18th century, but Kula implies that it holds as an average for the whole period from the 16th to the 18th centuries. The index of commercialization of any given harvest was perhaps 35–40 per cent of the net product. The share of exports in the total *market* for grain was thus 25–40 per cent, which as Kula points out, was very considerable.

24. Blum, 'The Rise of Serfdom in Eastern Europe', p. 830.

25. Kamen, *The Iron Century*, p. 47.

26. A. Maczak, 'The Social Distribution of Landed Property in Poland from the 16th to the 18th Century', *Third International Conference of Economic History*, Paris 1968, p. 469; A. Wyczanski, 'En Pologne. L'Economie du Domaine Nobiliaire Moyen (1500–1580)', *Annales ESC*, January–February 1963, p. 84.

of manufactured goods, without the inconveniences of politically autonomous cities on their doorsteps. They now merely had to ensure that the existing towns were by-passed for direct deals between foreign merchants and local landowners. This in fact they proceeded to do. Dutch shipping soon dominated the whole rye traffic. The final result was an agrarian system which gave rise to units of production that in certain regions were much larger than the original feudal demesnes in the West, which had always tended to crumble away at the edges into rented plots: the windfall profits of the export trade in the century of the price revolution in the West could sustain the costs of domainial supervision and organization of production on a superior scale. The centre of the production complex shifted from the petty producer upwards to the feudal entrepreneur.[27] But the eventual perfection of this system should not be confused with the original structural response of the Eastern nobility to the agrarian depression of the 14th and 15th centuries, which was determined by the whole balance of class forces and the issue of a violent social struggle within the Eastern European social formations themselves.

The manorial agriculture which was consolidated in Eastern Europe during the early modern epoch was nevertheless in certain critical respects very distinct from that of Western Europe in the early mediaeval epoch. Above all, it proved economically much less dynamic and productive as an agrarian system – the fatal consequence of its greater social oppression of the rural masses. The main progress it registered over the three or four centuries of its existence was extensive. From the 16th century onwards, land clearances proceeded slowly and irregularly across most of the East – the equivalent of the reclamations of the mediaeval West. This process was greatly protracted by the problem, specific to the region, of the Pontic steppe-lands jutting into Eastern Europe, the notorious habitat of predatory Tartars and roaming Cossacks. The Polish penetration of Volhynia and Podolia in the

27. S. D. Skazkin, 'Osnovnye Problemi tak Nazyvaemovo 'Vtorovo Izdanii Krepostnichestva' v Srednei i Vostochnoi Evrope', *Voprosy Istorii*, February 1958, pp. 103–4 – a scrupulous and acute essay. Because of the numerical mass of small squires, the statistically average Polish estate was not very large – some 320 acres in the 16th century: but the scale of magnate properties, concentrated in a few aristocratic families, was enormous – sometimes hundreds of thousands of acres, and equivalent numbers of serfs.

16th and early 17th centuries was probably the most profitable single agrarian expansion of that epoch. The final Russian conquest of the vast wilderness further to the east, with the agricultural colonization of the Ukraine, was not achieved until the late 18th century.[28] The Austrian settlements of the same period put large areas of Transylvania and the Banat under the plough for the first time. Much of the Hungarian *puszta* was actually untouched by arable farming until the mid 19th century.[29] The sowing of South Russia eventually represented the largest quantitative reclamation in the history of the continent, and the Ukraine was to become a corn-basket of Europe in the age of the industrial revolution. The extensive spread of feudal agriculture in the East, although very gradual, was thus ultimately imposing. But it was never matched by any intensive gains in organization or productivity. The rural economy remained technologically backward, never generating any significant innovations of the type that marked the mediaeval West, and often revealing prolonged resistance even to the adoption of these early occidental advances. Thus crude *podseka* assartage remained predominant in Muscovy down to the 15th century; it was not until the 1460's that the three-field system was introduced.[30] Iron ploughs with mouldboards were long unknown in those regions of the East unaffected by German colonization; the simple ard or *soka* – a wooden scratch-plough – was a normal tool of the Russian peasant down to the 20th century. No new crops were developed, amidst a constant shortage of fodder, until the importation of maize into the Balkans in the epoch of the Enlightenment. The consequence was that the productivity of Eastern feudal agriculture was in general miserably low. Cereal yields were still in the region of 4:1 as late as the 19th century, or in other words at levels which had been reached in Western Europe in the 13th century, and surpassed by the 16th century.[31]

28. For the import of its eventual settlement, see the remarks in McNeill, *Europe's Steppe Frontier 1500–1800*, pp. 192–200.

29. Den Hollander, 'The Great Hungarian Plain', pp. 155–61.

30. A. N. Sakharov, 'O Dialektike Istoricheskovo Razvitiya Russkovo Krest'yantsva', *Voprosy Istorii*, 1970, No. 1, p. 21; Hellie, *Enserfment and Military Change in Muscovy*, p. 85.

31. See the analysis in B. H. Slicher Van Bath, 'The Yields of Different Crops (Mainly Cereals) in Relation to the Seed c. 810–1820', *Acta Historiae Neerlandica*, II, 1967, pp. 35–48 ff. Van Bath classifies wheat yields into four historical levels of

Such was the epochal retardation of Eastern Europe. The fundamental cause of this primitive performance, by inter-feudal standards, was to be found in the nature of Eastern serfdom. Rural relations of production never permitted the determinate margin of peasant autonomy and productivity that had existed in the West: the uniform concentration of economic, juridical and personal lordship that characterized Eastern European seigneurialism precluded it. The result was often a proportion of demesne to tenant acreage quite unlike anything in the West; the Polish *szlachta* systematically achieved ratios double or treble those of the mediaeval West, pushing the extension of their *folwarky* to the limits of rural exhaustion. Labour services were likewise forced up to levels unknown in Western Europe – in principle often 'unlimited' in Hungary, and in practice sometimes 5 or 6 days a week in Poland.[32] The most striking effect of this seigneurial super-exploitation was to reverse the whole productivity pattern of previous feudal agriculture. Whereas in the West, yields were always typically higher on the demesne than on peasant plots, in the East peasant plots frequently achieved higher rates of productivity than aristocratic demesnes. In 17th century Hungary, peasant yields were sometimes twice those of dominical reserves.[33] In Poland, demesnes that were more than doubled in size by engrossing squires might increase their actual income by little more than a third, so sharp was the drop in output once their serfs were pressed down in this fashion.[34] The limits of Eastern feudalism – which constricted and defined its whole historical development – were those of its social organization of labour: rural forces of production remained trapped within comparatively narrow confines by the type and degree of exploitation of the direct producer.

Engels, in a famous phrase, referred to the manorial reaction of

productivity: Stage A registers average yields of up to 3:1, Stage B from 3:1 to 6:1, Stage C from 6:1 to 9:1, and Stage D above 9:1. The transition from B to C occurred before 1500 in most of Western Europe; while most of Eastern Europe was still in Stage B in the 1820's.

32. Zs. Pach, *Die ungarische Agrarentwicklung im 16–17 Jahrhundert – Abbiegung von Westeuropäischen Entwicklungsgang*, Budapest 1964, pp. 56–8; R. F. Leslie, *The Polish Question*, London 1964, p. 4.

33. Kamen, *The Iron Century*, p. 223.

34. De Maddalena, *Rural Europe 1500–1750*, p. 41.

Eastern Europe in the late Middle Ages and early Modern epoch as a 'second serfdom'.[35] It is necessary to clarify the ambiguity of this formulation, in order finally to set the Eastern path of feudalism in its full historical context. If it is taken to mean that serfdom was a revenant in Eastern Europe, which arrived for a second time to haunt the poor, the term is simply incorrect. Serfdom proper had never previously existed in the East, as we have seen. On the other hand, if it is taken to mean that Europe knew two separate waves of serfdom, first one in the West (9th to 14th centuries) and then one in the East (15th to 18th centuries), it is a formula that fits the real historical development of the continent. With it, we can *reverse* the normal angle of vision from which the Eastern enserfment is viewed. Conventionally, it is presented by historians as an epochal regression, from the prior liberties that existed in the East before the manorial reaction. But the truth is that these liberties themselves were an *interruption* of a slow indigenous process of servile feudalization in the East. For what Bloch called the 'growth of ties of dependence' was well under way when the Western expansion across the Elbe and the Russian transmigration to the Oka and the Volga suddenly and temporarily arrested it. The manorial reaction in the East from the late 14th century onwards can thus be seen, in a longer perspective, as a *resumption* of an autochthonous journey towards an articulated feudalism that had been externally blocked and deviated for two or three centuries. This journey had started later, and was much slower and more halting than in the West: above all, as we have seen, because it had no original 'synthesis' behind it. But the unravelling line of its march appeared to point ultimately towards a social order not dissimilar to that which had once existed in the less urbanized and more backward regions of the mediaeval West. From the 12th century onwards, however, no purely endogenous evolution was ever again possible. The destiny of the East was altered by the intrusion of the West, initially and paradoxically towards a greater emancipation of the peasantry, and subsequently into the common ordeal of a long depression. Finally, the native return to

35. Marx-Engels, *Selected Correspondence*, p. 355. Engels alludes here to his essay on the Mark, in which he clearly inclines to the first interpretation of the phrase, by – wrongly – including the whole of Germany in the process so described. (*Werke*, XIX, pp. 317-30).

manorialization was itself determined and marked by the whole intervening history, so that it was henceforward irrevocably other than it would have been if it had developed in relative isolation. Nevertheless, the basic distance between East and West remained throughout. Eastern European history was from the outset immersed in an essentially distinct temporality, from Western European development. It had 'started' much later, and hence even after its intersection with that of the West, it could resume an earlier evolution towards an economic order that had been lived out and left behind elsewhere in the continent. The chronological coexistence of the opposite zones of Europe, and their increasing geographical interpenetration, creates the illusion of a simple contemporaneity of the two. In fact, the East had still to run through a whole historical cycle of servile development just when the West was escaping from it. This is in the end the deepest reason why the economic consequences of the general crisis of European feudalism were to be diametrically opposite in the two regions: commutation of dues and withering away of serfdom in the West, manorial reaction and implantation of serfdom in the East.

5

South of the Danube

A distinct sub-region remains to be discussed, whose historical evolution separated it from the rest of Eastern Europe. The Balkans might be said to represent a zone typologically analogous to Scandinavia, in its diagonal relationship to the great divide running across the continent. There is, indeed, a curious inverse symmetry between the respective destinies of North-West and South-East Europe. We have seen that Scandinavia was the one major region of Western Europe which was never integrated into the Roman Empire, and therefore never participated in the original 'synthesis' between the dissolving slave mode of production of Late Antiquity and the disrupted primitive-communal modes of production of the Germanic tribes that overran the Latin West. Nevertheless, for reasons examined above, the far North eventually entered the orbit of Western feudalism, while preserving the durable forms of its initial distance from the common 'occidental' matrix. A converse process can be traced in the far South of Eastern Europe. For if Scandinavia ultimately produced a Western variant of feudalism *without* benefit of the urban-imperial heritage of Antiquity, the Balkans failed to develop a stable Eastern variant of feudalism *despite* the long metropolitan presence of the sucessor state to Rome in the region. Byzantium maintained a centralized bureaucratic Empire in South-East Europe, with major cities, commodity exchange and slavery, for seven hun red years after the battle of Adrianople.

In that time repeated barbarian invasions, border conflicts and territorial shifts occurred in the Balkans. Yet the final fusion of two worlds, such as occurred in the West, never took place in this region of Europe. Far from accelerating the emergence of a developed feudalism, the Byzantine legacy actually appeared to brake it: the entire area of Eastern Europe south of the Danube, with its seemingly more advanced starting-point, fell economically, politically and culturally behind the vast, empty lands north of it, where there was virtually no prior experience of urban civilization or state formation at all. The whole centre of gravity of Eastern Europe came to rest on its northern plains; so much so that the long subsequent epoch of Ottoman rule over the Balkans was to lead many historians tacitly to exclude them from Europe altogether, or reduce them to an indeterminate margin of it. Yet the long social process that finally ended in the Turkish conquest is of great intrinsic interest for the 'laboratory of forms' that European history provides, precisely because of its anomalous outcome: secular stagnation and regression. Two questions are posed by the particularity of the Balkan zone. What was the nature of the Byzantine State that survived the classical Roman Empire for so long? Why did no durable feudal synthesis of the Western type ever occur in the clash between it and the Slav and Turanian barbarians who overran the peninsula from the late 6th century onwards, and thereafter settled there?

The fall of the Roman Empire in the West was fundamentally determined by the dynamic of the slave mode of production and its contradictions, once imperial expansion was halted. The essential reason why it was the Western Empire that crumbled away in the 5th century, rather than the Eastern, was that it was there that extensive slave agriculture had found its native habitat, with the Roman conquests of Italy, Spain and Gaul. For in these territories, there was no mature anterior civilization to resist or modify the new Latin institution of the slave latifundium. Thus it was always in the Western provinces that the remorseless logic of the slave mode of production achieved its fullest and most fatal expression, ultimately weakening and bringing down the whole imperial edifice. In the Eastern Mediterranean, on the other hand, Roman occupation was never superimposed on a comparable *tabula rasa*. On the contrary, there it encountered a coastal and maritime environment that had already been densely peopled with commercial cities by the great wave of Greek expansion in the Hellenistic epoch. It was this prior Greek colonization that had settled the basic social ecology of the East, much as the later Roman colonization settled that of the West. Two critical features of this Hellenistic pattern – as we have seen – were the comparative density of the towns and the relative modesty of rural property. Greek civilization had developed agrarian slavery, but not its extensive organization in a latifundium system; while its urban and commercial growth had been more spontaneous and polycentric than that of Rome.[1] Quite apart from this original divergence, trade was anyway inevitably much more intense along the frontiers of the Persian Empire and the Red Sea than on the confines of the Atlantic, after the Roman unification of the Mediterranean. The result was that the Roman institution of the large slave estate never took root in the Eastern provinces to the same general extent as in the Western: its introduction was always tempered by the persistent urban and rural pattern of the Hellenistic world, in which small peasant property had never been so savagely weakened as in post-Punic Italy, and municipal vitality had a longer and more indigenous tradition behind it. Egypt, the granary of the Eastern Mediterranean, had its colossal Apion slave-owners: but it nevertheless remained predominantly a region of small-holders. Thus when the time of crisis came for the whole slave mode of production and its imperial superstructure, its effects were far more mitigated in the East, just because slavery had always been more limited there. The inner solidity of the social formation of the Eastern provinces was consequently not so shaken by the structural decline of the dominant mode of production of the Empire. The development of a colonate from the 4th century onwards was less marked; the power of large landowners to undermine and demilitarize the imperial state was less formidable; the commercial prosperity of the towns was less eclipsed.[1] It was this internal configuration that gave the East the political compactness and resilience to resist the barbarian invasions that felled the West. Its strategic advantages, so often cited to explain its survival in the age of Attila and Alaric, were in fact very precarious. Byzantium was better fortified than Rome because of its sea-defences: but it was also within much closer range of barbarian attacks. The Huns and Visigoths started their incursions in Moesia, not in Gaul or Noricum, and the first shattering defeat of the imperial cavalry was in Thrace. The Goth Gainas achieved a position in the Eastern military command

1. See above, pp. 97–100.

as prominent and perilous as that of the Vandal Stilicho in the Western. It was not geography that determined the survival of the Byzantine Empire, but a social structure which proved capable of successfully expelling or assimilating external foes, unlike that of the West.

The decisive test for the Eastern Empire came at the turn of the 7th century, when it was nearly overwhelmed by three great assaults from different points of the compass, whose concatenation represented a far more formidable threat than anything the Western Empire had ever had to confront: the Slav-Avar invasions of the Balkans, the Persian drive right into Anatolia, and finally the definitive Arab conquest of Egypt and Syria. Byzantium withstood this treble ordeal by means of a social galvanization whose exact extent and nature is still a matter for dispute.[2] It is clear that the provincial aristocracy must have suffered greatly from the disastrous wars and occupations of this period, and that the existing pattern of medium and large property was probably disrupted and disorganized: this may even have been especially true of the usurper reign of Phocas, product of a mutineers' revolt in the ranks of the army.[3] It is equally evident that peasant adscription to the soil, implanted by the late Roman colonate system, progressively dwindled away in Byzantium, leaving behind a large mass of free village communities, composed of peasants with individual private plots and collective fiscal responsibilities to the State.[4] It is possible, although far from certain, that a further radical division of landed property was promoted by the imperial establishment under Heraclius of a military system of soldier-smallholders, who received farms for their maintenance from the State, in exchange for war service

2. The classical interpretation of this period is to be found in G. Ostrogorsky, *History of the Byzantine State*, Oxford 1968, pp. 92–107, 133–7; P. Charanis, 'On the Social Structure of the Later Roman Empire', *Byzantion*, XVII, 1944–5, pp. 39–57. Key aspects of it have been seriously challenged in recent years: see below, note 5.

3. For the impact of the invasions, see Ostrogorsky, *History of the Byzantine State*, p. 134. Soviet historians have singled out the episode of Phocas for emphasis: see, for example, M. Ya. Siuziumov, 'Nekotorye Problemy Istorii Vizantii', *Voprosy Istorii*, March 1959, No. 3, p. 101.

4. E. Stein, 'Paysannerie et Grands Domaines dans l'Empire Byzantin', *Recueils de la Société Jean Bodin, II, Le Servage*, Brussels 1959, pp. 129–33; Paul Lemerle, 'Esquisse pour une Histoire Agraire de Byzance: Les Sources et Les Problèmes' *Revue Historique*, 119, 1958, pp. 63–5.

in the Byzantine *themata*.[5] At all events, there was a substantial military recovery, which achieved first the defeat of the Persians and then – after the initial Islamic seizure of Egypt and Syria, whose loyalty to Byzantium had been sapped by religious heterodoxy – the arrest of the Arabs at the barrier of the Taurus. In the next century, the Isaurian dynasty built the first permanent imperial navy, capable of giving Byzantium maritime superiority against Arab fleets, and started the slow reconquest of the Southern Balkans. The social foundations of this political renewal manifestly lie in the broadening of the peasant

5. This is the major *vexata quaestio* of meso-byzantine studies. Stein's and Ostrogorsky's thesis – long an accepted orthodoxy – that Heraclius was responsible for an agrarian reform which created a soldier-peasantry by establishing the *thema* system, is now widely doubted. Lemerle has subjected it to a three-fold critique, arguing firstly that there is no real evidence that Heraclius created the *thema* system at all (which gradually emerged after his reign in the 7th century), secondly that the 'military lands' or *strateia* were an even later development for which there is no documentation before the 10th century, and thirdly that the holders of these lands were never soldiers themselves anyway, but merely had the fiscal duty of financially supporting a cavalryman in the army. The effect of this critique is to divest Heraclius's reign of structural importance in either the agrarian or military field, and to project a greater degree of continuity in Byzantine rural institutions than had hitherto been supposed. See P. Lemerle, 'Esquisse pour une Histoire Agraire de Byzance', *Revue Historique*, Vol. 119, 70–4, Vol. 120, pp. 43–70, and 'Quelques Remarques sur le Règne d'Heraclius', *Studi Medievali*, I, 1960, pp. 347–61. Similar views on the military problem are developed in A. Pertusi, 'La Formation des Thèmes Byzantins', *Berichte zum XI Internationalen Byzantinisten-Kongress*, Munich 1958, pp. 1–40, and W. Kaegi, 'Some Reconsiderations on the Themes (Seventh–Ninth Centuries)', *Jahrbuch der österreichischen byzantinischen Gesellschaft*, XVI, 1967, pp. 39–53. Ostrogorsky has riposted in his *Korreferat* to Pertusi's 1958 report, cited above (*Berichte*, pp. 1–8), and in 'L'Exarchat de Ravenne et l'Origine des Thèmes Byzantins', *VII Corso di Cultura sull'Arte Ravennate e Bizantina*, Ravenna 1960, pp. 99–110, which argues that the creation of the Western Exarchates of Ravenna and Carthage in the late 6th century presaged the establishment of the *thema* system shortly afterwards. Ostrogorsky has received some flanking support from the Soviet Byzantinist A. P. Kazhdan, who has rejected Lemerle's views in 'Eshchyo Raz ob Agrarnykh Otnosheniyakh v Vizantii IV–Xi vv', *Vizantiiskii Vremennik*, 1959, XVI, 1, pp. 92–113. The dispute over the origin of *thema* system turns largely on the meaning of a single phrase in Theophanes, a historian writing two hundred years after the epoch of Heraclius, and is consequently unlikely to be resolved as such. It should be said that Lemerle's own suggestion that increased peasant freedom in the meso-byzantine epoch was basically due to the Slav migrations, which solved labour shortages within the Empire and so rendered adscription redundant, is much less persuasive than his criticism of explanations tracing it to the *thema* system.

base of village autonomy within the Empire, whether it was directly facilitated by the *thema* system or not: the extreme concern of later Emperors to preserve small-holder communities for their fiscal and military value to the State leaves no doubt about this.[6] Byzantium thus survived through the Dark Ages of the West, with a shrunken territory but with virtually the whole superstructural panoply of classical Antiquity intact. There was no drastic cessation of urban life;[7] luxury manufactures were maintained; shipping if anything slightly improved; above all, centralized administration and uniform taxation by the imperial state subsisted – a remote pole of unity visible from afar in the night of the West. Coinage furnished the clearest index of this success: the Byzantine gold besant became the most universal standard of the time in the Mediterranean.[8]

Yet a crippling price was paid for this revival. The Byzantine Empire, in effect, unloaded enough of the burden of Antiquity to survive into a new epoch, but not enough to develop dynamically across it. It remained transfixed between slave and feudal modes of production, unable either to return to the one or advance to the other, in a social deadlock that could only eventually lead to its extinction. For, on the one hand, the path back to a generalized slave economy was closed: only an immense imperial programme of expansion could have created the captive labour force necessary to recreate one. In fact, the Byzantine State did perpetually attempt to reconquer its lost territories, both in Europe and Asia, and whenever its campaigns were successful, the stock of slaves within the Empire promptly increased as soldiers brought their booty home: most significantly with the

6. Ostrogorsky, *History of the Byzantine State*, pp. 272–4, 306–7.

7. The fate of the towns from the 7th to the 9th centuries is another focus of controversy. Kazhdan has maintained that there was an effective collapse of the cities in this epoch: 'Vizantiiskie Goroda v VII–IX vv', *Sovietskaya Arkheologiya*, Vol. 21, 1954, pp. 164–88; but this portrayal has been successfully modified by Ostrogorsky, 'Byzantine Cities in the Early Middle Ages', *Dumbarton Oaks Papers*, No. 13, 1959, pp. 47–66, and Siuziumov, 'Vizantiiskii Gorod (Seredina VII – Seredina IX v.)', *Vizantiiskii Vremennik*, 1958, XIV, pp. 38–70, who have shown that it is much overdrawn.

8. R. S. Lopez, 'The Dollar of the Middle Ages', *The Journal of Economic History*, XI, Summer 1951, No. 3, pp. 209–34. Lopez points out that Byzantine monetary stability, while it testified to balanced budgets and well-organized trade, did not necessarily mean much economic growth. The Byzantine economy in this epoch may well have been largely stationary.

Bulgarian conquests of Basil II in the early 11th century. There were also, moreover, the convenient markets of the Crimea, through which barbarian slaves were steadily exported southwards, to both the Byzantine and Arab Empires, and which probably provided the main supply for Constantinople.[9] But neither source could compare with the great swoops that had made the fortunes of Rome. Slavery by no means disappeared from Byzantium, but it never became predominant in its agriculture. Yet at the same time, the rural solution which had saved the East from the fate of the West – the consolidation of small landed property beneath the large estates – inevitably proved only a provisional one: the in-built pressure exerted by the provincial ruling classes towards a dependent colonate was pushed back in the 6th and 7th centuries, but by the 10th it had reasserted itself relentlessly once more. The decrees of the 'Macedonian' dynasty denounce again and again the implacable appropriation of peasant lands and subjection of the poor by the rural potentates of the time, the *dunatoi* or 'powerful ones'. The concentration of land in the hands of local oligarchies was fiercely resisted by the central imperial State, because it threatened to destroy its recruiting and tax-collecting reserves, by subtracting the agrarian population from the domain of public administration in the same way that the late Roman *patrocinium* and colonate had done: a para-seigneurial system in the countryside meant the end of a metropolitan military and fiscal apparatus capable of enforcing imperial authority throughout the realm. But the attempts of successive Emperors to check the tide of *dunatoi* power proved necessarily vain; for the local administration that was entrusted with the implementation of their decrees was itself overwhelmingly manned by the same families whose influence they were intended to limit.[10] Thus not only did economic polarization proceed in the countryside, but the military

9. A. Hadjinicolaou-Marava, *Recherches sur la Vie des Esclaves dans le Monde Byzantin*, Athens 1950, pp. 29, 89; R. Browning, 'Rabstvo v Vizantiiskoi Imperii (600–1200 gg)', *Vizantiiskii Vremennik*, 1958, XIV, pp. 51–2. Browning's article is the best synthesis on the topic.

10. The growth of the economic and political power of the *dunatoi* is a theme common to all modern Byzantine historians: one of the best discussions is still one of the earliest, C. Neumann, *Die Weltstellung des byzantinischen Reiches vor den Kreuzzügen*, Leipzig 1894, pp. 52–61 – a pioneering study in many respects.

network of the *themata* was itself increasingly captured by local magnates. Its very decentralization, initially the condition of its robust vitality, now assisted its confiscation by coteries of provincial potentates, once its original small-holder basis was undermined. The stabilization of late ancient forms achieved in the Byzantine renewal of the 7th and 8th centuries was thus increasingly compromised by tendencies towards a proto-feudal disintegration in rural economy and society.

On the other hand, if any durable reversion to the type of social formation characteristic of Antiquity was impossible, progression towards a developed feudalism was equally thwarted. For the supreme bureaucratic apparatus of the Byzantine autocracy remained essentially intact for five hundred years after Justinian: the centralized State machine in Constantinople never relinquished its overall administrative, fiscal and military sovereignty over the imperial territory. The principle of universal taxation never lapsed, although after the 11th century there were more and more frequent departures from it in practice. The economic functions of the late Ancient State thus never disappeared. Significantly enough, indeed, hereditary slavery remained dominant in the state manufacturing sector, as it had in the Roman Empire, and this sector in turn enjoyed monopoly privileges which made it pivotal both for the Byzantine export trade and procurements industry.[11] The peculiarly intimate connexion between the slave mode of production and the imperial state superstructure which had marked Antiquity was thus retained right down to the closing centuries of Byzantium. Moreover, slave-labour in the private sector of the economy was by no means negligible either; not only did it continue to provide the bulk of domestic service for the wealthy, but it was also used on large estates down to the 12th century. If the statistical extent of agricultural slavery in the Byzantine Empire is impossible to determine today, it is nevertheless possible to surmise that its structural impact on rural relations was not a negligible one: for both the relatively low level of labour dues paid by the dependent tenant *paroikoi* throughout later Byzantine history, and the relatively large scale of demesne cultivation, may well have been a function of the availability of slave labour to the rural magnate class, even where its actual incidence was

11. Browning, 'Rabstvo', pp. 45–6.

isolated.[12] Thus a prepotent imperial bureaucracy and residual slave economy constantly acted to block the spontaneous tendencies of class polarization in the countryside towards a feudal exploitation of the land and seigneurial separatism. Moreover, for the same reasons, the cities too never had an opportunity to develop towards a mediaeval communalism. The municipal autonomy of the towns which had once been the cellular basis of the early Roman Empire was already in far-reaching decline by the time the Western Empire fell, although it still retained some reality in the East. The establishment of the Byzantine *thema* system, however, led to a political demotion of the cities locally, while their civic life was anyway progressively stifled by the weight of the capital and the court. All vestiges of municipal autonomy were formally abolished by a decree of Leo VI which merely consummated a long historical process.[13] Against this background, Byzantine cities – having once lost ancient forms of privilege – were never able to regain feudal forms of liberty, within the imperial system. No municipal freedoms emerged inside the constricting framework of the autocratic State.

Given the absence of any radical parcellization of sovereignty, an urban dynamic of the Western type was structurally impossible. The unfolding of a feudal path of development was barred in Byzantium both in the country and city, by the countervailing force of its late-classical institutional complex and commensurate infrastructure. A revealing symptom of this deadlock was the juridical nature of the very aristocracy and monarchy of the Byzantine Empire. For to the bitter end, the imperial purple never became the hereditary property of an anointed dynasty, no matter how strong popular legitimism eventually became; it always technically remained what it had begun by being in the far-off days of the Augustan Principate – an elective office over which the Senate, Army and people of Constantinople exercised formal or factual rights of investment. The semi-divine summit of the imperial bureaucracy was the site of an impersonal function, cognate with that

12. Browning, 'Rabstvo', p. 47.

13. Ostrogorsky, 'Byzantine Cities in the Early Middle Ages', *Dumbarton Oaks Papers*, No. 13, 1959, pp. 65–6. The same legal recodification abrogated ancient rights of the Senate and curial class, systematizing the administrative centralization of the Byzantine imperial bureaucracy: Ostrogorsky, *History of the Byzantine State*, p. 245. Leo VI ruled from 886 to 912.

of the uniform officialdom beneath it, and by the same token separate from that of personal kingship in the feudal West. The nobility which ruled through this administrative State was no less distinct from the seigneurial lords of the West. No hereditary system of titles ever crystallized in Byzantium: honours were basically conferred for official duties in the Empire, as they had been in the late Roman epoch, and did not pass to a second generation. In fact, even an aristocratic family name system was slow to develop (in pointed contrast to the more genuinely seigneurial society of Armenia and Georgia in the adjacent Caucasus, with its full-blown ranking system).[14] The entrenched *dunatoi* dynasties of Anatolia, which increasingly came to disrupt the fabric of the metropolitan State, were a comparatively late development: most of the famous families – Phocas, Sclerus, Comnenus, Diogenes and others – did not rise to prominence before the 9th and 10th centuries.[15] Moreover, Byzantine landowners – like Roman latifundists before them – always characteristically resided in towns,[16] in a pattern sharply contrasting with the rural domiciles of the Western feudal nobility, with its much more direct original role in agrarian production. The ruling class of Byzantium thus itself remained half-way between the clarissimate of Late Antiquity and the baronage of the early Middle Ages. In its own body was inscribed the frustrated tension of the State.

It was this deep inner impasse within its whole economy and polity which accounts for the strangely barren and immobile character of the Byzantine Empire, as if the very feat of its longevity drained it of vitality. The deadlock of rural modes of production led to a stagnant agrarian technology, which registered virtually no significant advances over a millennium, apart from the introduction of a few specialized crops in the Heraclian age. The primitive and constricting harnesses of

14. See the perceptive comments of C. Toumanoff, 'The Background to Manzikert', *Proceedings of the XIIIth International Congress of Byzantine Studies*, London 1967, pp. 418–19. The clarissimate was, of course, technically hereditary in the later Roman Empire, but simultaneously lost much of its significance to new bureaucratic titles, which were not transmissible: Jones, *The Later Roman Empire*, Vol. II, pp. 528–9.

15. S. Vryonis, 'Byzantium: the Social Basis of Decline in the Eleventh Century', *Greek, Roman and Byzantine Studies*, Vol. 2, 1959, No. 1, p. 161.

16. G. Ostrogorsky, 'Observations on the Aristocracy in Byzantium', *Dumbarton Oaks Papers*, No. 25, 1971, p. 29.

Antiquity were preserved down to the end of Byzantine history: the mediaeval shoulder-collar was never adopted. The heavy plough was equally ignored, for the use of the ineffective traditional ard. At most, the water-mill – belated gift of the Roman Empire itself – was accepted.[17] The great cluster of innovations which transformed Western agriculture in the same period were never acclimatized in its arid, thin-soil Mediterranean environment: and no native improvements occurred in their stead. One major manufacturing breakthrough was achieved in the reign of Justinian: the introduction of a silk industry in Constantinople, where state plants henceforward enjoyed a monopoly role in the European export market until the ascent of the Italian mercantile towns.[18] Even this was a technical secret purloined from the Orient rather than an indigenous discovery; and apart from it, little of note was ever developed in the workshops of Byzantium. Similarly, the great cultural florescence of the 6th century was succeeded by an increasingly narrow and rigid hieratism, the relative monotony of whose forms of thought and art presents a mournful contrast with those of late Antiquity. (It is no coincidence that the first real intellectual and artistic reawakening should have occurred when the Empire finally slid into irreversible crisis, because only then was its social logjam broken.) The underlying truth of Gibbon's famous judgment of Byzantium, here as elsewhere, is only confirmed by posterior explanations that were inaccessible to him.[19]

17. For the harness, see Lefebvre des Noettes, *L'Attelage et Le Cheval de Selle à Travers Les Ages*, Paris 1931, pp. 89–91; for the plough, A. G. Haudricourt, M. J-B. Delammare, *L'Homme et la Charrue a Travers le Monde*, Paris 1955, pp. 276–84: for the water-mill, J. L. Teall, 'The Byzantine Agricultural Tradition', *Dumbarton Oaks Papers*, No. 25, 1971, pp. 51–2. Teall's paper evinces what appears to be an unwarranted optimism about Byzantine agriculture, which its own evidence is too limited to support.

18. R. S. Lopez, 'The Silk Trade in the Byzantine Empire', *Speculum*, XX, No. 1, January 1945, pp. 1–42, stresses the international importance of the Byzantine monopoly of precious cloths.

19. *The Decline and Fall of the Roman Empire*, Chapter XLVIII. Naturally, Gibbon's language is greatly exaggerated ('A tedious and uniform tale of weakness and misery'), to the displeasure of subsequent historians, among whom no passages of his work are more unfashionable. But Gibbon's treatment of Byzantium was in fact governed by the whole architecture of his *History*: whereas the fall of Rome was 'a revolution that will ever be remembered by the nations of the Earth', the fate of Byzantium was merely '*passively* connected' with 'revolutions which

In one single domain, however, Byzantine history is restless and accidented throughout: its combat record. Military conquest – or rather, reconquest – remained a leitmotif of its existence, from the epoch of Justinian to that of the Paleologues. Universal territorial claims, as the successor of the *Imperium Romanum*, were the permanent principle of its foreign policy.[20] In this respect, the conduct of the Byzantine State was centrally and unceasingly governed by its matrix in Antiquity. From its very birth as a separate imperial entity, it tried to recover the lost lands which had once owed obedience to Rome. But literal realization of this ambition had been emptied of any meaning by the whole intervening passage of time, since Byzantium could never now hope to repeat the triumphant tour of conquest and enslavement that had taken Roman legions from one end of the Mediterranean to the other: the slave mode of production had long since been surpassed in the West, and become recessive in the East. There was thus no social or economic charge to its military expansion; it could kindle no historically new order into existence. The result was that the successive waves of Byzantine expansionism each time broke back on the imperial base from which they had started, and ended by washing over and weakening it. An uncanny fatality visited virtually every one of the great reigns of reconquest. Thus Justinian's grandiose recovery of Italy, North Africa and Southern Spain in the 6th century was not only wiped out by the Lombard and Arab invasions: within the next generation, the Balkans, Syria and Egypt had fallen. Likewise, the impressive advances of the 'Macedonian' Emperors in the late 10th and early 11th centuries were followed, equally suddenly and disastrously, by the collapse of Byzantine power in Anatolia before the Seljuks. In the 12th century, the renewed expansion of Manuel Comnenus, who

---

have changed the state of the world' (his italics: I, p. 1; V, p. 171). The implicit conceptual distinctions indicated here are perfectly rational and modern.

20. This theme of Byzantine history has been most forcibly emphasized by H. Ahrweiler, *Byzance et la Mer*, Paris 1966: see especially pp. 389–95. Ahrweiler's own insistence that it was basically the naval ambitions of the Byzantine Empire which were most responsible for its eventual collapse, by overstretching its resources and distracting it from consolidation of its land power, is much more doubtful. It was rather the total military effort involved in successive reconquests, in which armies always bulked far larger than fleets, that was critical for the ultimate fall of the State.

led his troops into Palestine, Dalmatia and Apulia, once again capsized into catastrophe, as the Turks cantered towards the Aegean and the Franks sacked Constantinople. Even in the final epilogue of its existence, the same pattern is visible: the Paleologue repossession of Byzantium itself in the 13th century led to the abandonment of Nicaea and ultimate shrinkage of the Empire into a petty area of Thrace, tributary to the Ottomans for a century before their entry into Constantinople. Each phase of expansion was thus succeeded by a more drastic contraction, the unfailing penalty for it. It is this jagged rhythm which makes the course of Byzantine history so different from that of Rome, with its comparatively smooth curve of ascent, stabilization and decline.

It is clear, of course, that within the sequence enumerated above there was one, truly decisive crisis which settled the fate of the Empire irrevocably: the period from the Bulgarian campaigns of Basil II to the Seljuk victory of Manzikert, in the 11th century. This has been widely seen as a phase in which, after the brilliant military successes of the last Macedonian Emperor, the 'civilian' bureaucracy of Constantinople systematically dismantled the provincial armies of the Empire, in order to check the ascent of the rural magnates who had come to control their command, and thereby threaten the integrity of the central imperial administration itself.[21] The rise of these provincial oligarchs was, in turn, a reflection of the dispossession of the small peasantry which was now gaining an increasingly irresistible momentum. A savage outbreak of court conflicts and civil wars ensued, which critically weakened Byzantine defences that had already been gravely damaged by the demilitarizing policies of the bureaucratic cliques in the capital. The *coup de grâce* was then delivered by the arrival of the Turks in the East. This general line of explanation is certainly correct as far as it goes, but its presentation often implies a deceptive contrast between the triumphs of Basil II's reign and the setbacks which succeeded it, and so fails to provide a persuasive account of the reasons why the political groups which dominated the Constantinople court after 1025 acted in the apparently suicidal fashion that they did. In fact,

21. See, *inter alia*, Ostrogorsky, *History of the Byzantine State*, pp. 320–1, 329–33, 341–5 ff., Vryonis, 'Byzantium: the Social Basis of Decline in the Eleventh Century', pp. 159–75.

it was the long strain of the Bulgarian wars of Basil II, with their great expense and huge casualties, that probably prepared the way for the precipitate collapse of the next fifty years. Byzantine armies had traditionally been held at what were overall relatively modest troop strengths. Ever since the 6th century, the average size of an expeditionary corps was only about 16,000; the total military apparatus of the State in the 9th century was perhaps some 120,000 – a figure well below that of the later Roman Empire, which probably helps to explain the greater internal stability of the Byzantine State.[22] But from the reign of John Zimisces in the mid 10th century, the size of the imperial armies increased steeply, to an unprecedented peak during Basil's rule.

This burden had to be scaled down after his death; there were already menacing signs of inflation and incipient devaluation, after centuries of price stability within the Empire. The coinage depreciated rapidly from the reign of Michael IV (1034–41) onwards. The domestic policies of the 'Macedonian' Emperors had been to curb the economic greed and political ambitions of the provincial *dunatoi*: the 'civilian' rulers of the mid 11th century continued this tradition, but gave it a perilously novel edge.[23] For they sought to whittle down the local *themata* that had gradually become the military arm of magnate power, above all in Anatolia. By doing so, they aimed both to relieve the exchequer and to control the outlying nobles whose ambition and insubordination were always a political threat to civil peace anyway. The introduction of the heavily-armoured cataphract in the late 10th century had increased the financial burden of *themata* units on the provinces, and rendered the old local defense systems more difficult to maintain. The new bureaucratic regimes in Constantinople, which succeeded the war-like 'Macedonian' dynasty, thus switched to a much

22. J. Teall, 'The Grain Supply of the Byzantine Empire, 330–1025', *Dumbarton Oaks Papers*, No. 13, 1959, pp. 109–17. The change was probably connected in part with the development from Roman legionary infantry to Byzantine heavy cavalry.

23. N. Svoronos, 'Société et Organisation Intérieure dans l'Empire Byzantin au XIe Siècle: Les Principaux Problèmes', *Proceedings of the XIIth International Congress of Byzantine Studies*, pp. 380–2, hazards that the new civilian Emperors also tried to elevate the role of the commercial 'middle classes' in the towns, by democratizing access to the Senate, in order to create a counter-weight to the rural magnates – a doubtful hypothesis, resting on inappropriate categories.

greater reliance on the crack *tagmata* regiments which were stationed near the capital, and had a higher professional and foreign component. The *tagmata* cavalry units had always provided the firmest military nucleus of the imperial armies, with the best discipline and training. Disbanded *themata* soldiers were now probably to some extent brigaded with these professional regiments, which were increasingly dispatched for provincial or frontier duties; at the same time the proportion of foreign mercenaries in them steadily grew. The total size of the Byzantine military establishment was much reduced by these 'civilianist' policies, which sacrificed strategic strength to the economic and political interests of the court bureaucracy and metropolitan dignitaries. The result was to cleave the whole unity of the Byzantine state in a conflict between civilian and military branches of the imperial order, strikingly similar to the fatal split which had preceded the fall of the Roman Empire.[24] For *dunatoi* resistance to the new course was fierce, and by now the balance of power in the countryside had shifted too far for such a solution to be successfully imposed. Its only effect was to provoke a grinding series of civil wars in Anatolia between 'military' and 'bureaucratic' factions of the ruling class, which demoralized and disorganized the whole Byzantine defence system. Religious and ethnic persecution of the Armenian communities who had recently been reincorporated into the Empire created further disarray and ferment along the vulnerable eastern frontier. The stage was thus set for the debacle of Manzikert.

In 1071, the Seljuk Sultan Alp Arslan, making his way south from

24. The most obvious and important difference between the two conflicts was that the late Byzantine military elite was primarily a provincial landowning class from Anatolia, while the late Roman army command was mostly composed of professional officers, first Balkan and then increasingly barbarian (see above, pp. 85–90, 100–2). The change was probably to a large extent due to the introduction of heavy cataphract cavalry, after the implantation of the *thema* system, which created local military potentates in the Byzantine Empire. The lines of division were consequently divergent in the two cases: in Rome, the apparatus of the high command was centred on the cities, the power of civilian landlords in the countryside, while in Byzantium military magnates dominated the provinces, and civilian bureaucrats the capital. Hence the outbreak of actual civil war between the two sides in the Greek Empire, and the much greater consciousness of the nature of their antagonism among contemporaries (compare Psellos with Ammianus). The structural resemblances between the processes in Rome and Byzantium were otherwise revealingly close.

the Caucasus towards Egypt, brushed into the armies of Romanus Diogenes IV, and annihilated them, capturing the Emperor himself. On the battle-field, Armenian auxiliaries, Frankish and Petcheneg mercenaries, and Byzantine regiments commanded by a 'civilianist' rival, had all deserted or betrayed the imperial standards. Anatolia was left an undefended vacuum, into which Turcoman nomads steadily drifted over the next decades, without any serious effort to oppose them.[25] Byzantine rule in Asia Minor was broken, neither by the eruption of a mass *Völkerwanderung* of the Gothic or Vandal type, nor by an organized military occupation of the Persian or Arab type, but by the gradual migration of clusters of nomads into the highlands. The fragmentary and anarchic character of successive Turkic incursions, however, was no token of their ephemerality. On the contrary, the growing nomadization which resulted from it proved far more durably destructive of Greek civilization in Anatolia than the centralized military conquest of the Balkans by later Ottoman armies. Chaotic Turcoman raiding and savage pillaging slowly de-urbanized region after region, dislocating settled agrarian populations and destroying Christian cultural institutions.[26] The nomadic disruption of the rural economy eventually tailed away with the rise of the Seljuk Sultanate of Konya in the 13th century, which restored peace and order to most of Turkish Anatolia; but the respite was to be only temporary.

Meanwhile, the very informality of the Turcoman settlements in the interior allowed the Byzantine State of the later 11th century to survive and counter-attack from the coasts of Asia Minor: but never to regain the central plateaux. Under the Comneni, the provincial military oligarchies that had been accumulating power on their estates and at the head of their local levies, finally gained control of the imperial state. The major magnate groups were not elevated to court office by

25. Claude Cahen, 'La Première Pénétration Turque en Asie Mineure (Seconde Moitié du XIe Siècle)', *Byzantion*, 1948, pp. 5–67.

26. There is now a comprehensive documentation and discussion of this process in S. Vryonis, *The Decline of Mediaeval Hellenism in Asia Minor and the Process of Islamization from the Eleventh through the Fifteenth Century*, Berkeley-Los Angeles 1971, pp. 145–68, 184–94 – a major study. Vryonis perhaps tends to overstate the responsibility of the civilian-military conflicts within the Byzantine ruling class for the Greek collapse at Manzikert and after ('The single most fateful development', pp. 76–7, 403), but his account of the social mechanisms of the subsequent Turkification of Anatolia is authoritative.

Alexius I, who reserved these for his own ramified family connections, to ensure against powerful *dunatoi* rivals: but the medium and lower gentry now came into its own. The barriers to feudalization were now progressively swept aside. Administrative benefices or *pronoiai* were granted to gentry landowners, which gave them fiscal, judicial or military powers over fixed territories in exchange for specific services to the State: multiplied by the Comneni, they eventually became hereditary under the Paleologues.[27] Nobles gained 'immunities' or *ekskousseiai* from the jurisdiction of the central bureaucracy, and received donations of monastic or church lands for their personal use (*charistika*). None of these institutional forms acquired the logic or order of the Western feudal system; they were at best partial and broken versions of it. But their social trend was clear. Free peasants were now increasingly degraded into dependent tenants or *paroikoi*, whose condition gradually came to approximate to that of serfs in Western Europe.

The urban economy of the capital, with its state manufactures and luxury export wares, was meanwhile sacrificed to diplomatic bargains with Venice and Genoa, whose merchants soon enjoyed absolute commercial supremacy within the Empire because of the privileges lavished on them by the Chrysobull of 1084, which exempted them from the imperial sales tax. Reversing its traditional trade balance, Byzantium in its economic decline now lost its monopoly of silks and became a net importer of Western cloths and other finished manufactures, and in exchange exported primary commodities such as wheat and oil to Italy.[28] Its administrative system decayed to the point where regional governors often resided in the capital and merely forayed to their provinces to collect taxes, in thinly-disguised looting expeditions.[29] Mercenaries and adventurers filled the ranks of its armies; crusaders

27. G. Ostrogorsky, *Pour l'Histoire de la Féodalité Byzantine*, Brussels, 1954, pp. 9–257, is the classic study of the institution of the *pronoia*. Ostrogorsky maintains that: 'The *pronoia* in Byzantium and the South Slav lands, like the fief in the West and the *pomest'e* in Russia, is the manifestation of a developed feudality' (p. 257) – a debatable contention that is discussed below.

28. M. Ya. Siuziumov, 'Borba za Puti Razvitiya Feodal'nykh Otnoshenii v Vizantii', *Vizantiiskie Ocherki*, Moscow 1961, pp. 52–7.

29. J. Herrin, 'The Collapse of the Byzantine Empire in the Twelfth Century: A Study of a Mediaeval Economy', *University of Birmingham Historical Journal*, XII, No. 2, 1970, pp. 196–9, a vivid cameo of the time.

surveyed it with confident avarice. The seizure and sack of Constantinople by a Veneto-Frankish expedition in 1204 finally smashed the unity of the remaining imperial state from the outside. A complete Western feudal system of fiefs and vassalages was now imported, above all into Central and Southern Greece, where French lords introduced a pattern similar to that of Outremer. But this artificial implantation did not last long. The Greek successor regime in Nicaea, left on the periphery of the former Empire, was able painfully to reassemble the broken remnants of Byzantine territory and reconstitute a shadow imperial State once again in Constantinople.

The *pronoiar* landowning class had now become hereditary holders of their benefices; the mass of the peasantry were *paroikoi*; vassal relationships were assimilated into the political conceptions of local state-craft, and appanages granted by the ruling Paleologue family; foreign merchant communities possessed autonomous enclaves and franchises. In the countryside, monastic estates multiplied, while secular landowners frequently resorted to extensive pastoralism, to be able to shift their property during Turcoman raids.[30] But this final apparent 'feudalization' of the Byzantine social formation never achieved an organic or spontaneous coherence.[31] Its institutions were a simulacrum of Western forms entirely lacking the historical dynamic that had produced the latter: a signal warning against any attempt to read off modes of production by atemporal comparison of their elements. For late Byzantine feudal forms were the end-result of a

30. Ernst Werner, *Die Geburt einer Grossmacht – Die Osmanen (1300–1481)*, Berlin 1966, pp. 123–4, 145–6.

31. The problem of whether a true Byzantine feudalism ever emerged, in the twilight of the Greek Empire, has been a traditional dividing-line among Byzantinists. Ostrogorsky has lent the weight of his authority to the view that late Byzantine society was essentially feudal: most recently, see 'Observations on the Aristocracy in Byzantium', pp. 9 ff. Soviet historians have likewise always asserted the existence of a Byzantine feudalism (often tending to date its appearance somewhat earlier). A recent Bulgarian restatement of this position can be found in Dimitar Angelov, 'Byzance et L'Europe Occidentale', *Etudes Historiques*, Sofia 1965, pp. 47–61. Lemerle, on the other hand, has categorically denied that feudalism ever became implanted in Byzantium, and most Western scholars have agreed with him. Boutruche's comparative study, conceptually more refined, also rejects the notion that the *pronoia-ekskousseia-paroikoi* complex ever constituted an authentic feudal system: *Seigneurie et Féodalité*, Vol. I, pp. 269–79.

secular *decomposition* of a unitary imperial polity that had lasted largely unaltered for seven centuries: in other words, they were the product of a process that was the diametric opposite of that which gave birth to Western feudalism – a dynamic *recomposition* of two dissolved anterior modes of production, in a new synthesis which was to unleash productive forces on an unprecedented scale. No increase in demographic density, agrarian productivity or urban trade was registered in the dusk of Byzantine rule. At best, the disintegration of the old metropolitan state system released a certain intellectual effervescence and social turmoil in the shrinking perimeter of its sway in Greece. The economic capture of the capital by Italian merchants led to a devolution of native commerce to a few of the better-protected provincial cities; increased cultural traffic with the West diluted the grip of Orthodox obscurantism.

The last significant episode of Byzantine history – ultimate, dying flare-up of vitality – paradoxically combined the manifestation of new ferments generated by the incipient feudalism of the Greek East, with the influence of processes derived from the crisis of descendant feudalism in the Latin West. In Thessalonika, second city of the Empire, a municipal revolt against the imperial usurpation of the magnate Cantacuzene mobilized anti-mystical and anti-oligarchic passions among the urban masses, confiscated and distributed the property of the monasteries and rich, and for seven years held at bay the attacks of the bulk of the landowning class, backed by the Ottomans.[32] The inspiration of this ferocious social struggle, unexampled in nine hundred years of Byzantine history, was perhaps provided by the Genoese communal revolution of 1339, one of the great chain of urban upheavals during the late mediaeval crisis in Western Europe.[33] The

32. P. Charanis, 'Internal Strife in Byzantium during the Fourteenth Century', *Byzantion*, XV, 1940–1, pp. 208–30, analyses the character and course of the revolt.

33. Siuziumov claims that the model for the revolt of Thessalonika was, on the contrary, Cola di Rienzo's 'national' revivalism in Rome, not the merely 'municipal' revolt in Genoa, and that it only became a communal affair at the end, in its closing phase. For him, the insurrection was essentially the work of an urban entrepreneurial class, whose aim was the restoration of a central imperial State, capable of defence against Turkish and Western threats. Such an interpretation of the Thessalonika Zealots seems unduly forced, in an otherwise stimulating essay: 'Borba za Puti Razvitiya Feodal'nykh Otnoshenii v Vizantii', pp. 60–3.

suppression of the Zealot 'republic' in Thessalonika was, of course, inevitable: the dwindling Byzantine social formation was incapable of sustaining any such advanced urban form, which presupposed an altogether different economic and social tonus. With its defeat, independent Byzantine history effectively petered out. From the late 14th century onwards, renewed Turcoman nomadism devastated Western Anatolia and overran the last footholds of Hellenism in Ionia, while Ottoman armies moved north from Gallipoli. Constantinople spent the last century of its existence a forlorn tributary of Turkish power in the Balkans.

The question can now be posed: why, throughout this long history, did no dynamic fusion ever occur in the Balkans between barbarian and imperial social orders, such as might have produced an ascendant feudalism of the Western type? Why was there no Helleno-Slav synthesis comparable in scope and effects to the Romano-Germanic synthesis? For it must now be recalled that tribal invasions over-ran the vast bulk of the lands stretching from the Danube to the Adriatic and Aegean, in the late 6th and early 7th centuries; and that thereafter Slav and Byzantine borders shifted back and forth across the Balkan Peninsula, for over 700 years of constant contact and conflict. The fate of the three major regions within it was variant, of course, and can be briefly summarized as follows. The tidal Avar-Slav wave of 580–600 swept over the whole Peninsula, submerging Illyricum, Moesia and Greece, down to the southernmost Peloponnese. The loss of Illyricum to Slav migration and settlement cut the historic overland linkage of the Roman imperial world; no single event was to be so decisive for the rupture of unity between Eastern and Western Europe in the Dark Ages. To the south, it was two centuries before Byzantium was capable of starting the systematic reconquest of Thrace and Macedonia in the 780's: an additional twenty years before the Peloponnese was finally subdued. Thereafter, most of Greece proper was ruled without interruption from Constantinople until the Latin conquest of 1204. Slav-settled Moesia, on the other hand, was invaded by the Bulgars, Turanian nomads from Central Russia, who established a khanate there in the late 7th century. By the end of the 9th century, the Bulgar ruling class had become Slavicized, and presided over a powerful Empire whose control extended well into Western Macedonia. After a series of epic military struggles with Byzantium, the Bulgar State was overwhelmed by John Zimisces and Basil II, and was incorporated into the Greek Empire from 1018, for over a hundred and fifty years. But in 1186 a Bulgar-Vlach revolt successfully threw off Byzantine occupation, and a Second Bulgarian Empire emerged, which again dominated the Balkans until it was hit by the Mongol invasions of the 1240's. The former Illyrian zone, by contrast, vegetated beyond the orbit of Byzantine politics for four centuries, before being partially regained and partially reduced to clientage by Basil II in the early 11th century. Greek rule here was thinly and precariously established only for a century, punctuated by numerous rebellions, until a united Serb kingdom emerged in 1151. In the mid 14th century, the Serbian Empire in its turn became the paramount Balkan power, humbling that of Bulgaria and Byzantium, before itself disintegrating on the eve of Turkish conquest.

Why did this alternating pattern fail to generate any robust feudal synthesis – indeed any durable historical order at all? The soil of the whole zone proved a quicksand for social organization and state formation alike: nothing is more striking than the ease with which the Ottomans finally took possession of it, after every local power had sunk into a common abeyance by the end of the 14th century. The answer to the question surely lies in the peculiar stalemate between the post-barbarian and late-imperial orders in the Balkans. The Byzantine Empire, after the loss of the Peninsula in the 6th and 7th centuries, was still too strong to be destroyed from without, and was able partially to recover its ground there, after an interval of two hundred years. But in the supervening epoch, the Slav and Turanian peoples who had settled the Balkans had conversely themselves become too developed or numerous to be assimilated, when they were eventually in turn reconquered: so that Greek rule never succeeded in integrating them into Byzantium, and in the end proved ephemeral. The same equation can be formulated negatively. The Slav communities that formed the massive majority of the initial barbarian settlers in the Balkans were socially too primitive in the Heraclian epoch to be able to establish political systems of the type that the German tribes had created in the

Merovingian West. On the other hand, the Byzantine State – because of its own inner structure, as we have seen – was incapable of the type of dynamic subjection and integration of tribal peoples that had once been characteristic of Imperial Rome. The result was that neither force could permanently prevail over the other, while both could wreak repeated and lethal damage on the other. The clash between the two did not take the form of a general cataclysm from which a new synthesis arose, but of a slow, reciprocal trituration and exhaustion. The distinctive signs of this process, which set South-Eastern apart from Western Europe, can be registered in a number of ways.

To take two sensitive 'cultural' indices first: the whole pattern of religion and linguistic evolution in the region was very different. In the West, the Germanic invaders had been converted to Arian Christianity at the time of their conquest; they were then gradually won to the Catholic Church; and with few exceptions, their languages disappeared before the Romance speech of their Latinized subject populations. In the South-East, on the other hand, the Slavs and Avars who swamped the Balkans in the late 6th century were both pagan peoples, and for nearly three centuries most of the Peninsula remained dechristianized – the most dramatic single setback Christianity ever suffered in the continent. Moreover, when the Bulgars became the first barbarians to be converted in the late 9th century, they had to be granted an autonomous Orthodox patriarchate which was tantamount to an independent 'national' Church: the Serbs were eventually to win this privilege too, in the 12th century. At the same time, while Greece was slowly rehellenized linguistically after its reconquest by Byzantium in the late 8th and early 9th centuries, the whole interior of the Balkan Peninsula remained Slavonic in speech: so much so, that precisely to achieve the conversion of its inhabitants, the Greek missionaries Cyril and Methodius from Thessalonika (then still a bilingual border town) had to invent the Glagolitic alphabet specifically for the Slav language-group of the region.[34] Cultural 'assimilation' thus proceeded in exactly the reverse order in the Balkans: whereas in the West, particularist

34. G. Ostrogorsky, 'The Byzantine Background to the Moravian Mission', *Dumbarton Oaks Papers*, No. 19, 1965, pp. 15–16. For the character of the Glagolitic and subsequent Cyrillic scripts, see D. Obolensky, *The Byzantine Commonwealth*, London 1971, pp. 139–140.

heresy gave way to universalist orthodoxy and linguistic Latinism, in the South-East, paganism yielded to separatist orthodoxy enshrined in linguistic non-Hellenism. Later Byzantine military conquest was in no way able to alter this basic cultural datum. The great mass of the Slav population of the Peninsula had in this respect crystallized outside the radius of Byzantine control. Greater demographic density of settlement may in part account for the contrast with the Germanic invasions. But there is no doubt that the nature of the initial Byzantine environment was also a prime determinant.

If at the cultural level, barbarian/Byzantine relations reveal the relative weakness of the latter, at the political and economic levels, they indicate no less the peculiar limits of the former. The general problems of early Slav state formation have already been discussed earlier. The particular Balkan experience throws them into sharp relief. It seems clear, in fact, that it was the nomadic Avar military organization that commanded and led the original barbarian drive into the Balkans which made possible their conquest. The Slavs, who fought as their auxiliaries, greatly outnumbered them and stayed behind in the new lands, while the Avar hordes wheeled back into their base in Pannonia, to emerge again for periodic mobile raids against Constantinople, but not to settle in the Peninsula.[35] Slav migrations were now spread across territories which had for centuries been an integral part of the Roman imperial system, and which even included the cradle of classical civilization itself – Greece. Yet for over three centuries after their invasions, these peoples produced no trans-tribal polity of which any record remains. The first actual State to be created in the Balkans was the work of another Turanian nomadic people, the Bulgars – whose military and political superiority over the Slavs enabled them to create a powerful khanate below the Danube that soon challenged Byzantium frontally. The 'Proto-Bulgar' ruling class of boyars dominated a mixed social formation, the bulk of whose population were free Slav peasants, paying tribute to their Turanian overlords, who composed a two-tier military aristocracy still organized on a clan basis. By the end of the 9th century, the proto-Bulgar language had disappeared and the khanate

35. P. Lemerle, 'Invasions et Migrations dans les Balkans depuis la Fin de l'Epoque Romaine jusqu'au VIIe Siècle', *Revue Historique*, CCXI, April–June 1954, pp. 293 ff.

had been formally christianized: the clan system and paganism fell together, as elsewhere, and soon the whole boyar class had become Slavicized, if with a certain Greek cultural veneer.[36] The early 10th century witnessed a formidable and direct attack on Byzantium by the new Bulgarian ruler Simeon, who seized Adrianople twice, raided down to the Gulf of Corinth and laid siege to Constantinople. Simeon's declared ambition was nothing less than to become ruler of the Eastern Empire itself, and in pursuit of this goal he succeeded in wresting the grant of an imperial title of 'Tsar' from Byzantium. Eventually, after prolonged campaigns, his armies were defeated by the Croat ruler Tomislav, and Bulgaria lapsed into weakness and unrest under his son Peter.

The first unmistakably radical religious movement of Christian Europe, Bogomilism, now sprang up, an expression of peasant protest against the enormous cost of Simeon's wars and the social polarization that had accompanied them.[37] The Bulgarian State received a further setback from the destructive Russo-Byzantine wars which were then waged across it. A major military and political revival under the Tsar Samuel at the end of the 10th century, however, led to renewed and all-out conflict with Byzantium, which lasted for twenty years. It was this protracted, pitiless struggle, as we have seen, that finally over-reached the Byzantine imperial system and paved the way for its collapse in Anatolia. Its consequences, of course, were even more disastrous for Bulgaria, whose independent existence was extinguished for over 150 years. Byzantine occupation during the 11th and 12th centuries led to a rapid augmentation of large estates and intensification of both Greek and Bulgar noble exactions and central fiscal pressures, on the peasantry. The institution of the *pronoia* was introduced into Bulgaria for the first time and *ekskousseia* immunities multiplied. Increasing numbers of formerly free peasants sank into dependent *paroikoi* status, while slavery was contemporaneously extended via the

36. S. Runciman, *A History of the First Bulgarian Empire*, London 1930, pp. 94–5; I. Sakazov, *Bulgarische Wirtschaftsgeschichte*, Berlin/Leipzig 1929, pp. 7–29.

37. An Orthodox priest of the time summed up Bogomil social doctrines: 'They teach their own people not to obey their lords, they revile the wealthy, hate the tsar, ridicule the elders, condemn the boyars, regard as vile in the sight of God those who serve the tsar, and forbid every servant to work for his master.' Obolensky, *The Byzantine Commonwealth*, p. 125.

captivity of local war-prisoners.[38] Bogomilism now predictably revived. There were repeated popular revolts against Byzantine rule, and in 1186 two Vlach chieftains, Peter and Asen, led a successful insurrection which routed the Greek punitive expeditions sent against it.[39] A 'Second' Bulgarian Empire was now constructed, whose administrative hierarchy, court protocol, and tax system were all closely modelled on that of Byzantium: the number of free peasants continued to decline, while the upper boyar stratum consolidated its power. In the early 13th century, Tsar Ioannitsa (Kalojan) veered back once again to the traditional goal of Bulgarian dynasties – the assault on Constantinople and assumption of the universal imperial title that went with control of it. His troops defeated and killed the Latin Emperor Baldwin shortly after the Fourth Crusade, and his successor carried the Bulgarian standards victoriously to the Adriatic. But within a decade, this enlarged State has crumpled before the onslaught of the Mongols.

The Slav populations in the former region of Illyricum were by and large much slower to develop a post-tribal political system, in the absence of an initially superordinate nomadic military class: social differentiation proceeded more gradually and clan organization proved very tenacious. The early Croat kingdom (900–1097) was absorbed by Hungary and played no further independent role. To the south, hereditary *župani* governed local territories from their fortified settlements as family patrimonies, which were divided among their kinsmen for administration.[40] The first princedoms to emerge were those of Zeta and Rascia in the 11th century, anti-Byzantine creations which were suppressed with only partial success by the Comneni Emperors.

38. Dimitar Angelov, 'Die bulgarische Länder und das bulgarische Volk in der Grenzen des byzantinischen Reiches im XI–XII Jahrhundert (1018–1185)', *Proceedings of the XIIth International Congress of Byzantine Studies*, pp. 155–61. While Byzantine *ekskousseiai* were virtually never 'integral' immunities, because always retaining public charges on the *paroikoi*, equivalent Bulgar grants in this period conferred much more comprehensive seigneurial powers over the peasantry. See G. Cankova-Petkova, 'Byzance et le Développement Social et Economique des Etats Balkaniques', *Actes du Premier Congrès International des Etudes Balkaniques et Sud-Est Européennes*, Sofia 1969, pp. 344–5.

39. The clearest account of this rising is R. L. Wolff, 'The "Second Bulgarian Empire". Its Origin and History to 1204', *Speculum*, XXIV, No. 2, April 1949, pp. 167–206.

40. Dvornik, *The Slavs. Their Early History and Civilization*, pp. 162–3.

In the later 12th century, the Grand Župan Stephen Nemanja united the two territories into a single Serbian kingdom, acquiring the royal title from the Pope. But although Byzantine efforts to reconquer Serbia were checked, it was another hundred years before its fragmented clan notables had undergone a sufficient annealing process to form a unified landowning class, with seigneurial rights over a servile peasantry, and a military capacity to expand the territory of the Serbian monarchy. But the eclipse of Bulgaria and Byzantium by the early 14th century gave it the opportunity to win dominance of the Balkans. Stephen Dushan annexed Macedonia, Thessaly and the Epirus and proclaimed himself Emperor of the Serbs and Greeks at Skoplje in 1346. The social and political structure of the Greater Serbian Empire is documented by the comprehensive law-code or *Zakonnik* which was drawn up under Dushan just afterwards. The ruling nobility possessed hereditary allodial estates, which were worked by dependent *sebri* – the Serb equivalent of the Byzantine *paroikoi* – peasants owing labour services, who were formally bound to the soil by royal decree. The monarch had wide autocratic powers, but was surrounded and advised by a permanent council of magnates and prelates. Dushan abolished the title *župan*, with its clan overtones, and substituted it with that of the Greek *kefalija*, the Byzantine term for an imperial governor. The court, chancellery and administration were rough copies of those of Constantinople.[41] Some of the Danubian coastal towns exercised municipal self-government by reason of their close links with the Italian cities. The silver mines which provided much of the royal income were worked by slave-labour, and managed by Saxons. The Serbian Empire was undoubtedly the most advanced Slav state to emerge in the mediaeval Balkans: both Western and Byzantine cross-currents are visible in the mixed character of its political system, intermediate between an outright fief system and an autocratic bureaucracy. But the same heterogeneity of its elements condemned it to a very brief life. Within a few years of Dushan's death, it had disintegrated back into squabbling despotates and divided appanages. One last Slav power succeeded it. For fifty years in the latter half of the 14th century, it was

41. S. Runciman, 'Byzantium and the Slavs', in N. Baynes and H. Moss (ed.), *Byzantium: An Introduction to East Roman Civilization*, Oxford 1948, pp. 364–5; Dvornik, *The Slavs in European History and Civilization*, pp. 142–6.

the turn of Bosnia to predominate along the Adriatic: but the Bogomil faith of its dynasty and the elective character of its monarchy rendered this mountain outpost incapable of emulating the Serbian Empire which had preceded it.

The circular contest between Byzantium, Bulgaria and Serbia had thus ended in a common regression and decline by the end of the 14th century. The fragile state-system of the mediaeval Balkans was in general crisis before the Ottoman conquest overtook it. The structural reasons for the failure of the region to produce an indigenous feudal synthesis have already been indicated. The nature of the abortive Bulgar and Serb states only underlines them. For their most striking characteristic in any comparative European perspective is their recurrent and impossible imitation of the imperial autocracy of Byzantium itself. They sought to be, not kingdoms, but empires; and their rulers aimed, not for any imperial title, but that of the universal Graeco-Roman *autokrator*. Thus the Bulgar and Serb Empires both attempted to mimic the internal administrative system of the Byzantine states, and take external possession of it by direct conquest and succession. Such a task was inherently unviable for them, and fatally led to social and political over-extension: a direct transition from local-tribal to imperial-bureaucratic rule was beyond the resources of any nobility in the region, and corresponded to no real economic infrastructure, in the absence of either an urban or slave economy. Hence the reciprocal ruin of the three-cornered struggle for an imperial dominion that was itself by now an illusory anachronism. Yet at the same time, the epoch in which this ruin was consummated was also that of the general depression throughout Europe. Documentation of the rural economy in the Balkans in this age is still too sparse, in part because of the subsequent Ottoman obliteration of its institutions, for any firm judgments now to be made as to its inward tendency. But here as elsewhere the great plagues took their toll. Recent calculations suggest that between 1348 and 1450 there was an overall demographic decline of 25 per cent, from some 6 million to 4.5 million, in what was anyway a thinly inhabited region.[42] Moreover, in the Balkans too, social revolts now erupted.

42. J. C. Russell, 'Late Mediaeval Balkan and Asia Minor Population', *The Journal of the Economic and Social History of the Orient*, III, 1960, pp. 265–74; *Population in Europe 500–1500*, p. 19.

The 'Commune' of Thessalonika has already been described. Simultaneous with it was a peasant insurrection on the Thracian plains, in 1342, against the provincial Byzantine landlords there. Along the Adriatic, Kotor and Bar were the scene of municipal upheavals. In Bulgaria, a rural rebellion in 1277 had briefly brought a plebeian usurper to power; in the 14th century, vagabondage and banditry spread, as land became increasingly concentrated. The strains of would-be imperial State construction by the various aristocracies of the peninsula had naturally led to greater fiscal and predial exactions on the poor, who responded with distrust and unrest.

It is noticeable that there was virtually no popular resistance in the countryside to the arrival of the Ottomans, except – significantly – in the primitive alpine fastnesses of Albania, where tribal and clan organization still checked large landed property and obstructed social differentiation. In Bosnia, where the Bogomil peasantry had been particularly persecuted by the Catholic Church as 'Patarene' heretics, and delivered over to slave-raiding by Venetian and Ragusan merchants,[43] the rural masses and sections of the local nobility welcomed Turkish rule and were eventually widely converted to Islam. Braudel, indeed, has written categorically: 'The Turkish conquest of the Balkans was only possible because it benefited from an astonishing social revolution. A seigneurial society that lay hard upon the peasantry was taken by surprise and collapsed of its own accord. The conquest, which eliminated the large landowners, was in certain respects a "liberation of the poor". Asia Minor had been conquered patiently and slowly, after centuries of obscure efforts by the Turks; the Balkan

43. Werner, *Die Geburt einer Grossmacht – Die Osmanen*, pp. 229–33.
44. F. Braudel, *La Méditerranée et Le Monde Méditerranéen à l'Epoque de Philippe II*, Paris 1949, p. 510. Braudel's contrast of the respective pace of conquest in Asia Minor and the Balkans is misleading, in so far as it implies that the critical variable was the relative vigour of Christian resistance. For Anatolia was gradually occupied by Turcoman tribal irregulars, in successive waves of spontaneous migration, while the Balkans were conquered by a highly organized military State, in the new shape of the Ottoman Sultanate. With his typical sense of scruple, Barudel has rectified the last sentence in the passage quoted above in the second, revised edition of his work. It now reads: 'the Balkan peninsula *seems* not to have resisted the invader' (his italics), and in a note he adds that if a study by Angelov is correct, Bulgarian resistance was more lively than his text allows. See *La Méditerranée et Le Monde Méditerranéen à l'Epoque de Philippe II*, Paris 1966, II, p. 11.

peninsula so to speak made no resistance to them.'[44] Such a judgment is, however, too summary. In fact, there was little sign of any spontaneous or outright collapse of the indigenous social order prior to the Turkish attacks. The noble class was everywhere increasingly oppressive, and its political systems were in crisis. But a subsequent recovery could not be excluded. It was the Ottoman assault which destroyed any possibility of a further autochthonous development in the Balkans. The fields of Maritsa and Kossovo, on which the Bulgarian and Serbian aristocracies went down to their defeat, were hard fought: there was no simple Turkish walkover. On the other hand, once the decisive Ottoman blows had been delivered, the precarious state structures of the Balkans had no reserves left to pursue the struggle against Islamic invasion. After the local princes and nobles had been routed, the sole remaining chance of stemming the Turkish tide lay with the defensive expeditions to save the Balkans organized by Western feudalism. Two international crusades set out from Vienna, and were successively crushed by Ottoman armies in 1396 and 1444 at Nicopolis and Varna. Western feudalism, now itself in full tribulation, was no longer capable of the victories of its prime. In these disasters, South-Eastern Europe fleetingly rejoined the general destiny of the continent, before departing from it again more radically than ever before.

The mediaeval world thus ended in generalized crisis. Both the homelands of feudalism in the West, and the territories of the East to which it had extended or where it failed to develop, were the scene of deep processes of socio-economic dissolution and mutation by the early 15th century. At the threshold of the early modern epoch, as the ramparts of Constantinople fell to Turkish cannon, the consequences of these changes for the political order of Europe still lay largely hidden. The dénouement of the State system that was to come into being from them, remains to be explored.

Index of Names

Index of Authorities